PUBLIC LIBRARY MOVEMENT

PUBLIC LIBRARY MOVEMENT

Kerala

DR. A. PASLITHIL

KALPAZ PUBLICATIONS
DELHI-110052

Public Library Movement: Kerala

Rs. 690

ISBN: 81-7835-579-5

Published in 2006 in India by
Kalpaz Publications
C-30, Satyawati Nagar,
Delhi-110052
E-mail: kalpaz@hotmail.com

Lassertype Setting by : Rudra Computer Graphic, Delhi
Printed at : Salasar Imaging System, Delhi

Dedicated to Library Workers of India

Contents

Preface 9

Acknowledgements 11

Abbreviations and Terms 13

1. **Introduction** 15

2. **The Early Stages of Library Movement** 23

3. **Spread of Library Movement and Socio-political Developments** 45

4. **Formation of Effective Library Organisations** 67

5. **United Travancore - Cochin Library Association** 89

6. **Library Movement After the Formation of Kerala State** 117

7. **Take Over of The Kerala Grandhasala Sanghom** 155

8. **The Structural FrameWork and Functional Details** 171

9.	**The Present Status Of The Kerala Grandhasala Sanghom.**	**195**
10.	**The Opinionnaire Survey**	**203**
11.	**Conclusion**	**217**
	Appendices	**235**
	Bibliography	**257**
	Index	**275**

Preface

The Kerala Grandhasala Sanghom – an apex body of the voluntary association of libraries in the state gave a charismatic leadership to the library movement in Kerala. It was a mass movement, which stood apart from other library movements in the country. For the last one hundred years the public libraries of the state have been serving the people of Kerala as nonformal educational institutions for enhancing educational, political, cultural, and social enlightenment throughout the state. It provides not merely an intellectual development, but diffuses as an integral part in the socio-cultural developments.

The present study is intended to evaluate the history of the public libraries, during the pre and post Grandhasala Sanghom period. The public libraries of the state have played a vital role in the social life of Kerala. The study is relevant and unique in the sense that, so far, no scientific and systematic studies have been conducted on the activities and contributions of this popular movement. The major objective of the study is to trace out the origin and development of this mass movement and assess its contributions in the socio-cultural fields.

The relevant data and information obtained from the primary sources – like Annual Report of the Kerala Grandhasala Sanghom, State Administrative Report, Diary of P.N. Panicker, Minutes of the Sanghom meetings, Government Orders, Official Files etc., and also from secondary sources – like News Papers, Journals, periodicals and published books related to the Kerala Grandhasala Sanghom, Socio – cultural history of Kerala etc. In addition to this some valuable data were collected by interviewing some important persons, who are mainly responsible for this movement. An Opinionnarie Survey was also conducted to understand and to arrive at general conclusions about the present position of the public libraries in the State. Moreover, many eminent personalities, who are strongly involved in this movement, have been contacted personally for the purpose.

It is really an inquiry into the public library movement in the state, which played a substantial role in the process of social transformation of the State. The study concentrates on the library movement from the inception to the year in which the Kerala Grandhasala Sanghom was changed its name as State Library Council in 1994.

Dr. A. Paslithil

Acknowledgements

I have great pleasure in placing on record my deep sense of gratitude to my Professor Dr. K.K. Kusuman, Former Head of the Department of History, University of Kerala for his valuable guidance and inspiration throughout my study; these few words are inadequate to express fully my gratitude to him.

I am also indebted to Dr. Samsanada Raj, Professor, Department of Psychology and Dr. Immanual Thomas, Reader of the same Department, University of Kerala, for their help in the preparation and analysis of the opinionnaire survey.

It is a pleasant duty to record my indebtedness to the doynes of the library movement in the State, Sri. P.N. Panicker and Sri. P.T. Bhaskara Panicker for their encouragement and help for completing my work. My sincere thanks are due to Sri. I.V. Das, the public library workers of the state and the K.G.S. Staff members especially Sri. K.A. Somashekara Kurup for providing all facilities and services to me.

I owe an extra measure of thanks to the Former State librarian Sri. N. Sukumaran Nair, Library Professionals of the University of Kerala, the Legislative library of the Kerala State, and the staff members of the Directorate of State Archives for their boundless help they extended to me.

Last but not the least, I record my thanks to my wife and colleagues for the splendid co-operation they rendered me in moulding this work to its final form.

A. Paslithil

Abbreviations and Terms

A.T.C.G.S	-	Akhile Thiruvithamcore – Cochin Grandhasala Sanghom
A.T.G.S	-	Akhila Thiruvithamcore Grandhasala Sanghom
D.P.I	-	Director of Public Instructions
C.P.I	-	Communist Party of India
C.P.I (M)	-	Communist Party of India (Marxist)
KANFED	-	Kerala Association for Non-Formal Education and Development
D.L.C	-	District Library Council
K.G.S	-	Kerala Grandhasala Sanghom
K.P.C.C	-	Kerala Pradesh Congress Committee
L.L.A	-	Local Library Authority
M.E	-	Malayalam Era

M.L.A	-	Member of Legislative Assembly
M.L.C	-	Member of Legislative Council
M.S	-	Memorial Souvenir
P.S.P	-	Praja Socialist Party
S.L.A	-	State Library Authority
S.L.C	-	State Library Council
S.P.C.S	-	Sahithya Pravarthaka Sahakarana Sanghom (Co-operative Society)
T.P.L	-	Trivandrum Public Library
T.L.U	-	Taluk Library Union
TVM	-	Trivandrum
UNESCO	-	United Nations Educational Scientific and Cultural Organization.
ed.	-	Editor
eds.	-	Editors
Mal.	-	Malayalam
Bharanasamiti	-	Board of Directors
Grandhasala Painkili	-	Library
Sahityam	-	Trash literature
Sanghom	-	Association
Vayanasala	-	Library

1
Introduction

Kerala,[1] the Spice Garden of India, is a small lush green state lying on the South West corner of the peninsular India. Being one of the smallest states in the Republic of India, it is embedded in between the mighty Sahyadri Hills[2] on the east and the Arabian sea on the west. The state lies between 8° 18′ and 12° 48′ North Latitude and between 74° 52′ and 77° 22′ East Longitude. It has an area of 38, 863 sq. kms. and a population of 31,838,619 crore[3]. Cut off from the Decan plateau by the mountainous belt of the Western Ghats, but with a long coastline that opens it to foreign intercourse, Kerala has evolved a unique culture of its own. It is a highly politicised region with different religious groups, but it has a long tradition of religious amity. The State of Kerala is educationally advanced state. The literacy percentage is 100% and this confers it the foremost position among the Indian States[4]. The State is the most humid tropical part of India and astoundingly beautiful in topography, and flora and fauna. Malayalam is the mother tongue of the people of Kerala.

In contrast to the rest of the country, Kerala has a distinct physical and cultural entity. The spectacular cultural mosaic of Kerala with its scenic splendours and age old traditions offer a lure of romantic fascination. It has been the cradle of varied cultures and ways of life through ages. At the dawn of history, it is believed that this land was occupied by Dravidians, who were in a semi-tribal state of civilization with casteless community and vertically divided into groups on the basis of topography and occupation[5]. During this period Kerala was a republic and later on it remained as a democratic monarchy till the early years of Christian Era when, aristocracy was the order of the world[6].

In the Sangam period[7] the present Kerala was part of a larger political unit, Tamilakam, and was crowned by the Kinds of the Chera line of rulers and minor Chieftains[8]. Though in the third and fourth centuries B.C Jainism, Buddhism and Brahminism had their sway in Kerala, majority of the people followed Dravidian practices[9]. But there was no rigorous caste and social exclusiveness. People enjoyed a large measure of social freedom and equality[10].

Education was widespread and there was high standard of literacy[11]. All people, irrespective of sect and sex, were entitled to get the benefit of education[12]. Libraries attached to Jain Pallis and Buddha Viharas[13] promoted education among the people. The books were in manuscript form and these were copied down from time to time[14]. Palmleaves were usually used for the purposes of writing and people has developed a tendency for keeping these written documents[15]. "Naladiar", one of the 36 famous Sangham works, sheds lustre on the fact that men gathered books in abundance and filled their house with them[16].

The early foreign trade contacts starting from the third millennium B.C. have left much impact on the social and cultural life of Kerala. The Arabs, the Babylonians, the Phoenecians, the Jews, the Greeks, the Romans and the Chinese had trade contacts with the people of Kerala which resulted in the dissemination of world religions, like Christianity (52 A.D.) Judaism (68 A.D.) and Islam (seventh or eighth century) in the soil of Kerala[17]. But since the fifth century, Aryan culture had begun to exercise its dominant influence in the society of Kerala.

By the eighth and ninth centuries, Kerala witnessed a great revival of Hindiusm under Sree Sankara (788-820 A.D.). Sankara, the greatest Hindu Saint of India, was born at Kalady in Central Kerala. His philosophy of *Advaita Vedanta* or monism purified Hinduism of its irrational formalities and laid down the foundation for cultural synthesis[18]. Sree Sankara has no match among his contemporaries in India in matters of scholarship. Kerala was in a position to breed a soul like Sankara whose profoundity in knowledge has been widely accepted.

But the process of Aryanisation of increasing hold of the caste system brought about a decline in the standards of general education and literacy. A revival of learning and literature took place during the reign of Kulasekharas (800-1102 A.D), when there was rich literary output in Sanskrit and Tamil. Education was imparted only in these languages[19]. Meanwhile, almost all the temples of Kerala were great centres of learning and different kind of arts. Imitating the Buddhists, health centres and libraries were started in the Hindu temples[20]. Apart from regular education institutions attached to the temples, like *Salai* and *Sabhamuttu,* village educational institutions and social education were also promoted[21].

By the beginning of the ninth century, Malayalam as a distinct language was slowly evolving[22]. But as a language it reached a high standard of development only by the thirteenth century[23]. It was an offshoot of Tamil Language and was perhaps the daughter or younger sister of Tamil[24]. During this period the equality and democracy of pre-historic society had been completely destroyed. In its place a new society based on caste system had emerged, it lacked democracy and equality. Untouchability, the main feature of the caste based society of Kerala, became more complex than in the rest of India[25].

During this period, a social transformation was slowly taking place, which brought about a potent administrative hierarchy under the hegemony of an elite section of Brahmins. They contributed to the feudalistic society of Kerala a rigorous caste system, patrilineal succession and Devadasi system[26]. They also made substantial contributions to the field of science, philosophy, education and literature. Their writings were kept in palm leaves and later on papers collected from other parts of India were also used[27]. These written documents were roughly collected and kept for further use. These were largely preserved in the private libraries of *Illoms, Kovilakams, Madams*[28] and palaces[29]. The other religious groups too had their respective place in the socio-political setup, but they were subordinated to the Brahmins[30].

After the fall of the Kulasekharas, three major native kingdoms Travancore, Cochin and Calicut came to prominence. The Kinds of these royal houses were great patrons of learning and literature. They had started many vernacular educational institutions and had collected large numbers of available written documents[31]. The Zamorins[32] of Calicut had rich collection of such documents for the preservation of which they maintained a separate palace. These documents were kept neatly in well-equipped and planned rooms. The length and width of the room was 40" × 20" where many big shelves, boxes and cloth bags were used for keeping them[33]. However, in 1513 and at the time of Tipu sultan these libraries caught fire and a good number of these precious documents were destroyed[34].

By the end of the fifteenth century literary activities in Kerala took a new turn. A family of Nayar scholars of Niranam (Niranam Poets) translated many Sanskrit classics into Malayalam while other scholars wrote several work in

Sanskrit language[35]. The literary revival of the period found its consummation in Thunchathu Ezhuthachan (mid sixteenth century), the greatest doyen of Malayalm literature[36]. Meanwhile, the European powers began to exert influence and to establish their supremacy over Kerala society and politics. The Portuguese, the Dutch and the English had made significant contributions to the cause of education and learning in Kerala. The Portuguese founded seminaries and colleges at Cochin, Cranganore and Vaipinkotta for the purpose of training Christian priests and thus helped to spread the knowledge of Portuguese and Latin among the local people[37]. They were also responsible for the establishment of printing press in Kerala. Joannes Gonzalves, a Spanish Jesuit, made cut-out of types for printing books in Malayalam in 1577[38]. Cochin and Vaipinkotta were the two centres where the Portuguese initially setup printing press, and they were among the earliest printing presses in the whole of India[39]. Likewise, the Christian missionaries started educational institutions and printing press which also contributed much to the development of language and literature in Kerala. The first printing press in Kerala was established on the Malabar coast by Christian missionaries. They prepared a dictionary and a grammar book for Malayalam language[40].

As a result of the introduction of printing technology in Kerala, there was a spurt in the publication of books, newspapers and journals. The title of the first Malayalam book printed in India was a "Grammer of Malayalam Language" (1799) which was printed by Curier Press in Bombay[41]. Before the publication of this book two other books named 'Hortus Malabaricus' (1688) 'Samkshepta Vedartam' (1772) had been printed in Malayalam, but they were printed in Amsterdam and Rome respectively[42]. The advent of printing and the publications of reading materials steadily developed the interest in books and the reading habit among the people of Kerala.

Thus, from very ancient time onwards the people of Kerala were blessed and graced from various quarters in developing a zest for learning and reading. This natural incentive was properly utilised by the people. With the result that they came to occupy the premier position in literacy and learning, outshining all other states in India.

Notes and References

1. Malabar was the popular expression used by the travellers of ancient and medieval periods to delineate the Malayalam speaking area of Kerala. Historically, the term Kerala too is very old, but politically this region was fragmented into numerous petty states and kingdoms which existed within the frame of this historical expression. By the close of the medieval period three kingdoms emerged prominently, outshining or devouring all the others - Travancore, Cochin and Calicut (Malabar). But after the State Reorganization on linguistic basis in 1956 these three political units came together and assumed the name, Kerala.
2. Western Ghats.
3. *Census of India - 2001* , Provisional Population Totals Series – 33 Kerala, Paper-2 of 2001, Trivandrum: Sheela Thomas, Director, Census Operations, Kerala, p.1.
4. *Ibid*
5. M.G.S. Narayanan, *Cultural Symbiosis in Kerela*, Trivandrum: Kerala Historical Society, 1972, p.1.
6. L.A. Krishna Iyer, *Kerala and Her People*, Palghat : Educational and Supplies Depot, 1961, p.125.
7. The first five centuries of Christian Era.

8. A. Sreedhara Menon, *A Survey of Kerala History*, Kottayam : National Book Stall, 1967, p. 64.
9. A. Sreedhara Menon, *Legacy of Kerala*, Trivandrum : Government Press, 1982, pp. 3-10.
10. *Ibid.*, p. 80.
11. K.A. Nilakanta Sastri, *A History of South India from Pre historic Times to the Fall of Vijayanagar*, Madras : Oxford Press, 1966, p. 322.
12. *Ibid.*
13. *Palli* and *Vihara* mean centers of worship of the Jains and Budhists respectively.
14. T.K. Velu Pillai, *The Travancore State Manual*, Vol.I, Trivandrum : Government of Travancore, 1940, p. 444.
15. M. Thomas, "Annathe Grandhasalakal". *Grandhalokam*, Trivandrum, (Mal.), Vol.I(1), 1948, p. 77.
16. G.G. Pope & F.W. Ellis, *Naladiar : 318*, Madras : South India Siva Sidhanta Works Publishing Society, Tirunelveli, 1958, p.139.
17. L.A. Krishna Iyer, No.6, pp.7-10.
18. A. Sreedhara Menon, No.8, p.5.
19. A. Sreedhara Menon, *Cultural Heritage of Kerala : An Introduction*, Cochin : East West Publication, 1978, pp.161-162.
20. Elamkulam Kunjan Pillai, *Keralathinte Iruladanja Edukal*, (Mal.), Kottayam : National Book Stall, 1953, p.46.
21. A. Sreedhara Menon, No.8, pp.153-168.
22. P.K. Balakrishnan, *Jathivyavasthayum Kerala Charithavum*, (Mal.), Kottayam: S.P.C.S. Limited, 1983, p.228.
23. K.M. Panikkar, *History of Kerala – 1498-1801*, Annamalai Nagar : Annamala University, 1960, p.426.
24. Ullor S. Parameswara Iyer, *Kerala Sahitya Charithram*, (Mal.), Vol.I, Trivandrum : Kerala University, 1952pp.39-40.
25. E.M.S. Namboodiripad, *Kerala Society and Politics : A Historical Survey*, New Delhi : National Book, 1984, p.41.

26. Elamkulam Kunjan Pillai, No.20, pp.75, 194.
27. K. Raghavan Pillai, "Kerala Sarvakalasala Hasthalikhita Grandhasala". *Kerala Grandhasala Directory – 1964,* (Mal.), Trivandrum : Kerala Grandhasala Sanghom, 1964, p.59.
28. Ilom, Kovilakom and Madam refer to Brahmin houses of various social status.
29. *Publication of Malayalam Manuscripts; Administrative Reports – 1104,* Trivandrum : Government Press, 1929, p.2.
30. E.M.S. Namboodiripad, No. 25, p.42.
31. K.V. Krishna Iyer, *Zamorins of Calicut,* Calicut : Norman Printing Bureau, 1938, p.311.
32. The Kings of Calicut were known as Zamorins.
33. K.V. Krishna Iyer, No.31, pp.315-317.
34. N.M. Namboothiri, *Zamoothiri Charitharathintea Kanappurangal,* (Mal.), Edapal : Vallathol Vidyapeedam, 1987, p.2.
35. K.M. Panikkar, No.23, pp.426-27.
36. *Ibid.,* p.427.
37. A. Sreedhara Menon, No.19, p.169.
38. *Ibid.,* p.170.
39. *Ibid.*
40. K.P. Padmanabha Menon, *History of Kerala,* Vol.IV, Cochin: Cochin Government Press, 1937, p.530.
41. K.M. Govi, "Aadimudranam – Banbayeparavam", *Mathrubhoomi Weekly,* (Mal.), Vol.51 (68), Calicut : Mathrubhoomi Press, February – March, p.10.
42. A.D. Hari Sharma, "Malayalamachadi". *Kerala Grandhasala Directory* – 1984, (Mal.), Trivandrum : Kerala Grandhasala Sanghom, 1964, pp.12-13.

2

The Early Stages of Library Movement

In the second half of the eighteenth and nineteenth centuries Kerala witnessed tremendous changes in all spheres of life. This was mainly due to the western influences and the enlightened rule of the local kings. Later, the social reform movements and political awakening of the people played a vital role in these developments.

Travancore entered into an agreement with the East India Company in 1773 to ward off subsequent Mysorean invasion on Travancore. In 1795 a formal treaty was signed by which the Company agreed to protect Travancore from all foreign enemies[1]. A Civil Office was opened under the East India Company in 1788 at Trivandrum and it served, for thc first time, as a medium of communication between the Maharaja of Travancore and the Madras Government[2]. An officer was appointed as Resident who served as a political agent of the Company in Travancore. He began to influence the policies and administrative matters of the state as per the provisions contained in the treaty. Gradually the paramount power became mandatory with regard to the foreign policy and advisory, in respect of home affaris[3].

During the reign of Gouri Lakshmi Bai (1810-1814),[4] the Resident, Col. Munro was appointed the Dewan of

Travancore, and he initiated the spread of English education and a number of administrative reforms[5]. By a Royal Proclamation, she abolished slave trade in Travancore on 5 December 1812. This was actually a milestone in the history of social transformation in Travancore, nay Kerala. Gouri Parvathi Bai (1815-1829),[6] the Regent Queen, laid the foundation of modern education policy and formulated a budget to support it. Her Highness resolved that "the State should defray the entire cost of education of its people, in order that there might be no backwardness in the spread of enlightenment among them, that by a diffusion of education they might become better subjects and public servants and that the reputation of the State may be advanced thereby"[7]. Vernacular Primary Schools were established in all parts of the State and qualified person were appointed as teachers who were paid by the State[8]. Christian Missionaries who were responsible for the spread of English education in Kerala made their own contribution in the field of education during that time. The first printing press in Travancore was installed by them at Nagercoil in 1820, followed by the installation of presses at other places like Kottayam (1821) and Neyyur[9]. In 1815, Rani Parvathi Bai made a donation of Rs. 20,000/- to the college (C.M.S College) which was started by the Church Mission Society at Kottayam[10]. Following her, Maharaja Swati Tirunal came to power in Travancore.

Maharaja Swati Tirunal, a great scholar, linguist endowed with rare artistic gifts, reigned Travancore from 1829 to 1847[11]. Though steeped in Indian tradition, he had imbibed western ideas of liberalism and elightenment. He was instrumental to the introduction of many sweeping reforms in Travancore. He wanted to give the benefit of the best features of both systems to the people. He was a great patron of art and men of letters. He continued to encourage and patronize science and education even to his last days[12].

In order to reorganize and modernize Travancore he established an Engineering Department with a special irrigation section to provide adequate facilities to agriculturists. For the first time the survey of the paddy lands and preparation of land records were made. In 1012 M.E. (1873 A.D) the first census was held in Tranvacore. He also established certain new institutions like a Government Press, an Observatory, Menagerie of wild animals[13]. He laid the foundation for modern education in the State by the establishment of an English School in 1834 and declared it as Raja's Free School in 1836[14]. After this, a number of new schools sprang up in different parts of the State.

During his reign the western concept of Public Library trickled into Travancore. Before that a number of private libraries existed in different parts of the country. But these libraries kept written documents for their own purpose and did not allow the public to make use of them. A public library is capable of extending its services to all groups and it helps to share the opinions in the community, irrespective of age, religion, profession, sex, political conviction and economic level[15]. It can claim a dynamic part in community life; it can shape the thought process of a community. Libraries give light and people find their way to become good citizens of world, endowed with a deep desire to secure peace and progress[16].

Swati Tirunal was primarily instrumental for the library movement in Kerala[17]. The Trivandrum Public Library was established during his reign. "This library is the oldest of its kind in India. It was started in 1829 by the then British Resident Col. Edward Cadogan, the grand son of Sir Hans Salane, the founder of British Museum. The Maharaja and the British Resident took an active interest in the affairs of the library. The former being the patron and latter the president. The library was managed by an association known as Trivandrum Public Library Committee"[18]. This library was founded by a few prominent individuals, some of whom were Britishers and some Civilians. There were military men, a few Indians, and some local residents of Trivandrum. They were given high status entitling them to be invited to the 'Darbars' of the Maharaja. They managed it as a private club, though it was called a Public Library[19].

In 1836 at the request of Trivandrum Public Library Honorary Secretary J. Robert an amount of Rs. 1000/- was sanctioned to the library (See Appendix-A)[20] . Even though the British officers used this library the doors were opened to the natives also. The natives were allowed to read books in the library by paying Re.1/- as monthly subscription. The Public of Trivandrum could not easily afford it at that time[21].

The objective of the library was the gradual formation of an extensive library of books of general reference for the use and the benefit of the people of Trivandrum[22]. It was established in a pattern similar to the British Book Clubs and Private Subscription Library of the early nineteenth century. In 1847 it had acquired its own land and building which was near the present public library building. The members had also constituted themselves formally into Trivandrum Public Library Society with proper constitution and body of rules[23]. The Tranvancore Government recognized the library and an agreement was reached between the Government and subscribers of the library on 28 February 1856. According to this agreement the government agreed to pay Rs. 13/- per mensum for office expense, and to shift the library to museum after constructing a suitable building[24] In 1865, when this institution was transferred to the museum complex it had enriched itself by a good collection of scientific books[25].

While the Trivandrum Public Library was thus slowly coming up a new library called People's Library came into existence in Trivandrum near the Police Stadium on 18 October 1862. John Allan Brown, the Astronomer to the Travancore Sircar and Director of the Observatory during 1852-65 was mainly responsible for this[26]. Thus in 1038 M.E (1862-63) there were two public libraries for the people in Trivandrum, and the circulation of English and vernacular newspapers and periodicals visibly increased[27]. Two years later, two reading clubs were opened in the town and they were maintained by private subscription[28].

In 1894, Trivandrum Public Library was registered under Trvancore Joint Stock Companies Regulation, in the name of Trivandrum Public Library Society and it was taken over by the Government in 1898, when the People's Library merged with this[29]. After the Government's take over, the library was opened to the public. "Thus in 1898, fifty years before the dawn of independence, the common people of Trivandrum were allowed entry into the temple of knowledge, during the reign of Sree Mulam Tirunal, which is an event as unique as the Temple Entry Proclamation"[30].

By the close of the eighteenth century Tipu Sultan of Mysore had succeeded in establishing his political hegemony over Malabar and Cochin[31]. Soon after the departure of Tipu Sultan from cochin, the king of Cochin openly discarded his allegiance to him and joined the English. By the formal treaty signed on 6 January 1791, the King agreed to throw off all allegiance to Tipu Sultan and became a tributary to the East India Company[32]. The English men settled in Cochin started English Schools. The first English School was opened at Mattancheri in 1818 and followed by a number of schools and a second grade college affiliated to Madras University were opened[33].

The erstwhile Cochin State kept pace with Travancore in the case of vernacular education. By a Royal Proclamation issued in 1818 at the instance of the Resident, Colonel Munro, thirty three vernacular schools were established by the Cochin Government[34]. In 1877, District Schools were opened in all Taluks, and in 1889 grant-in-aid was given to private schools which attracted private agencies to start educational institutions[35].

After the fall of Tipu Sultan (1792), Malabar slipped into the hands of East India Company by the treaty of Srirangapatnam (18 March 1792)[36]. For years that followed Malabar remained a part of the Bombay Presidency and by and by it became a part of the Madras Presidency in which it remained till the birth of independence in 1947. It was ruled by the English till India attained independence in 1947. But the spread of education and the growth of literacy were at a low pace when compared to the other two Princely States of Kerala. The enactment of the Madras Local Boards Act of 1834 gave an impetus in the field of education[37], They has started many schools in different parts of Malabar. The Government provided liberal grant-in-aid to those private agencies and missionaries who were ready to start schools consequent on the acceptance of the principle of free education[38]. Five Municipalities were opened in Malabar under the Town Implementation Act of 1865. These Municipalities and District Boards encouraged and administered the educational affairs of Malabar[39].

In 1855, all kinds of slavery was abolished in Travancore and education was opened to backward classes too[40]. Missionaries of Kerala, and the Government of Travancore took keen interest to educate people of backward classes. After 1856 the Travancore Government showed much interest in improving the vernacular education of the State. As a result of this, the number of vernacular educational institutions increased in Travancore and the Travancore Educational Rule was drawn up in 1894 and it was issued for grant-in-aid[41]. In 1866 the Raja's Free School (as the name indicates the levy of fee was not insisted on) of Trivandrum was raised to the status of a colleges[42]. An important change was made in the year by the abolition of the system of free education and compulsory levying of fees. However, in 1904 the Government of Travancore accepted the responsibility of providing free primary education irrespective of caste, creed or race[43].

Non-formal education also had its modest beginning in Kerala by that time. Night schools were opened in different parts of the country. The proper hailing from various walks of life like the labourers, coolies, traders, merchants, people of backward classes and artisans took to adult educational facilities available.

Table 1. Literates in thousands

Political Units	*Males*	*Females*
Cochin	324	45
Travancore	215	31
Malabar	89	63

Along with the increase in the number of night schools, the number of illiterate people receiving instruction also increased[44]. Till the development of library movement, it played an important role in the development of literacy. Later on, night schools were replaced by libraries and reading rooms as agencies of social education[45]. The literacy rate in the three political units of Kerala in 1911 was as follows[46].When literacy increased, the reading habit of the people also increased. The growth of reading habit helped the birthof libraries in different parts of the state. Along with the spread of education and literacy the vernacular press and its publications too began to make headway. Journals and periodicals in Malayalam were first started by the Missionaries and in most cases, they were for proselytisation purpose. *Rajya Samachara* (1847) published from Tellichery was the first printed news paper in Malayalam language[47]. Paschimodayam (1847) and *Jananishapam* (1848) are the other early Malayalam newspapers published from Tellicherri and Kottayam respectively[48]. The *Malayali* (1866) published from Trivandrum, *Nazarani-Deepika* (1887) and *Malayala Manorama* (1888) from Kottayam, *Swadeshabhimani* (1905) from Trivandrum and Mitavadi (1907) from Tellicherry are the other important newspapers[49].

In Travancore, some of the newspapers criticized the wrong policies of the authorities[50]. As a result of such criticism of Royal Proclamation was issued on September 1910 by which the *Swadeshabhimani* Press was confiscated and the editor of the daily, K. Ramakrishna Pillai, was sentenced to be exiled for life[51]. The other dailies like *Mitavadi* (1907) and *Kerala Kaumudi* (1911) stood for social reforms and development of backward classes[52]. All these newspapers caught the attention of the literate as well as illiterate. They found it necessary to meet at a common place for reading, hearing and discussing items appeared in the newspapers. They thought that library and reading rooms would be the proper places for this purpose.

The nineteenth century saw the beginning of a cultural renaissance in Kerala. The desire for basic change was reflected in the field of culture[53]. The rulers of Travancore and Cochin undertook several cultural pursuits. The Malayalam literature reached its highest peak during this time. The spurt was noticeable in its variety. They were not merely translations of weak adaptations or imitations of some Sanskrit works, but genuine and original[54]. The style and technique of writing of these classical works attracted the vast majority of reading public. Some writers concentrated on social evils which prevailed in Kerala

Society. The situation goaded the ordinary people to think on the line of centres of reading where these works could be made use of.

The upsurge in the field of literature culminated in an upheaval in the social life of Kerala[55]. In the caste dominated feudalistic society of Kerala, institutions like Joint Family, Polyandry and *Marumakkathayam*[56] were peculiar. The low caste people who constituted the bulk of the population, were denied almost all the rights which were enjoyed by the high caste[57]. Though slavery was abolished in Trivandrum a large number of slaves were condemned to agrestic slavery in the state, with the result they could be brought and sold like cattle by the land owning classes[58]. The codes of untouchability and unapproachability were observed in an irrational manner. The caste tyranny created havoc in the Kerala Society till the end of the nineteenth century. As a result of the spread of modern education, and when the rulers underwent moderation, changes had begun to be seen in Kerala society[59]. The missionaries offered opportunities to the depressed classes for their upbringing. The educational activities of the missionaries rapidly advanced the social conditions of the backward classes[60]. It gave them hope and aspirations of a better living.

The slumbering depressed communities gradually woke up the their own organisations, educational institutions, temples, libraries and industries[61]. Popular socio-religious reform movements of the depressed communities in Kerala played a vital role in the social transformation of Kerala. Social reform movements led by Chattampi Swamikal (1853-1934), Srinarayana Guru (1854-1928), Ayyankali (1861-1941), Vaghadananda (1885-1940) and A. Ayyappan (1889-1968) helped the people of Kerala to taste the sweetness of modern development[62].

Srinarayana Guru was the most outstanding social reformer in Kerala. His active campaign was in favour of socio-economic and educational advancement of the Ezhava Community, which constituted a dominant section in Kerala society. He was strongly opposed to caste system, primitive religious practices and traditional social systems. He was an advocate of formal schooling as well as informal education. He advised the teachers of his community to build libraries and cultural societies in every village which could enlarge the educational horizon[63]. In course of time he founded several temples, educational institutions, industrial enterprises and libraries[64].

Chattampi Swamikal, another important social reformer, raised his voice against the existing social order in which the Brahmins had superiority over the members of the depressed castes. He also gave incentive to start educational institutions and libraries for the social development. He selected for his *Samadhi* the C.P.P. Library at Panmana near Quilon[65]. The other social reformers of Kerala also gave encouragement for starting educational institutions and libraries. They found that social changes can be brought out through these institutions. Due to the interest evinced by these pioneer social reformers schools and libraries were established all over Kerala[66]. It was this trend that ultimately brought Kerala in the forefront of education, outstanding all other states. These social reformists accepted library as an important social institution and it not only enriched the knowledge of the people but also acted as a nucleus for promoting social reform movements.

Literary renaissance coincided with social renaissance and both were instrumental for the growth of political consciousness in Kerala[67]. The first manifestation of political consciousness was the submission of a mammoth petition "Travancore Memorial ' signed b y 19,308 people to Maharaja Sri Moolam Thirunal on 18 June 1891. It gave vent to the pent-up feelings of dependency, indignation and disappointment of the non- Brahmin subjects of the Maharaja due to the denial of the right of employment under the State service[68]. The Memorial claimed to express the grievance of all *Malayalies* eventhough it was not so. However, what is relevant is that a section of the people had become conscious of their political right, and for its enjoyment they were prepared to move to the path of open protest and agitation [69] . The incentive behind this, it must be said, was certainly the education they got and the enlightenment they attained.

In order to prepare an 'Explanatory Memorial' and select a six member deputation to discuss the memorandum with the Maharaja a meeting was held. The petitioners preferred Kottayam Public Library (1882) as the venue of the meeting. The memorializes held the view that the 'Travancore Memorial' had the representation of all the subjects of the Maharaja and as such the venue chosen must be suitable for the participation of all[70]. On 3 July 1891 a big crowd had assembled in the Library to discuss the 'Travancore Memorial' and select delegates[71]. Thus the library got the rare opportunity to witness the matters of 'Travancore Memorial'. It was the first direct constitutional protest of the people against discriminatory rule[72].

The spurt in learning naturally led to the formation of a number of public libraries in various parts of Travancore. In this connection reference can be made of Sugunaposhni Library at Vanchiyoor in Trivandrum (1884), Janapradayani Library at Neyyattinkara, Munthankara Sankaravilasom Library at Chengannoor (1913), Y.M.C.A Library at Kizhakara (1913), Sree Chitra Thirunal Library at Trivandrum (1914), Raja Raja Library at Oachira, Lalithavilasom Library at Padmanabhapuram (1916) and the two rural Library at Oachira, Lalithavilasom Library at Mavelikkara (1916) and the two rural libraries at Elenial and Thodupuzha (1917 [73]. Sugunaposhini Library which started with a collection of Malayalam books during the reign of Visakam Thirunal (A.D 1880-85) in 1884 was a unique one. It was the first rural library in Travancore and the collections were mainly in Malayalam. But it functioned only for two years[74].

In addition to the above libraries, another library, namely, Ernakulam Public Library was founded on 1 January 1870, in a small thatched shed, which originally a part of the high school behind the present building of the Maharaja's College. The stalwarts who helped the growth of the library in its rudimentary states include A.F. Sealy, the Head of the Education Department, Cochin State, Lock, the Chief Judge, Cochin Chief Court, Thomas Manjooran, Chief Justice, Court of Cochin and M. P. Padmanabha Menon[75].

The other important Public Library in Cochin State was Trichur Public Library formed in 1873[76]. After the formation of this Library Irinjalakuda Victoria Jubilee Library and Reading Room started functioning. In 1889 many new institutions came into existence in Cochin and this was one among them. H.M. Appadura was mainly responsible for the formation of this library[77]. Following this Cherai Public Library (1914), Kodungaloor Public Library (1912) and Yogaskshema Library and Reading Room (1915) also began to function[78]. Some of these libraries were started by different caste organisations as part of their social reform movements. The Arayas (Hindu fisherman) of Kerala formed an Association in 1908 for their social and educational development. They started a library called Vinjana Sandayani Library at Cheriyazhikkal as part of their social development programme. Though the Sanghom disappeared after two years of library survived and is still in existence[79].

The Tellichery Public Library, formed in 1901 was the earliest of public libraries in Malabar[80]. Two more libraries founded later were the Rural Library at Engandiyoor (1914), the Sreenarayan Vilasom Library and Reading Room at Panagode (1919)[81]. The social reformer Vaghbadanandan and his *Athmavidhya Sanghom* had also started many rural libraries during that period[82]. The organizers of these libraries were educated young men with some literary talents.

It is noteworthy that the progressive socio-cultural movements and the political awareness attained by the people resulted in the starting of new libraries in different parts of Kerala by the end of nineteenth century. The libraries in the schools and colleges were actually incentives to the students to work for the formation of public libraries , when they came out of those institutions, after completing their studies[83].

When the libraries sprang up in different parts of Kerala, the rulers began to look upon them as inevitable social institutions. For instance, applications for grant to libraries and Reading Rooms were invited by the Assistant Inspector of Vernacular Schools of Travancore in 1917[84]. Accordingly thirty seven well-organised reading rooms and libraries were entitled to receive grant-in-aid during 1917-18[85]. Krishnavilasom Mahila Vayanasala, functioned during that period at Balaramapuram, Trivandrum was exclusively for the women folk. This library too received grant from the Government[86].

The first proceeding regarding the libraries of Travancore was issued on 23 September 1917[87]. As per the proceeding a library means a collection of books that may be issued to persons for reading. Reading room means, in addition to all that is included by 'library', the existence of a room in the premises in which a person may, read.' Such libraries and reading rooms were the repositories of current books and newspapers. It was not essential that such reading rooms should possess news papers[88]. This order had also put down certain conditions for getting grants from the government [89].

Though the libraries sprang up profusely, some of them were short- lived. This was mainly due to the uninterested of the public and the lack of educated men and in sufficient literature in mother tongue.

In the meantime an All Travancore Library Workers' meeting (the first ever Library Conference in the State) – was held at Neyyattinkara under the Chairmanship of C.V. chandrasekharan in 1101 M.E. (1925- 26). Neyyattinkara Jnanapradayani Library was mainly responsible for this meeting which helped to project the seriousness and importance of the public libraries[90]. It gave an opportunity to the library workers to exchange their ideas about the functioning and prospect of this movement. The meeting passed the following resolutions[91]:

1. Grant to libraries may be fixed to a minimum of Rs. 100- and maximum of Rs. 500/-
2. Sites for the libraries may be granted freely.
3. All Government publications should be supplied to library freely.
4. Rules of affiliation to the Public Library, Trivandrum may be revised.
5. An Officer for libraries may be appointed to inspect all libraries.

As a result of this, library grant was raised to a maximum of Rs. 200/- Government publications were freely supplied to Libraries. Library building materials and furniture were granted as per the Travancore Educational Code to the public libraries of Travancore. The Government had also decided not to establish a particular library department or an officer, but instead an Inspector of Vernacular Schools to look after the affairs of the State libraries An Assistant Inspector of English Schools was put charge of the libraries from the beginning of 1928[92].

The political and social developments in Kerala as mentioned earlier, had been primarily responsible for the growth of libraries. The period between the partition of Bengal and the outbreak of the First World War (1904 - 1914) witnessed tremendous changes in the political chess board of India[93]. On 4 May 1916 Malabar District Congress meeting was held under the chairmanship of Annie Besant in Palghat. One of the important resolutions passed in the meeting was to establish autonomous panchayats which would have full freedom to establish schools and libraries in each village[94]. In other words the participants considered libraries as very powerful instrument for arousing political consciousness among the masses.

At that time, in Travancore, most of the politicians were actively engaged themselves in library works too. They made it a point to support and supplement all popular uprisings. Their support to the students strike of 1918-1921 in Travancore was conspicuous. Many library workers were arrested and one of the charges levelled against them was that they were actively involved in library activities[95].

The annual meeting of the Kerala Pradesh Congress Committee (K.P.C.C) was held at Ernakulam on 24 July 1924. The meeting decided to spread the ideas of Congress through libraries which would be set up by each village committee of the Congress party[96]. In 1927, along with the annual meeting of the Congress, a library movement[97]. These attempts helped the rise of new libraries in different parts of the State.

The *Atmavidya Sanghom* founded in 1920 by Vagbhadananda has been a major force of social change in Malabar. The cultural enlightenment created by the wiritings and speeches of Vagbhadanandan gave an inspiration to start many libraries after his name and by the Sanghom.

Pattiyam Gurudeva Vilasam Vayanasala, Azhikkode Sree Vagbhadanandan Gurudeva Grandhasala and Ernajipalam Desabandhu Library had their origin, from initiative taken by the Sanghom[98].

At the dawn of the twentieth century Malabar witnessed several conflicts between the rural people and the British authorities. A powerful expression of this conflict was the repeated uprisings of the Mappila peasantry against land lords and the colonialists[99]. The early uprisings were of isolated nature with limited participants, but subsequent uprisings gained momentum and it culminated in the massive show of 1921[100]. After the Mappila revolt of 1921, many individuals and voluntary organisations rendered their service for the rehabilitation of the people. Devadar Malabar Reconstruction Trust (DMRT) under the leadership of G.K. Devadar was one important voluntary organization of that kind. According to them, lack of education was mainly responsible for this revolt. In order to spread literacy, they started many libraries in the present Malappuram District[101].

Thus during this period the public libraries were started to function in almost all parts of the state, and they received the social recognition and recognition and political support as an integral part for the strength and capacity to lead the library movement for enhancing socio-cultural progress in the society.

Notes and References

1. P. Shungonny Menon, *History of Travancore from the Earlier Times*, Vol.I, New Delhi : Cosmo Publication;, reprint 1084, pp. 239, 252.
2. *Ibid.*, p. 218.
3. S. Ramanath Iyer, *Progressive Travancore*, Trivandrum : Anantharaman Press, 1923, p.125.

4. T.K. Velu Pillai, *The Travancore State Manual,* Vol. II, Trivandrum : Government of Travancore, 1940, p.501.
5. P. Shungonny Menon, No.1, Vol. II, p. 371.
6. *Ibid.*, p. 383.
7. Travancore, Maharani Parvathi Bai, Nittu, Trivandrum : Directorate of State Archives, 19 Edavam 992 M.E. [30-5-1817].
8. A. Sreedhara Menon, *Cultural Heritage of Kerala : An Introduction,* Cochin : East West Publication, 1978, p. 173.
9. M.J. Koshy, The History of the Growth of Legislature in Travancore and Cochin upto 1956, Unpublished Doctoral Thesis, Trivandrum : Kerala University, 1966, p. 31.
10. V. Nagam Aiya, *The Travancore State Manual,* Vol. II, Trivandrum : Travancore Government Press, 1906, p.447.
11. T.K. Velu Pillai, No.4, p. 545.
12. P. Shungonny Menon. No.1, Vol.II, p. 441.
13. Sooranad Kunjan Pillai, *Sree Swati Tirunal Rama Varma Maharajavu,* (Mal.), Trivandrum : Department of Cultural Publications, 1989, pp. 32-38.
14. V. Nagam Aiya, No.10, p. 448.
15. C.N. Viswanath, *An Introduction to Public Library Organization with Special Reference to India,* Bombay : Agricultural Publishing House, 1961, p. 4.
16. Edward Syalvey, *Delhi Public Library Project,* New Delhi : Ministry of Education, UNESCO Project, 1953, p. 65.
17. Pirapancode Murali, "Keralathile Grandhasala Prasthanam". *Grandhalokam,* Trivandrum, (Mal.), Special issue, September 1990, p. 50.
18. A. Sreedhara Menon, (ed.), *Kerala District Gazetteers : Vol.1, Trivandrum District,* Trivandrum : Government of Kerala, 1962, p. 690.
19. V.K.M. Menon, "Early years : From Darbaris to People, The Trivandrum Public Library". *Trivandrum Public Library Platinum Jubilee Souvenir,* Trivandrum : Government of Kerala, 1974, p. 15.

20. Travancore, Maharaja Swathi Thirunal, *Nittu,* Trivandrum: Directorate of State Archives, 5 Kanni 1012 M.E.[18-5-1836].
21. P.V. Vargheese, *Souvenir of the XXV All India Library Conference,* Trivandrum : Geo Printers, 1979, p.135.
22. Trivandrum Public Library, Minutes of Special General Meeting, 15 October 1854, Trivandrum : Public Library, pp.1-4.
23. V.K.M. Menon, No.19, p.15.
24. An Agreement between the *Sircar* of Travancore and the Subscribers of the Trivandrum Public Library, Trivandrum: Public Library, 1856, p.1.
25. V. Nagam Aiya, No.10. Vol.III, p. 530.
26. Kurian K. Thomas, *Trivandrum Public Library : Historical Perspective,* Kottayam : Archana Printers, 1987, p. 32.
27. V. Nagam Aiya, No.10, Vol.III, p. 530.
28. T.K. Velu Pillai, No.4, Vol.I, p.750.
29. V.K.M. Menon, No.19, pp.16-17.
30. P.V. Varghese, No.21, p.136.
31. The King of Mysore (1782-1792) who conquered Kerala.
32. C. Achutha Menon, *The Cochin State Manual,* Ernakulam : Cochin Government Press, 1911, p.132.
33. *Ibid.,* 291-292.
34. *Ibid.,* p. 291.
35. *Ibid.,* p. 292.
36. William Logan, *Malabar,* Vol.I, Trivandrum : Charithram Publication, Reprinted, 1981, p.534.
37. *Kerala State Administrative Report – 1957-58,* Trivandrum : Government Press, 1939, p.246.
38. *Ibid.,* p. 246.
39. C.A. Innes, and F.B. Evans, (ed.), *Madras District Gazeteers,* Madras : Government Press, 1951, pp.296-298.
40. V. Nagam Aiya, No.10, pp.481-82.
41. *Ibid.,* pp.457-459.
42. A. Sreedhara Menon, No.8, p.172.

43. *Government Proceedings*, Current No.E 115M, Trivandrum : Directorate of State Archives, 15 August 1904, p.1.
44. *Report of the Director of Public Instruction*, 1073 M.E. (1897-1898), Ernakulam : Cochin Government Press, 1898, p.8.
45. *Administrative Report, Education Department – 1120 M.E.* (1944-45), Ernakulam : Cochin Government Press, 1946, p.13.
46. C. Achutha Menon, No.32, p.296.
47. G. Priyadersan, *Pathrapravarthanam : Prarambha Swaroopam*, (Mal.), Trichur : Kerala Sahitya Academy, 1982, p.31.
48. *Ibid.*, p.31.
49. Government of Kerala, *The Press in Kerala*, Trivandrum : Department of Public Relations, 1977, p.14.
50. *Ibid.*, p.15.
51. Muhamed Kannu, *Vakkom Maulavi*, (Mal.), Biography, Kottayam, National Book Stall, 1981, p.45.
52. Government of Kerala, No.49, pp.14-15.
53. A. Sreedhara Menon, No.8, p.174.
54. E.M.S. Namboodiripad, *Kerala Society and Politics : A Historical Survey*, New Delhi : National Book, 1984, p.104.
55. T.K. Ravindran, *Asan and Social Revolution in Kerala : A Study of his Assembly Speeches*, Trivandrum : Kerala Historical Society, 1972, p.XVII
56. Matrilineal Inheritance.
57. A. Sreedhara Menon, No.8, p.186.
58. *Ibid.*, p.208.
59. L.A. Krishna Iyer, *Kerala and Her People*, Palghat : Educational and Supplies Depot, 1961, p.47.
60. V. Nagam Aiya, *Report of the Census of Travancore* – 1891, Vo.1, Madras : Addition & Co., 1894, pp.437-471.
61. P.K. Gopalakrishnan, *Keralathinte Samskarika Charithram*, (Mal.), Trivandrum : State institute of Languages, 1974, p.509.

62. K.K.N. kurup, *Modern Kerala : Studies in Social and Agrarian Relations,* Delhi : Mittal Publication, 1988, p. 93.
63. P.K. Balakrishnan, *Narayana Guru,* (Mal.), Kottayam : N.B.S., 1954, p. 161.
64. Jerald J. Pereira, *Narayana Guru : A Social education,* Varkala : R.R. Publishers, 1989, p.157.
65. M.K. Kumaran and T.Bhaskaran, (ed.), *Sree Narayana Yuga Prabhavam,* (Mal.), Varkala : Sree Narayana Guru Propagation Committee, 1978, p. 37.
66. P.K. Gopala Krishnan, No. 61, p. 518.
67. T.K. Ravindran, No. 55, p. XVII.
68. T.K. Ravindran, No. 55, p. LXXI.
69. Robin Jafferry, *The Decline of Nayar Dominance : Society and Politics in Travancore – 1847-1908,* New Delhi : Vikas Publishing House, 1976, p. 168.
70. John Pellishery, "Malayali Memoriyalum Librariyum", *Kottayam Public Library Souvenir,* Kottyam : Indian Press, 1967, p. 22.
71. "Kottayam Vayanasalayil Oru Janasanghom". *Malayala Manoram,* Kottatam, (Mal.) Daily, 3 June 1891.
72. T.K. Ravindran, No. 55, p. IXXI.
73. Kerala Grandhasala Sanghom, *Grandhasala Directory – 1964,* (Mal.), Trivandrum : Kerala Grandhasala Sanghom, 1964, pp. 351-378.
74. Akhila Thiruvithamcore Grandhasala Sanghom, *Grandhasala Manual,* (Mal.), (Trivandrum : Akhila Thiruvithamcore Grandhasala Sanghom, 1948), p. 72.
75. "Centenarian Library", *Indian Express,* (Cochin), 14 July 1990.
76. K. Sivadasan Pillai, (ed.), *Kerala Grandhasala Sanghom,* Trivandrum : Kerala Grandhasala Sanghom, 1981, p. 55.
77. C. Achutha Menon, "Mahatma Vayanasala", *Grandhalokam,* Trivandrum (Mal.), Special Issue, September 1990, p. 52.
78. Kerala Grandhasala Sanghom, No. 73.

79. P.S. Velayudan, (ed.), *Kerala Charithram,* (Mal.), Vol.I, (Cochin : Kerala History Association, 1973), p.1296.
80. K. Sivadasan Pillai, (ed.), No.76, p.2.
81. K.M. Lenin, "Aadyakala Sankatanakalum Grandhasalakalum" Keralathile Grandhasala Prasthanam, (Mal.), Trivandrum : Steps, 1982, p.23.
82. P. Udayabhanu, "Prasthanathinte Adiverukal", *Keralathile Grandhasala Prasthanam,* (ed.), Trivandrum : Steps, 1982, p.31.
83. *The Kerala Public Library Bill 1985 : Background materials,* Trivandrum : Secretariat of Kerala Legislature : 1986, p.13.
84. *Proceedings of Her Highness Maharani,* Regent of Travancore, G.O.No.E2157, Trivandrum dated 18 August 1917, Trivandrum : Directorate of State Archives, Kerala.
85. T.K. Velupillai, No.4, Vol.III, p.742.
86. Akhila Thiruvithamcore Grandhasala Sanghom, No.74, p.347.
87. *Travancore Gazette,* 23 September 1917, Trivandrum : Directorate of State Archives, Kerala.
88. *Ibid.*
89. I. (1). They shall be under the management of a Committee and Office Bearers to approved by the Director; (2) They shall be freely opened to the public for purposes of reference; (3) They shall be entirely undenominational; (4) The rent of the library and reading room should be approved by the Director; (5) Each library and reading room shall contain a minimum of 200 approved books; (6) The minimum guaranteed annual income from subscription should not be less than Rs.40/- II. Separate buildings are necessary to accommodate libraries and reading rooms. Each library and reading room shall possess complete registers and records. The concerned Assistant Educational Officer should be allowed to verify them. III. Books and periodicals vetoed by the Director shall not find a place in any library or reading room aided by Government.

90. English Records, File No.149/29 Edn. 28 January 1929, Trivandrum : Directorate of State Archives, Kerala, p.76.
91. *Ibid.*
92. *Ibid.*, pp.76-78.
93. E.M.S. Namboodiripad, No.54, p.106.
94. A.K. Pillai, *Congressum Keralaum,* (Mal.), Trivandrum : Kerala State Congress Committee, 1982, p.16.
95. Sree Chithira Thirunal Library, *Sree Chithira Thirunal Grandhasala Golden Jubilee Souvenir - 1966,* (Mal.), Trivandrum : Sree Chithira Thirunal Grandhasala, 1966, p.32.
96. A.K. Pillai, No.94.
97. P.K. Narayana Pillai, "Grandhasala Prasthanam Annum Innum". *Grandhalokam,* Trivandrum, (Mal.), Vol.4(1), 1952, p.16.
98. P. Udayabhanu, No.82, p.31.
99. K.N. Panicker, *Against Lord and State : Religion and Peasant Uprising in Malabar – 1836-1921*, (Delhi : Oxford University, 1989), p.IX.
100. *Ibid.*, p.IX.
101. *P.* Udayabhanu, No.82, p.32.

3

Spread of Library Movement and Socio-political Developments

The Cochin Government has as a part of their adult education programme, established rural libraries in different parts of the State as an experimental measure since 1926[1]. In the following years, the number of libraries increased. They were directly under the control of Minister of Village Development, who was elected by the people on the basis of adult franchise. In the Fourth All India Library Conference held at Madras during December 1927, representative from the State had participated. Prominent Malayalies like K.C. Chacko, Ambat Sivarama Menon and Chenkulath Gopala Menon were included in the meeting of the Library Committee. They later inspired and encouraged the growth of library movement in Malabar and Cochin States[2]. Ambat Sivarama Menon was one of the first elected Ministers of Cochin State who made significant contributions to the development of library movements in this area. *Village Sevak Sanghom* (Village Service Society) was formed during that period for the development of the villages. As a part of their programme they also started many libraries in Cochin area[3].

At that time, a literary organisation named *Samastha Kerala Sahitya Parishath* (1927) was formed by the writers of Kerala, at Cochin. Ever since, it has been contributing for the development of Malayalam language and literature. It also made its own contributions for the growth of library movement; and in later periods, the annual meetings of both the library and this literary organisation were held together[4].

After the civil-disobedience movement (1931), the library movement gathered momentum in Kerala. The youth, who came out of jails, decided to strengthen the freedom movement by organising the agriculturists and labourers. They were the leftists in the Congress Party, and later, they formed a socialist group in the party itself. The pioneers of them were P. Krishna Pillai, E.M.S. Namboodiripad, A.K. Gopalan, K.P.R. Gopalan and K.A. Keraleeyan who opened a number of libraries in different parts of Malabar[5]. Most of these leaders were workers of library movement in the 1930's and later they became prominent leaders of the Communist Party of India[6]. In those days libraries received one or two newspapers and somebody would read it aloud and others, especially illiterates, listened to it . Most of the people gathered in reading room, leaders would comment on the news in the newspapers. Doubts would be raised and cleared, it would sometimes lead to political discussions[7]. These libraries attracted labourers, agriculturists and educated men. They used these institutions as centres for the social and political activities of that place[8].

The visit of S.R. Ranganathan, the great Library Scientist of India and President of Indian Library Association, gave inspiration to the people of Malabar for starting new libraries. He made appealing speeches in Palghat in September 1930[9]. Likewise the arrival of Ambat Sivarama Menon to Malabar on first June 1931 gave encouragement to the Library Movement in Tellicherry, Calicut, Tirur Palghat and many other places, and gave shape to many programmes regulating the development of libraries[10].

As a result of this, the idea of library movement began to spread in every nook and corner of Malabar. The leftists in the Indian National Congress had started a new library called Sree Harshan Library at Mangattu in Kannur District, and libraries were also set up at Bakkalam, Parassinikkadavu, Anchampeedika, Keecheri, Kolencheri, Karivalloor, Ellarani, Blathoor, Kalliyad, Vadakara, Tellicherry, Mattannur, Eranjoli and other places. The pioneers behind this were kundajerry Kunjuraman, M.K. Kelu, Sugreevan Kunjuraman, K.A. Keraleeyan and so on[11]. These libraries were great centres of political, social and cultural activities in Northern Malabar. Under the auspices of Sree Harshan Library, a manuscript magazine called 'Sree Harshan' was published during that period. E.K. Nayanar, the former Chief Minister of Kerala (1980-82, 1987-91,1996-2001), used to contribute poems and articles to this journal. He writes: "many who read the Sree Harshan journal in Kalliasserry had predicted a bright future for me. I have worked as writer and editor in my life"[12]. These libraries started adult education programmes and night classes[13]. They also helped to spread the spirit of nationalism among the people[14]. But the library workers received severe opposition from the landlords who feared that they were organizing the labourers and educated men to voice their rights[15].

It was in 1931 that library movement got a firm footing in North Kerala. In March 1931 an all Kerala library committee was formed with Trichur as Head Quarters. Subsequently, an all Kerala Library Meet was held at Trichur and formed the *Samastha Kerala Pusthakalaya Samithy*. Chenkulath Cheirya Kunjuraman, a social worker was mainly responsible for this[16]. This meeting decided to do the following activities for the development of library movement[17]:

1. The Council will give publicity to 6000 villages of Kerala for establishing libraries in each village.
2. It will convince its importance to the Government, local bodies and rich people of the society.
3. A committee shall be formed to select books and periodicals from the Publishers for the libraries.
4. Different publishers may be summoned to one place and arrangements made to purchase books by the libraries.
5. Publicity shall be given for starting new libraries and family libraries.
6. A new book depot on the name of University shall be opened.
7. It was decided to form a branch of this council in Trivandrum and Calicut.

This Samithi also started a quarterly called *'Grandha Vijar'* (April 1931) for propagating the ideas of library movement[18]. But the Samithi could not continue to function due to the non-cooperation of the people[19]. In the meantime another professional association called All Travancore Library Association was formed in Travancore in 1933 under the initiation of Malloor Govinda Pillai. It also disappeared very soon without making any significant contribution to this field[20].

In Travancore, the years after 1930 was periods of political awakening, when the under represented throughout life, company and companionship with good book"[27].

The Second Library Conference was held at Trivandrum under the auspices of Sree Chithira Tirunal Library on 25 July 1934. The conference was presided over by P.K. Narayana Pillai, one of the great literary men of Travancore and inaugurated by Sir C.P Ramaswamy Iyer,[28] the Constitutional Adviser to the Maharaja, who later became the Dewan of Travancore. They highly appreciated, the movement and passed the following resolutions:[29]

1. To start more libraries throughout the state as a part of library movement .
2. To increase the grant-in-aid of the libraries.
3. To supply the Government publications to all libraries.
4. To request the Government to supply, the library furniture free of cost, and to meet the expenses of the library (expenses incurred by its setting up and the purchase of land for the purpose).

This meeting proposed a Library Bill and sent it to the Government for legislation. It also laid the foundation for the formation of *Akhila Thiruvithamcore Grandhasala Sanghom* in 1945 which has spearheaded the library movement in Kerala since its formation[30].

The Travancore Government chalked out many new schemes and programmes regarding the library movement during this time. In the light of the report of the Travancore Education Reforms Committee (1932) under the Chairmanship of K.M. Statham, the Director of Public Instructions presented a scheme in 1110 M.E. (1935) for the establishment of a central circulating library and a large number of rural libraries [31]. He also recommended the setting up of public libraries along with village schools and use of Motor Vans for resource sharing from the central library.

The government approved the proposals of the Director of Public Instructions and decided to open rural libraries attached to the department primary schools in 15 centers with one in every division[32].

Another very important recommendation of the Director of Public Instructions was the establishment of the State Library System and the legislation for the setting up a large number of libraries and local library authorities[33]. The government considered the steps to be taken to develop and expand library movement in the State with a view to prevent neo-literates from relapsing into illiteracy and provide facilities for adult education. "Necessary funds were to be provided by the Director of Public Instructions, and rural library section attached to schools would be started. Arrangements should be made for the transfer of excess books and old magazines from the public library to the rural library. The government did not deem it necessary to have any legislation in connection with the library movement."[34]. These steps of the Government were severely criticised by the public. The leading Malayalam news paper Kesari wrote that the rulers of Travancore have no idea about the basic principles of library movement. A library legislation, an imposition of library cess and establishment of library department, are inevitable for the development of library movement[35].

Travancore had the lead in establishing public libraries which proved to be an aid to education. But the proposal for establishing a library department, and for making a network of well-equipped and well-supervised library system in the state was delayed. However on 6 March 1935, Muhammed Habeebulla, the Dewan, forwarded a draft letter to His Highness for the reorganisation of Trivandrum Public Library and the establishment of State Library System[36].

In the meantime, Travancore Government took more enthusiasm in the development of rural libraries. In 1934,

37 rural libraries received grants from the Travancore Government. The grant received in the previous years was as follows:[37]

Table 2. Rural Libraries and Grants

Year	*Number of Rural Libraries*	*Total Sum Distributed*
1106 M.E / 1931 A.D.	33	Rs. 2,655/-
1107 M.E / 1932 A.D.	28	Rs. 2,594/-
1108 M.E / 1933 A.D.	30	Rs. 2,673/-

In 1936 a Rural Library System was introduced to develop and extend library movement in the state and to promote adult education (See Appendix-B)[38]. In the same year, 60 libraries were started among which 57 were Malayalam libraries and remaining were Tamil libraries. An allotment of Rs. 100/- was made for each library for furniture[39]. The Headmasters of Primary Schools acted as honourary secretary of libraries and they were assisted by a local committee consisting of three members. Each library, Secretary received Rs. 3/- as remuneration. A set of 200 books was purchased and supplied to each library. Besides this, 4700 books were distributed by Text Book Committee free of cost. A daily newspaper and a magazine were also supplied to each library. The movement was duly appreciated by the local people[40].

The Third Library Conference was held at Neyoor under the auspices of Dewan Nanu Pillai Memorial Library in 1111 M.E. (1936). Malloor Govinda Pillai, one of the leading advocates of Travancore, presided over the meeting. After this meeting, the people and the Government began to evince more interest towards the library movement[41].

The libraries expanded their nature of functioning during this time. They began to act as institutions of social service in each village. Many social service programmes like night classes, literary associations for discussions, public activities and sanitation works were conducted by the libraries. These programmes greatly attracted people to the libraries[42].

At that time certain libraries with specific aims and objectives were organized in Malabar. Among these the important were the Sanmargha Darshini Library (1929), (which aimed at the promotion of good morality) Aikya Kerala Grandhasala (1934), (which stood for the creation of a United Kerala), Chowa Thozhilali Library (1934), (which was for the cultural and social elevation of labourers and peasants), and Deshaposhini Library (1936) and Sen Gupta Library (1937) (primarily which stood for promoting national integration)[43]. These libraries spread the noble ideas for which they stood.

The first peasant organization of Kerala called Kolacherry Karshaka Sanghom (Kolacherry Kisan Union) was formed in July 1935 at Thalipparambu in North Malabar with V.M. Vizhnu Bharatheeyan as President and K.A. Keraleeyan as Secretary[44]. In order to expose the socio-economic grievances of the peasants, Sree Harshan Library Workers staged a drama written by K.Damodaran, "Pattabaki",in different parts of Malabar. Sree Harshan Library workers were mainly responsible for the formation of this Kisan Union and drama troop. The union expanded its area of work throughout Malabar by 1937 and formed Akhila Malabar Kisan Sanghom which succeeded in organizing peasant revolts in Kerala which awakened the whole of India [45]. The union organized a number of libraries in different parts of Malabar and conduced night classes for peasants and labourers in order to eradicate illiteracy and superstitious belief. In most of these places, the libraries were centres of peasant and labour movements[46].

Likewise in South Malabar, a number of new libraries sprang up for which P.C. Raghavan Nair, P.V. Kunjiknnan Nair and E.P. Gopalan were mainly responsible[47].

Though several libraries sprang up in the rural areas of the state they were short lived. Inspite of there being enough library workers, financial problems and non-cooperation of the public, were the real reasons for the ill fate of the institutions. In order to overcome these difficulties, a meeting of library workers was convened under the leadership of K. Damodaran, a veteran communist leader, at Tirur Grama Bandhu Library on 20 April 1937. It decided to conduct a big library meeting at Calicut in May 1937 with the participation of two members each from the library of Malabar area[48]. A Committee consisting of K. Damodaran as Secretary, Mathuravanam Krishna Kurup as Chairman and Ravi Varma Raja, V. Sankaran Nair and Mukundan Kartha as members was also formed for the future course of actions[49]. Accordingly, a large meeting of the representatives of library workers was held at Calicut and a reception committee was formed for Malabar Vayanasala Conference, (Malabar Library Conference), that was to be held on 11 July 1937. The following were the Committee members:[50]

1. Mathuravanam Krishna Kurup (Chairman)
2. K. Damodaran (Secretary)
3. E.P. Chathu (Joint Secretary)
4. A. Balagopal (Treasurer)
5. C.K. Ravi Varma Raja
6. V. Sankaran Nair
7. A. Damodaran
8. Mukundan Kartha

9. P.T. Eradi
10. N.C. Shekharan
11. P.T. Narayan Nair
12. T. Appu
13. P. Gopalan
14. K. Achuthan Nair

The conference was held at Calicut and it led to the formation of the Malabar Vayanasala Sanghom (Malabar Library Association)[51]. The meeting was presided over by K. Kelappan, a prominent freedom fighter, and attended by more than three hundred delegates representing different libraries of Malabar. K. Kelappan said in his presidential address that the role and responsibility of library was greater than formal educational institutions and that this movement should work for the eradication of illiteracy among the people and increase the awareness of the people about foreign countries[52]. The following resolutions were passed in the meeting[53]:

1. To form an All Malabar Library Association.
2. To form a Committee to carry out the functions of the Association.
3. To send a message to Kerala Pradesh Congress Committee for forming libraries in each elementary unit of the Congress Party.
4. To request the Malabar Municipal Council and District Board to form a Central Circulating Library by uniting all the libraries run by these local bodies.
5. To request the authorities of both the elementary schools and the higher elementary schools of Malabar to start libraries along with schools.

After the general meeting of the library workers. E. Raman Menon (President), Mathuravanam Krishna Kurup (Vice-President) K. Damodaran (Secretary), P.T. Narayanan

(Joint Secretary), A. Balagopal (Treasurer) were elected as office bearers of the Malabar Vayanasala Sanghom[54]. They were political activists and freedom fighters. In the first meeting of the office bearers of the Sanghom, it was decided to form a constitution for this organization and open an office at Calicut Oriental Engineering works building[55].

In Cochin, though libraries were mainly established under the departments of education and local administration, it received enough support only after 1938, when the new administrative reforms were introduced as per the Cochin Act of 1938. According to this Act, Ambat Sivarama Menon, a prominent leader and member of the Legislative Assembly of Cochin was elected as the Minister of Village Department. He was in-charge of Library Department as well and gave all kinds of support for the development of library movement[56].

Sivarama Menon was succeeded by A.R. Menon as the Minister who also agreed in principle to establish libraries and reading rooms in all villages[57]. Night schools and libraries were the principal models employed in the field of adult education.[58] Trained teachers in the filed of agriculture gave instructions through libraries to the public on improved scientific methods of cultivation[59]. Though Cochin Government's attitude towards library movement was appreciable, the amount spent for this movement was very small. They gave Rs. 50/- per year for purchasing books and Rs. 25/- for other purposes for each library. The libraries were inspected once a year along with school inspection. However, there was no satisfactory improvement in this movement[60]. The total number of public libraries and rural libraries were 15 and 23 respectively in 1938. Besides this there were Princes Libraries, Jail Libraries, libraries attached to colleges, and a mobile library. The amount spent on all the libraries together was Rs. 6,354/-[61]. A.R. Menon established 272 rural libraries throughout the Cochin State[62]. In 1943, 10 public libraries and 163 Rural libraries received grant from the State[63].

During this period, Kerala witnessed great socio-political developments. In addition to the social reforms mentioned earlier, the caste organizations and political parties like the *Sri. Narayana Dharma Paripalana Sanghom* (1903), *Yoga Kshema Sabha* (1908), *Nair Service Society* (1914), and the Indian National Congress and its regional leaders led the campaign for eradication of untouchability and other social evils prevailed in the Society[64]. These caste organisations declared war against some of the outdated social practices and pleaded the people to switch over to the track of modernism.

The major events in the agitation against untouchability were the *Vaikom Sathyagraha* (1924-25) and *Guruvayur Sathyagrayha (*1931-32)[65]. It attracted all India attention, and Mahatma Gandhi, the unquestionable leader of the National Movement, got involved in both. On 12 November 1936, the Maharaja of Travancore Sri. Chithira Tirunal Balarama Varma issued his historic proclamation throwing open temples in Travancore to all Hindus irrespective of caste[66].

Simultaneously, a series of Social Regulation Acts like Nair Regulation Act of 1925, Cochin Nair Act of 1937- 38 and Mappila Marumakkathayam Act of 1933 passed by the respective Government of Travancore, Cochin and Madras, broke the old Joint Family system and allowed the partition of Joint Family (Tharavad) property and legalised the inheritance from father to son, instead of uncle to nephew [67].

Likewise, the land reforms introduced in Kerala paved the way for a new socio-economic order during that time. The amendments of Janmi Kudiyan Regulation of 1932 by

Travancore Government had given full property rights to Kudiyans (tenants) subjected to the payment of Janmi Karam (Lord's rent)[68]. The Tenancy Act of 1915 and the Cochin Tenancy Act of 1938 granted fixity of tenure and imposed restrictions on eviction of tenants. The Madras Tenancy Act of 1930 provided security of tenure and enabled aggrieved parties to approach the Courts of Law for fixation of their fair rent[69]. The working class became more conscious of their rights and duties, and they formed their own unions for collective bargaining. The working class of Alleppey took the lead in this front and they organized a labour union on 31 March 1922[70]. During 1934 and 1935 a series of industrial strikes took place at Cannanore, Calicut Feroke, Trichur, Cochin and Alleppey respectively. As a result, the working class of Kerala got itself organized as a class[71].

The political atmosphere of Kerala also underwent changes at that time. By 1935, the left wing had gained predominance over the moderates and the rightists in the K.P.C.C. The leftists scored this upperhand over the rightists mainly owing to their public service, like conducting night classes, establishing libraries and organising labourers and peasants[72]. The first Conference of the All Kerala Trade Union Congress was held at Calicut on May 1935; which coincided with the formation of the Congress Socialist Party[73]. Meanwhile a secret meeting of the Communist Party of India was held at Calicut, where E.M.S Namboodiripad, P. Krishna Pillai, N.C. Shekhar, K. Damodaran and S.V. Ghate were present[74].

Apart from trade unions and kisan unions, unions for teachers and students were also formed by the middle of 1937[75]. The Malabar Aided Teachers' union helped the spread of library movement and owing to its initiation many libraries were formed[76]. Likewise the trade unions of Kerala took keen interest to spread literacy and social education among the labourers of Kerala. They conducted many libraries and night schools in different parts of the State. It was highly beneficial to their socio-cultural developments[77].

As per the Government of India Act of 1935 the Provincial Government was formed in Madras on 14 July 1937 under C. Rajagopalachari. Kongattil Raman Menon was the representative of the Malabar region in the Ministry. Likewise, on the election to the Malabar District Board (a local administrative unit), K. Kelappan was unanimously elected[78].

Meanwhile in Travancore, the Travancore State Congress was formed in February 1938 and declared that its object was the attainment of responsible government on the basis of adult franchise. The Dewan of Travancre, Sir C.P. Ramaswamy Iyer, adopted a policy of unprecedented repression towards the State Congree workers[79]. In 1939, a secret meeting of the Communist Party of India was held at Pinarai Vivekananda Libarary at Cannanore and resolved to come out into the open, and function in Kerala. It was also decided to convert the entire socialist group in the Congress Socialist Party to the Communist Party[80]. Thus one of the libraries of Malabar got a unique opportunity of witnessing the formation of the Kerala Unit of the Communist Party of India. Along with the formation of the Communist Party a number of new libraries were opened in Malabar area, and both celebrated their Golden Jubilee in 1989[81].

When the Second World War broke out in 1939, Indian National Congress decided to non-cooperate with the British Government in India and to start Individual Satyagraha. The Kerala unit of the Congress Party was also pleased by this decision and observed on 15 September 1939 as anti-imperialist day[82]. This was followed by a series of police firings and conflicts between police and activists of the

Communist Party in different parts of Malabar. Many people were killed and most of the leaders of the Congress and the Communist Parties were arrested. Certain public buildings and libraries were destroyed by the police. People even, feared to look at the place where once the libraries stood[83]. The authorities and police viewed the libraries as centres of propaganda of socialist and communist ideas. Soon the Communist Party was banned and the ban continued till the time of Quit India struggle in 1942[84].

In Cochin, though dual Government was introduced in 1938, people were not satisfied with this. On 26 January 1941 a political organization called Cochi Rajya Praja Mandalam was formed and it demanded responsible Government on the basis of adult franchise[85]. They had continued their agitation in order to achieve their final goal. During the time of Quit India Movement (1942), many political leaders and workers were arrested and tortured. At that time some of them went underground at certain places where they were provided with much reading materials. These secret places were later converted into public libraries. As a part of the anti-imperialistic movement many reading rooms were also opened at Malabar which later developed into good libraries of the State[86]. Further, when the national movement was in high peak, some young men met secretly at different places, where they read books and periodicals and conducted discussions on it. Later on it were developed into Young Men's Associations and Social Libraries at various places.

The literature of that time reflects the best thoughts and emotions of the people. The writers who influenced and led national movement were eager to break the shackles of traditions and establish a new order of society[88]. They were called progressive writers who formed the Progressive Literacy Union in 1944. They were ardent supporters of the library movement and whose works were made available in the libraries and reading rooms. The young generation read such materials and their influence began to act upon the society of Kerala[89].

The educational policy of the State, particularly in Trivandrum and Cochin, began to make giant leaps. The Dewan of Travancore, Sir C.P. Ramaswamy Iyer, substantially contributed towards the development of primary and higher education that led to the formation of Travancore University in 1937[90]. He had certain original ideas on educational innovations, which finally resulted in placing Travancore in the forefront among all native states and British India. With his initiation Travancore Government, the Dewan took measures for the speedy implementation of free and compulsory education in the State[91]. He also gave importance to the non-formal educational institutions like library and reading rooms. To mark his *Shashtiabtapurthi* (reaching the age of sixty) three libraries and two reading rooms were opened to the public[92].

Kerala also witnessed remarkable industrial growth during this time. On 17 August 1925, the Travancore Rubber Factory was opened at Trivandrum. Besides, in 1937, the Travancore Government nationalized the Road Transport Department[93]. The outbreak of the Second World War had accelerated the demand for many new products and the Governments of Travancore and Cochin States given special attention to promote oriental industries. Consequently, a variety of industries were established in Travancore and Cochin. When the World war was over, a fairly strong industrial base was set up in Travancore State while Cochin was following the example of Travancore, and Malabar remained undeveloped[94] .

In the field of communication media, new developments were brought about. A number of new magazines and newspapers were started. The number of libraries increased and a large number of people began to depend on this for getting of information of every kind. On 12 March 1943 the Travancore Broadcasting Corporation started to function. It was a milestone in the history of communication media in Kerala[95].

At that time library movements mushroomed in different parts of Indian States. The political parties like the Indian National Congress and some voluntary agencies took interest in this movement. Certain professional associations of libraries were formed in different parts of the country. In 1933, the first All India Library Congress was held at Calcutta and at the proposal of that Conference the All India Library Congress was formed for the development of library movement throughout the country. It conducted conferences once in every two years in different parts of India. In April 1942, 'Library Bulletin', a monthly special for libraries was published and recommended training courses for librarianship[96]. During that time two strong associations of libraries were formed in the South and the North of Kerala. Under the leadership of these associations, the library movement in Kerala seems to have gained a new orientation.

Notes and References

1. P. Ramanujan Nair, *The Library Movement in Kerala : The need for reform and legislation,* Trivandrum : Tvm Writers Club, 1974, p.11.
2. Akhila Thiruvithamcore Grandhasala Sanghom, *Grandhasala Manual,* (Mal.), Trivandrum : A.T.G.S., 1948, p.61.
3. Prajamandala Charithra Rachana Committee, *Cochin Rajya Prajamandalam* (Mal.), Kottayam : Current Books, 1985, pp.150-51.

4. C.P. Sreedharan "Kalathe Adijeevicha Sahithya Parishath". *Mangalam*, Kottayam, (Mal.), Dalily, 6 March 1990.
5. Interview with K.A. Keraleeyan, at his residence, Kuthiravattom . Calicut, on 7 December 1990, by the researcher (See Appendix – J).
6. K.M. Lenin, "Malabarileku". *Keralathile Grandhasala Prasthanam*, (Mal.), Trivandrum : Steps, 1982, p.140.
7. E.K. Nayanar, *My Struggle : An Autobiography*, New Delhi : Vikas Private House, 1982, p. 9.
8. A.K. Pothuval, "Vayanasala Prasthanam", *Keralathile Grandhasala Prasthanam*, (Mal.), Trivandrum : Steps, 1982, pp. 28-30.
9. Akhila Travancore Grandhasala Sanghom, No. 2, p. 61.
10. "Library Movement Towards a Gaint Leap", *Kerala Calling*, Trivandrum, Vol.9 (10), 1989, p. 7.
11. A.K. Pothuval, No. 8
12. E.K. Nayanar, No. 7, p.10.
13. A.K. Pothuval, No. 8, p. 29.
14. K.K.N. Kurup, (ed.), *Swathandriya Samaram Kasarkode Talukil*, (Mal.), Kottakat: Kalaniketan Publishers, 1984, p. xxxiv.
15. K.A. Keraleeyan, No. 5.
16. Venmani Memorial Committee, "*Libraries and Library Movement*", Venmani Shashtiapta Mahamaham, (Mal.) (Vellarapalli: Mangalodayam Press, 1120 M.E. 1944-45, p. 62
17. A. Balakrishnan, *Kesariyude Mukhaprasangangal*. (Mal.), Kottayam: N.B.S. 1961, p. 178.
18. Seethikumar, No.10, p. 7.
19. *Venmani Memorial Committee*, No. 16, p. 62.
20. K. Sunilkumar, "Library Legislation in Kerala – *A Survey*" *Public Library System in India*, New Delhi: Ess Ess Publication, 1980, p. 44.
21. K.K. Kusuman, *The Abstention Movement*, Trivandrum : Kerala Historical Society, 1976, p. 23.

22. *Ibid.*, p. 23.
23. P.K.K. Menon, *The History of Freedom Movement in Kerala,* (1885-1938), vol.II, Trivandrum : Regional Records Service Committee, Kerala State, 1970, p.VIII.
24. Secret Bulletin, No. 31, 25 July 1934, Trivandrum : Directorate of State Archives, Kerala, p. 2.
25. English Records, File No. R. Dis. 1633/34, Press Note, 14 April 1934 Edn, 2 October 1934, Trivandrum : Directorate of State Archives, Kerala, p. 31.
26. English Records, File No. C.F. of 3286/33 Edn., Trivandrum: Directorate of State Archives, Kerala, p. 3.
27. *Ibid.*, p. 9
28. Akhila Thiruvithamcore Grandhasala Sanghom, No.2, pp. 73-74.
29. English Records File C.F. of C 345/ 34 Edn., Trivandrum : Directorate of State Archives, Kerala, pp. 183-202.
30. *Sree Chitira Tirunal Grandhasala Golden Jubilee Souvenir* - 1966, (Mal.), Trivandrum :Sree Chithira Thirunal Grandhasala, 1966, p. 37.
31. P.G.S. Kumar, *Indian Library Chronology,* New Delhi: Metropolitan Book Company, 1977. p. 188.
32. File No. C.349/34 Edn., Trivandrum : Directorate of State Archives, Kerala), p. 15.
33. File No.1337/1936 Edn., Trivandrum : Directorate of State Archives, Kerala), p. 203.
34. File No.C.3286/33 Edn., Trivandrum : Directorate of State Archives, Kerala, p. 295, and the proceeding of the Government of His Highness of Travancore, 21 March 1931.
35. A. Balakrishna Pillai, *Kesariyude Mukha Prasangangal,* (Mal.) Kottayam: N.B.S., 1961, p. 177.
36. File No. C.F. of C. 349/ 34, Edn., Directorate of State Archives , Kerala, p. 249.
37. File No. C.F. of 3286/ 33, Edn., Trivandrum : Directorate of State Archives, Kerala, p. 9.

38. *Travancore Administrative Report*- 1936, Trivandrum: Travancore Government Press 1937, p. 136.
39. T.K. Velu Pillai, *The Travancore State Manual,* Vol. III, Trivandrum : Government of Travancore, 1940, p. 742.
40. *Ibid.*
41. Akhila Thiruvithamcore Grandhasala Sanghom, No.2, p. 75.
42. A.P. Nair, "Jnana Pradayani Library, Neyyattinkara," *Grandhalokam,* Trivandrum : (Mal.), Vol. III (1), 1950, p. 6.
43. A.K. Pothuval, No.8, p. 30.
44. A.K. Pothuval, *Keralathile Karshaka Prasthanathinte Oru Cheruvivaranam,* (Mal.), Trivandrum: Prabhath Printing, 1969, p. 23.
45. E.K. Nayanar, No. 7, p. 10.
46. K.A. Keraleeyan, No. 5.
47. P. Udayabhanu, "Prasthanathinte Adiverukal", *Keralathile Grandhasala Prasthanam,* (Mal.), Trivandrum: Steps, 1982, p. 31.
48. 'Libraries of Malabar', *Mathrubhoomi,* Calicut: (Mal.), Daily, 15 March 1936.
49. Pirappancode Murali, "Keralathile Grandhasala Prasthanam", *Grandhalokam,* Trivandrum : (Mal.), Special Issue, September 1990, p. 54.
50. *Ibid.*
51. Kerala Grandhalaya Sanghom, *Kerala Grandhalaya Sanghom : Oru Samkshiptha Vivaranam 1943 Muthal 1945 December Vare,* (Mal.), Calicut:Daily, 13 June1937, p. 2.
52. "Malabar Vayanasala Sanghom Conference", *Mathrubhoomi,* Calicut: (Mal.), Daily, 13 June 1937, p. 2.
53. *Ibid.*
54. *Ibid.*
55. *Ibid.*
56. P.K. Gopalakrishnan, *Keralathinte Samskarika Charithram,* (Mal.), Trivandrum : State Institute of language, 1974, p. 545.

57. *Library Movement in Kerala*, Trivandrum, Department of Public Relations, 1989, p. 2.
58. *Report on the Administration of Cochin- 1113 M.E*, 1938, Cochin: Cochin State Government, Cochin Press, 1939, p. 152.
59. *Ibid.*
60. Machad T. Neelakantan, "Grandhasala Sanghathinte Bhavi", *Grandhalokam*, Trivandrum: (Mal.), Vol. 11 (2), 1959, p. 59.
61. *Report on the Administration of Cochin*, No. 58, p. 152.
62. *Grandhasala Manual*, No. 2, p. 68.
63. *Report on the Administration of Cochin – 1118 M.E*, 1943, Cochin : Cochin State Government, Cochin Press, 1944, p. 70.
64. A. Sreedhara Menon, *Cultural Heritage of Kerala, An Introduction*, Cochin: East West Publication, 1978, pp. 225-226.
65. These Satyagrahas were organised against the prohibition that was in vogue in the approach roads of Vaikom temple and for securing entry in the Guruvayoor Temple by the lower caste people respectively.
66. *Souvenir of the Temple Proclamation Memorial*, Trivandrum: Temple Entry Proclamation Committee, 1942, p. 79.
67. A. Sredhara Menon, No. 64, pp. 230-231.
68. *Ibid.* pp. 232-233.
69. *Ibid.*
70. K.C. Govindan, *Memories of an Early Trade Unionist*, Trivandrum : Centre for Development Studies, 1986, p. 14.
71. E.M.S. Namboodiripad, *Kerala Society and Politics, A Historical Survey*, New Delhi: National Book, 1984, p. 129.
72. E.M.S. Namboodiripad, *Keralam Malayalikaluted Mathrubhoomi*, (Mal.), Trichur: Current Books, 1964, p. 335.
73. E.M.S. Namboodiripad, No. 72, p. 139.

74. N.C. Shekar, *Agniveedhikal*, (Mal.), Autobiography, Cannoor: North Kerala Printers and Publishing House, 1987, p. 327.
75. E.M.S. Namboodiripad, *National Question in Kerala*, Ernakulam : Prabhath Books, 1957, pp. 257-58.
76. K.M. Lenin, No. 6, p. 140.
77. R. Prakasam, *Keralathinte Trade Union Prasthanathinte Charithram*, (Mal.), Trivandrum : Prabhath Book House, 1979, p. 124.
78. A. Sreedhara Menon, *Aadhunika Keralam*, (Mal.), Kottayam: Indian Press, 1988, pp. 122-123.
79. M.J. Koshy, *Last Days of Monarchy in Kerala*, Trivandrum: Kerala Historical Society, 1973, pp. 1-5.
80. K.M. Mohan Das, "Anpatham Varshikam Innu Thudangunnu", *Deshabhimani*, Trivandrum : (Mal.), Daily, 19 august 1989.
81. "Varshikakhoshangal", *Deshabhimani*, Calicut, (Mal.), Daily, 30 August 1989.
82. A. Sreedhara Menon, No. 78, p. 124.
83. A.K. Pothuval, No.8, p. 30.
84. A. Sreedhara Menon, No. 78.
85. Prajamandala Charithra Rachana Committee, No. 3, p. 80.
86. Thayattu Sankaran, *Ente Anukalika Diary*, (Mal.), Kottayam: N.B.S., 1980, p. 45.
87. *Annual Report of the Young Men's Association and Social Library*, Trivandrum : Chakai, October 1980, p. 8.
88. P.K.K. Menon, No. 23, p. 158.
89. Interview with S. Guptan Nair, at his residence, Peroorkada, Trivandrum: on 19 September 1990 by the researcher.
90. G.R. Anil, Social and Economic Development of Travancore under Sir C.P. Ramaswamy Iyer, Calicut University : Department of History, Unpublished Doctoral Thesis, 1986, p. 82.
91. *Ibid.*
92. A. Padmanabha Iyer, *Souvenir of the Shashtiabtapurthi of Sachivottama Sir C.P. Ramaswamy Iyer*, Trivandrum : AVR Press, 1940, p. 62.

4

Formation of Effective Library Organisations

In the history of the library movement in Kerala, the formation of Kerala Grandhalaya Sanhom (Kerala Library Association) and the establishment of Akhila Thiruvithamcore Grandhasala Sanghom (All Travnacore Library Association) were remarkable events. In June 1943, a public library workers' meeting was held at Tellicherry where the library workers explored the feasibility of forming an all Kerala organization for a strong library movement[1]. Following this, the Malabar Vayanasala Sanghom passed a resolution on 26 September 1943, to convert it into the Kerala Grandhalaya Sanghom. Accordingly, on 6 December 1943, Kerala Ghandhalaya Sanghom was formed which brought the public libraries of Kerala under its control, and it was registered under the Charitable Act of (Act XXI of 1860) Madras Government[2].

The total number of libraries affiliated to the Kerala Grandhalaya Sanghom on 31 December 1944 was 134 of which 108 were ordinary members while 14 were permanent members and 12 were founder members[3]. The Sangom established relations with other contemporary library organisations in India like Madras Library

Association and Indian Grandhasala Association. It also took membership in these associations[4]. Soon it was recognized by the local bodies of Malabar like Malabar District Board, Palghat and Cannanore Municipal Councils, and they took membership in the Sanghom[5].

In order to propagate the idea of library movement, the office bearers of the Sanghom conducted extensive tours in different parts of the State, and arranged many programmes like, public meetings, library workers' conference, writing of articles and publishing of books dealing with various aspects of the library movement and so forth. They also opened certain branches of the Sanghom in Chirakkal, Kottayam, Calicut and Valluvanadu, but this move was a failure owing to the uninterest of the people. They also prepared a list of worthy books and sent it to all the libraries which helped them select proper books[6].

In the meantime, under the auspices of the Kerala Grandhalaya Sanghom, Sauhrdaya Samajam (Association for Friendship), a sister institution of the Sanghom, was formed at Calicut on 8 December 1943. Its main aims were encouraging the post - graduate studies in the subjects like literature, history, natural science, sociology, fine-arts and cultural developments. M.P. Sivadasa Menon (Chairman), M.K. Raj, T.P. Mathew (Secretaries) were the persons behind the setting up of this institution. They conducted many seminars and discussions under this institution. The birth days of eminent persons of Kerala like Thunchath Ezhuthachan and the centenary days of famous Malayalam writer Kerala Varma Valiya Koyithampuran were colourfully celebrated as a part of the programme. But this institution could not thrive owing to the lack of organizers. But attempts were often made to enliven this organisation, and to install similar institutions in other parts of the state, as centres of non-formal education for uneducated people, especially the downtrodden and illiterate[7].

In 1945, Kerala Grandhalaya Sanghom invites S.R. Ranganathan to visit the libraries of Kerala[8]. Accordingly he visited many libraries of Malabar and Cochin and gave valuable instructions to the library workers regarding the organisation of library movement in the State. His visit certainly inspired the library workers and it was considered as an important event in the history of library movement in Kerala[9].

The libraries of Malabar were centres of political activity too. But very often this created problems to the smooth functioning of the libraries. It was the timely guidance of the Kerala Grandhalaya Sanghom that saved the libraries from disunity. The leaders of the Kerala Grandhalaya Sanghom were also leaders of National Movement. So when they were imprisoned for political reasons, the functioning of the Grandhalaya Sanghom, naturally, faced difficulties[10].

It was proposed to have a central library at Calicut, through which all books published in Malayalam language and other important books published in different languages were made available to the affiliated libraries[11]. But it was not materialized due to the inactivity of the Sanghom.

When the thirty fifth State Education Conference was held at Calicut in May 1945, the Sanghom organized a Grandhasala (Library) Exhibition which attracted a large number of people. This was the first of its kind ever conducted in Kerala[12].

In Cochin, there was no central association, as in Malabar and Travancore, for the development of libraries. It was a part of Government department and so the policies and programmes of the libraries were directly conducted by the Cochin State Government. After the visit of S.R. Ranganathan in Cochin, in 1945, certain changes were effected in this field[13]. A step for forming a Central

Association for the libraries of Cochin was made by M.K. Raj who was an executive member of Kerala Grandhalaya Sanghom. When the Kerala History Conference was convened at Trichur on 21 August 1945 an attempt was made by him for forming an Association for the libraries of Cochin for their future development[14].

Accordingly an All Cochin Library Association was formed and the employees in the state were allowed to serve as the Committee members[15]. But no grant was made available to this Association for its functioning. M.K. Raja was elected as the President of the Association. Some of the suggestions forwarded by them to the Cochin government for improving the existing public library set up were accepted[16]. However, the venture in Cochin was a total failure[17].

In South Kerala, another library conference was convened at Ambalapuzha, (P.K. Memorial Library) which was considered to be the cultural centre of Travancore, on 16 September 1945, and it gave birth to the central organisation for the libraries of Travancore called Akhila Thiruvithamcore Grandhasala Sanghom. It was milestone in the history of library movement in Kerala. It was that day that the representatives on 47 libraries of erstwhile Travancore State met at the initiative of P.N. Panicker, the secretary of the P.K. Memorial Library at Ambalapuzha, and resolved to form an All Travancore Library Association[18]. Eminent library workers like Vettukattu G.N. Nair, V.N. Narayanakurup, P. Kunjan Kurup, Parthasaradhi Iyengar and Vayanasala Kesava Pillai rendered all helps to P.N. Panicker in his attempts[19].

P.N. Panicker narrates the formation of the Sanghom as follows: "Even though Ambalapuzha was advanced in education, there was no library worthy of its name in the area. The Sahithya Panchanan Library, which had been started in honour of the High Court Judge, Sahithya

Panchanan P.K. Narayana Pillai, could not survive even for six months. Meanwhile, I had to stay at Ambalapuzha as I was employed there as a teacher. I summoned a meeting of the people of the locality. Fortunately, a group , including K.K. Kunjan Pillai, a leading activist of the Travancore State Congress and others strongly supported me. According to their proposal, the Sahithya Panchanan Library was renamed P.K. Vilasam Library in 1937. It was functioning in a hired shed in the southern part of Srikrishna Temple, Ambalapuzha[20]." The name of the library was again changed into P.K. Memorial Library when Sahithya Panchanan P.K. Narayana Pillai died in 1938[21]. Then a double storeyed new library building was constructed with the help of eminent personalities of Travancore. The new library building was inaugurated by K.G. Parameswarn Pillai, the owner of the *Malayala Rajyam* daily, and the meeting was presided over by a famous advocate of Travancore, Malloor P.K. Govinda Pillai[22].

During this time, the Trvancore State Congress was very powerful in Ambalapuzha and the Congress leaders like K.K. Kunju Pillai and others were very active workers of the P.K. Memorial Library. The Government became antagonistic to this library and transferred P.N. Panicker to a remote hilly area, Peerumedu. But later it was cancelled due to the instruction of some influential person of Travancore State Services[23]. The P.K. Memorial Library took a keen interest in the literary and cultural activities, from the very beginning. It instituted an award for the best Malayalam writer in every year. Thus, M.R. Krishna Warrier a well known Malayalam writer received the first award from the P.K. Memorial Library. Every year a big cultural meeting was held under the auspices of the P.K. Memorial Library at Ambalapuzha in which prominent writers of Malayalam literature participated[24]. The smooth functioning of this library was made possible with the financial assistance rendered by the eminent persons of Travancore. In addition to this, a drama written by T.N. Gopinathan Nair, son of Sahithya Panchanan, was staged by the organizers of this library for the purpose of raising a fund. During that time A. Gopala Menon, the Director of Education of Travancore, paid a visit to the library. Even after this, no financial help or any other assistance was extended by the Government to this library[25].

According to P.N. Panicker, around this time he thought of the necessity of forming a library association to draw the attention of the Government on the problems of libraries. He held discussions with many people about it, and thus arrangements were made for a library conference at Ambalapuzha[26].

By this period, it was decided to invite Dewan Sir C.P. Ramaswamy Iyer for inaugurating a library conference at Ambalapuzha[27]. Some of the activists of the Travancore State Congress were opposed to the invitation extended to C.P. Ramaswamy Iyer, for the latter was known for his anti-state Congress posture. They made an attempt to raise black flag against him in order to register their protest. Ambalapuzha and surrounding areas like Punnappra and Vayalar were strong centres of the State Congress and Communist Party. The followers of both these parties were totally against him[28].

However, C.P. Ramaswamy Iyer inaugurated the library conference on 16 September 1945, with Director of Education of Travancore, A.N. Thampi presiding and N. Narayana Kurup, M.L.C. (Member of Tranvacore Legislative Council) welcoming the gathering[29]. In the inaugural speech the Dewan criticized the Catholic community of Kerala and the Communist Party, his two protagonists in politics[30]. Of the libraries he said, he could do nothing during his ten years in power mainly because nobody approached him with definite proposals. But he offered the maximum help from the part of the Government to the library movement[31].

The Ambalapuzha Library conference elected 14 members as office bearers of the Akhila Thiruvithamcore Grandhasala Sanghom and entrusted them with the task of preparing a constitution for the sanghom[32]. The following resolutions were passed in the conference[33]:

1. This meeting will show all kinds of piety and respect to the Travancore Maharaja and his Royal Family. (Resolution moved by the Chairman of the meeting.)
2. This conference proposed to form an All Kerala Travnacore Library Association by including all libraries of Travancore (Resolution moved by M.K. Kesavan, supported by T.A. Kasim Pillai.)
3. The libraries registered as members in this meetings by paying Rs.5/- each should be considered as members of the Sanghom. In future other libraries can join this Sanghom by paying membership fee. (Resolution moved by P.R. Sasthri seconded by P. Raghavan.)
4. A separate department as a part of the department of education may be formed for the unity and the efficient functioning of the libraries of the State. (Resolution moved by L. Vijayamma, seconded by K.C. Nair)
5. To purchase books, periodicals and furniture, and to meet the establishment charges, the Government should give a grant of fifty percent of the total amount required, or an annual grant equal to that of the annual income of a library as in the case of Charitable Institution. (Resiolution moved by P. Kunjan Kurup, Sec onded by J. Muthayya.)
6. Though the Government has agreed that all the Government publications would be made available free

of cost to the libraries, the meeting invited the attention of the Government to the fact that things were not actually so, and requested the Government that steps might be taken to make available all the Government publications in the libraries. (Resolution moved by Ananthasivayya, seconded by D.C. Kizhakkemuri).

Besides, the meeting took the following decisions whichwere to be carried out in the following years[34].

1. Enrole all the existing libraries and reading rooms.
2. Revive the libraries which have become inactive or defunct.
3. Help to start new libraries wherever is necessary.
4. Enrole individual members in this association.
5. Raise a working capital.
6. Publish pamphlets and organize campaigns.
7. Organise a preliminary survey of the libraries.

The organizers of the Sanghom got encouragement and assistance from the Government. To convey the matters of the Sanghom to the Government, a Committee, consisting of N. Narayana Kurup, K.P. Kumara Pizharady (Editor of *Chakravalam*), B. Narayana Pillai (Editor of *Dakshina Bharathi*), N. Kesavan Pillai, P.N. Panicker and P. Madhavan Pillai was constituted[35]. The delegation was received by the Dewan of Travancore on 6 August 1946. The Government carefully considered the proposals submitted by the Association for the betterment of the library movement, in the State. "In view of the usefulness of the movement, and of the good work done by the All Travancore Library Association, the Government considered that the Association deserved encouragement[36]." The Government, placed at the disposal of the Association an initial grant of Rs. 250 per mensem for supporting a body of enthusiastic workers. Government further proposed to enhance the maximum annual grant payable to a library from Rs. 200 to 240 , The actual amount to be paid to each library would be, decided on the basis of the continued usefulness of the institution as judged and certified by the Department of Public Instruction. "The Government wish to make it clear that it will be the duty of the Association to organize the library movement in the State on sound and up-to-date lines and to see that the libraries are well managed and properly equipped" (See Appendix-C)[37].

In view of the above, All Travancore Library Association appointed four organizers for organising libraries in the State. They were (1) P.N. Panicker (Chief Organiser), (2) S.K. Swamy (in-charge of Southern division of the State), (3) P. Madhavan Pillai (Central division), and (4) W.O. George (Northern division)[38]. The Chief Organiser P.N. Panicker was a Primary School Teacher who had been deputed from the Department of Education to the Grandhasala Sanghom. He continued to serve the Sanghom as General Secretary as well from 1945 to 1977, till it was taken over by the Government[39]. Later, two lady organizers, namely J. Thankam and L. Vijayamma were appointed by the Sanghom for inviting ladies also into this field[40].

A ten-point programme to be executed every month was chartered out for the organizers, and it was expected that they would act according to this programme. They were[41] (1) at least four non-members of the Association shall be made members of the Association (2) At least a new library or a reading room shall be established. (3) A new taluk Union shall be formed, and the meeting of the union shall be held twice a month. (4) A survey regarding each village shall be held. (5) At least one adult education centre shall be opened. (6) to visit each Taluk library and send a progress report to the Association office. (7) In different taluks public meetings were to be held for the spread of the idea of library movement. (8) Each organizer shall jointly work with the Chief Organiser for seven days in a month, the latter has to conduct his chartered work independently for ten days. The remaining days of the month may be used by both parties for the purpose of organising libraries in different parts of the State. (9) As per the instruction of the All Travancore Library Association, Library Conferences and exhibitions shall be organized. (10) According to the instruction of the Central Committee of the Association, the function of the affiliated libraries are to be improved.

In consequence of this planned programme and its meticulous implementation a large number of libraries sprang up in various parts of the State[42]. It was a healthy sign that people had come to recognize the usefulness of library and reading rooms, and had given unstinted support to library workers. Several local organisations and public spirited individuals had given lands and buildings to house libraries[43]. Many libraries began to set up their own buildings. Further developments were registered through the selfless efforts of enthusiastic library workers. Necessary funds were partly raised from the public. Popular enthusiasm has indeed gained momentum during the last few decades and the Government had given grants-in-aid to libraries which deserved support. However, apart from giving grants occasionally, (which also had not been done in the case of some libraries), the Government did not seem to have paid any attention to matters connected with the functioning of the library so as to make it really useful to the people[44].

The expansion of popular education and the changed conditions of life in the State, at that time, had made libraries and reading rooms a basic social need. It was the recognition of this fact and appreciation of the manifold problems confronting libraries in relation to the public on the one hand, and the authorities, on the other, that had led to the establishment of All Travancore Library Association.

Just before the formation of Akhila Thiruvithamcore Grandhasala Sanghom, another organisation called *Sahithya Pravarthaka Sahakarana Sanghom* [Co-operative society of men of letters (S.P.C.S)] was formed by some of the men of letters of the State at Kottayam[45]. It was actually the realization of along-cherished desire of the writers as well as readers of Kerala. It was registered as a co-operative society on 19 March 1945 and it opened its sale stall by the name of National Book Stall (N.B.S) at Kottayam on 15 June 1949[46]. Through this book stall, the sale of important books written by famous Malayalam writers was carried out[47]. The Malayalam literary men have got a rare opportunity for publishing their works through this co-operative society. Besides, they were properly rewarded. It was because of the formation of this society that most of the Malayalam writers now live with self-respect and proper means of subsistence. This libraries of Kerala purchased books published mainly by this Sanghom. The development of the *Sahitya Pravarthaka Sahakarana Sanghom* and the financial gains of the literary men were mainly due to the development of library movement in the State[48].

Ambalappuzha P.K. Memorial Library was the Headquarters of the All Travancore Library Assiociation for a year[49]. From these the organizers and the office bearers of the Association worked for the development of the libraries of the State. By their effort 320 new libraries were enrolled as affiliated libraries of the Sanghom. At that time 53 new libraries were established by the Sanghom while 140 defunct libraries were re-established. Moreover, twelve Adult

Education Centres were opened by the Sanghom in its affiliated libraries and thus the relationship between the libraries and adult education programmes was revealed to the public[50]. Thus, the attempts of the Sanghom bore fruit.

Meanwhile attempts were made to re-open those libraries of Travancore which had once been functioning properly, but were closed down during 1940's for various reasons. The members of the Akhila Thiruvithamcore Grandhasala Sanghom led by P.N. Panicker probed into the reasons for their closure. Neyyur Dewan Nanu Pillai Library, Thuravur Narasimhavilasam Library, Padmanabhapuram Lalithavilasam Library, Eattumannur Shashtiapthipurthy Memorial Library were reopened in such a way[51]. The Sanghom Library Association has helped many such libraries to increase their resources and improve the quality of their services[52].

On 27 May 1947 (13 Edavam 1122) the All Travancore Library Association was registered as per the Travancore Company Act as a Joint Stock company, [Act IX of 1114 M.E. (1938)][53] with the following objectives[54].

1. To function as the Central Organisation of all libraries of the State.
2. To work for the improvement of existing libraries.
3. To render all possible help for the promotion of adult education.
4. To prevent the neo-literates from relapsing into illiteracy and to provide facilities for the educated to read and acquire knowledge.
5. To work for the establishment of a library department in the State.
6. To conduct training courses for the library workers.
7. To start a central library in each Taluk.

On 3 and 4 February 1947, Second All Travancore Library Conference was held at Kottayam in which M.O. Thomas presided over the meeting. It was inaugurated by S.R. Ranganathan. A separate meeting for adult education was also held under Bishop Alexander Chulappara along with this meeting. Kottayam Muncipal Chairman Palampadan P.T. Thomas was the Chairman of the reception committee formed for this meeting. In the meeting a library exhibition was also held and technical training was given to library workers. Special speeches by library scientists were also included in the meeting[55].

The Kottayam Conference marked a turning point in the history of the Association. It passed some resolutions and forwarded them to the Government for necessary action[56].

The meeting extended special thanks to S.R. Ranganathan who prepared a library bill, and a scheme for the overall development of the libraries of the State. A Committee, consisting of M.O. Thomas (Madras University), Kodikal P. Balakrishnan Thampi, N. Narayana Kurup, D. Joseph and P.T. Thomas (President of A.T.G.S), was formed for modifying the Library Bill prepared by S.R. Ranganathan to suit the existing conditions in the Travancore State and submit the same to the Travancore Government[57].

S.R. Ranganathan felt that in spite of official lukewarmness, the people of Kerala have been running many libraries, and they were eager about the library service and library legislation[58]. He writes: "it was 3 February 1947, I went to open the Travancore Library Conference at Kottayam. Then the Education Minister of Cochin invited me for a talk on the library development of Cochin. I presented to him a draft library bill and a memorandum setting forth a thirty years' development plan. He was keen to implement them. But his Dewan was not. The Dewan of

Travancore, on the other hand, was keen. There was soon a change of Dewan. There was a consequential change in outlook. The Director wrote to me that there was no need for library legislation as we have many libraries already in our State[59]".

In this conference an important decision was taken on adult education programme[60]. A separate session was held for this purpose in the conference. It showed the interest of the Association for adult education, from the very beginning. In order to prepare strategies for the effective implementation of adult education programme, a Central Committee consisting of eminent educationalists of Travancore was formed. The Committee comprised of N. Gopala Pillai. P.C. Joseph, N. Narayana Kurup, Sooranand Kunjan Pillai, Kainikkara Kumara Pillai, P. Ulahannan Mappila, Mathew M. Kuzhiveli and N. Kesava Pillai[61]. Another Sub Committee consisting of P.S. Abraham and K.M. Kesavan were formed to report on this matter within three months. The timely help rendered by these educationalists were always used by the All Travancore Library Association for the development of adult education programme through libraries[62]. Besides, decisions on a few technical and functional matters were also taken in the conference[63].

In the conference a new fifteen members' Committee was elected as office bearers of the All Travancore Library Association in which P.T. Thomas and P.N. Panicker were elected as President and Secretary of the Association respectively[64].

The resolutions of the Kottayam conference were considered by the Travancore government. But the Government felt that it was not necessary to have either a separate department for libraries, or an Act exclusively for it. The rules containing in the then Educational Code for the maintenance of libraries were adequate. The supervision of libraries would be conducted by the education department in future. The government grant to libraries was raised. With regard to the distribution of grant to libraries the Government thought that the existing rule would be enough. The Government did not think it necessary to give grant for the purchase of books and other items used in the libraries. Maintenance grant was mainly meant for this purpose. Building grant was given still to those who deserved it. It was not exigent that land must be purchased on *Ponnum Panam*[65] for the libraries. It would be done on the basis of merit. In section 194(14) of the Education Code, the free cost publications list was attached. In every request of the libraries the recommendation of the Education Director would be considered by the Government. The government did not think it relevant to publish the library development plan prepared by S.R. Ranganathan[66].

Politically C.P. Ramaswamy Iyer, could not conform with the Travancore State congress activities for the establishment of responsible government in the State. According to the founders of the Sanghom, he was very helpful to the library movement despite the fact that he was opposed to the Travancore State Congress, the pioneer political party championing the cause of self Government[67]. Following a threat to his life, on 9 August 1947 he resigned Dewanship and left the State. After his resignation P.G. Narayanan Unnithan was appointed as Officiating Dewan of Travancore[68].

On 10 October 1947, a Committee consisting of P.T. Thomas, K.R. Elankathu, N. Augustalinga Pillai, N. Kesava Pillai, S. Parameswaran Pillai and P.N. Panicker visited Dewan P.G.N. Unnithan, and gave him a memorandum[69]. It sought the approval of the Government for the Association. The major other issues raised in the memorandum were enhancement of grant to the Sanghom, recognition of the Sanghom as the spokesman of libraries, removal of conditions for sanctioning grant to libraries, bringing of all libraries under the administrative control of the Association and the starting of Library Science Course in the University of Kerala[70] (See appendix-D).

It resulted in the setting up of a Committee consisting of Sooranad Kunjan Pillai, Mathew M. Kuzhiveli, Sivarama Subramoni Iyer by the Government. The Committee was intended to review the work done by the Association, and also to recommend feasible assistance and encouragement[71].

The committee reported as follows: "Our inspection of libraries has given abundant proof of the great goodwill and support that we can expect from all classes of people for the movement, and also of the benefits of an organized endeavour to make public libraries play and essential and important part in the social scheme. We came back with the conviction that the time has really come for a big leap to library expansion in the State"[72]. The Sanghom had made successful effort to unite all persons interested or engaged in library work in the State, and to demonstrate the benefit of team work based on an intelligent appreciation of the present needs and future possibilities[73].

The Committee strongly recommended the formulation of a planned library policy to be adopted by the Government in collaboration with non-official agencies, obviously meaning Akhila Thiruvithamcore Grandhasala Sanghom. It also recommended the doubling of the annual grant to the Sanghom, and authorizing the Sanghom to inspect libraries, including the department libraries. All Thiruvithamcore Grandhasala Sanghom may be allowed to conduct training to the librarians[74].

In 1946, the office of the Sanghom was shifted from Ambalapuzha to Trivandrum for activising its programme; Sree Chithira Tirunal Library at Vanchiyoor provided a temporary room for the Sanghom. Later on a room was rented out near the University College, Trivandrum for its functioning. After a prolonged discussion with the University Authorities, on 26 June 1948, a room was allowed to house the Sanghom Office in the Sanskrit College, Trivandrum[75]. Thus it, began to function from the capital city of the State and this enabled the Sanghom to catch the immediate attention of the Government and attract the elite section in the capital.

Notes and References

1. Library movement Towards a Gaint Leap", *Kerala Calling,* Trivandrum : Vol.9 (10), 1989, p. 7.
2. Kerala Grandhalaya Sanghom, *Kerala Grandhalaya Sanghom: Oru Samkshiptha vivaranam 1943 Muthal 1945 December 31 Vare,* (Mal.), Calicut: Mathrubhoomi Press, 1946, p.2.
3. *Ibid.*
4. *Ibid.*
5. Government Memorandum No. 44, 472-A (Edn.), 21 September 1944, Trivandrum: Directorate of State archives, Kerala.
6. Kerala Grandhalaya Sanghom, No. 2, p.1.
7. *Ibid.*, p. 6.
8. Kerala Grandhalaya Sanghom, No. 2, p. 5
9. Kerala Grandhalaya Sanghom, No. 2, p. 5.
10. *Ibid.*, p. 6.
11. *Ibid.*, pp. 3-4.
12. *Ibid.*, p. 6.
13. Thayat Shankaran, *Ente Aanukalika Dairy,* (Mal.), Kottayam: National Book Stall, 1980, p.43.
14. Kerala Grandhalaya Sanghom, No.2, p.8.
15. *Report of the Director of Libraries – State of Cochin, Cochin:* Government Press : 1949, pp. 9-10.

16. *Ibid.*
17. K.M. Lenin, "Kochiyile Grandhasalakal", *Keralathile Grandhasala Prasthanam,* (Mal.), Trivandrum : Steps, 1982, p. 109.
18. Akhila Thiruvithamcore Grandhasala Sanghom Working Committee's note, (Mal.), Ambalapuzha: P.K. Memorial Library, 1946, pp.1-2.
19. *Ibid.,* pp. 3-4.
20. P.N. Panicker, *KANFED'S 13th Anniversary Souvenir,* (Mal.), Trivandrum : Saksharatha Bhava, 1990, p.11.
21. P.K. Vilasam Library Yoga Natapadi Book, (Minutes Book), Ampalapuzha: P.K. Memorial Library, 1938, p.1.
22. P.N. Paniker, No. 20, p.11.
23. K.M. Lenin, "Puthiya Pravarthanashyil", *Keralathile Grandhasala Prasthanam,* (Mal.), Trivandrum : Step, 1982, p.46.
24. *Ibid.,* pp. 47-49.
25. K.N. Lenin, "Sir C.P. Enna Vivathapuruzhan", *Keralathile Grandhasala Prasthanam,* (Mal.), Trivandrum: Steps, 1992, p.51.
26. Interview with P.N. Panicker on 9 July 1990 at Saksharatha Bhavan, Sasthamangalam, Trivandrum by the researcher.
27. *Kerala Grandhasala Sanghom Rajatha Jubilee Souvenir,* (Mal.), Trivandrum: Kerala Grandhasala Sanghom, 1971, p.24.
28. Interview with Chakrapani Warrier on 10 February 1990 at Ambalapuzha at his residence who is staying near to the P.K. Memorial Library and the participated the Ambalapuzha Libarary Conference in 1945.
29. Akhila Thiruvithamcore Grandhasala Sanghom Working Committee's note, (Mal.), No.18, pp.75-77.
30. Pirappancode Murali, "Keralathile Grandhasala Prasthanam", *Grandhalokam,* Trivandrum : (Mal.), Special issue, September 1990, p.58.

31. P. N. Panicker, *KANFED's 8th Anniversary souvenir*, (Mal.), Trivandrum : Saksharatha Bhavan, 1985, p. 12.
32. *Kerala Grandhasala Sanghom Rajatha Jubilee Souvenir*, No. 27, P. 26 The Office bearers of the Akhila Thiruvithamcore Grandhasala Sanghom were : 1. K. M. Kesavan, President (Representative of Aroor Grandhasala); 2. P.N. Panicker, Convener (P.K. Memorial Library); 3. N. Kesava Pillai, Treasurer (Sree Chithira Thirunal Library, Vanchiyoor, Trivandrum); Committee Members: 4. P. Madhavan Pillai, Swadeshabhimani Library, Neyyattinkara; 5. Ananthanarayana Iyer, Sri. Karthiyani Vilasam Library, Kilimanoor; 6. K. J. Thomas, Sauhradaya Grandhasala, Kanjirappally; 7. V. P. Karunakaran Nair, Sree Sethu Parvathi Bai Library, Kudamaloor; 8. T.A. Kasim Pillai Vinjana Vilasini Grandhasala, Elampalloor, Kundra; 9. K. Kesava Pillai, Sree Chithira Thirunal, Kiridadharana Grandhasala , Adoor; 10. K. Raman, Vinjanodayam Library, Edakkadam; 11. P. N. Bhaskara Pillai, Sankara Vilasam Library, Mudankavu, Chengannoor; 12. K. Kesava Pillai, Kawdiar Kshetra Praveshna Grandhasala, Trivandrum; 13. L. Vijayamma, Sree Chithira Thirunal Vanitha Vayanasala, Kottayam; 14. M. D. Mammon, good Shephered Grandhasala, Thottakkadu.
33. Pirappancode Murali, No. 30, pp. 57-58.
34. K. Sivadasan Pillai, (ed.), *Kerala Grandhasala Sanghom*, Trivandrum : Kerala Grandhasala Sanghom, 1981, p. 14.
35. *Kerala Grandhasala Sanghom Rajatha Jubilee Souvenir*, No. 27, p. 27.
36. *Proceedings of the Government of His Highness, the Maharaja of Travancore*, Order No. 12, D.C. No. 6065/45/ Edn., 12 September 1945, Trivandrum : Directorate of State Archives, Kerala.
37. *Ibdi.*
38. Akhila Thiruvithamcore M.S. Book, Ambalapuzha : P.K. Memorial Library, 1948. pp. 20-22.

39. Interview with P.N. Panicker on 9 July 1990 and English Records, File No. G.O. Rt. 418, 18 February 1958, and G.O. Rt. No. 2793 / 67 Edn., 31 October 1962, (Kerala Government Secretariat.
40. Akhila, Thiruvithamcore Grandhasala Sanghom, *Grandhasala Manual,* (Mal.), Trivandrum : A.T.G.S., 1948, p. 76.
41. Pirappancode Murali, No. 30, pp. 60-61.
42. *Report submitted by the Committee appointed to inspect the work done by the All Travancore Library Association,* Trivandrum : 1948, p.2, (Letter No. 9003/ 111 of D.P.I. dated 21 Dec. 1947, a Committee under Sooranad Kunjan Pillai was constituted.
43. *Ibid.*
44. *Ibid.*
45. Thekkinkad Joseph, (ed.), *Souvenir Published in connection with 40 Anniversary Celebrations of Sahitya Pravarthaka Cooperative Society,* (Mal.), Kottayam : College Book House, December, p. 98.
46. *Ibid.,* p. 9.
47. Thekkinkad Joseph, (ed.), No. 45, p.45.
48. Speech delivered by D.C. Kizhakkemuri on 15 September 1990 in connection with 45 Kerala Grandhasala Sanghom State Conference held at Ernakulam, Mariya Complex. He was the founder member of the Sahitya Pravarthaka Sahakarana Sanghom and the Manager of National Book Stall from June, 1949 to 1965, and Secretary to Sahitya Pravarthaka Sahakarana Sanghom from 1 July 1965 to 1 January 1974.
49. Akhila Thiruvithamcore Grandhasala Sanghom Yoga Nadapati Book, Ambalapuzha : P.K. Memorial Library, 1945, p. 7.
50. Akhila Thiruvithamcore Grandhasala Sanghom, No. 40.
51. K.M. Lenin, "Punarudharana Pravarthanangal", *Keralathile Grandhasala Prasthanam,* (Mal.), Trivandrum, Steps, 1982, pp. 69-70.

52. *Report submitted by the Committee appointed to inspect the work by the All Travancore Library Association,* No. 42, p.3.
53. Akhila Thiruvithamcore Grandhasala Sanghom Pravarthaka Report- 1947, (Mal.), Ambalapuzha: P.K. Memorial Library, p. 1.
54. *The Kerala Public Library Bill, 1985, Background Materials,* Trivandrum : The Secretariat of the Kerala Legislature, 1987, p. 14.
55. K.M. Lenin, "Randam Sammelanam", *Keralathile Grandhasala Pravarthanam,* Trivandrum, Steps, 1982, p.71.
56. 1. The Government may enact a library legislation for the manifold scientific development of the library movement; 2. A library department may be organised for the development of libraries; 3. The amount sanctioned for the library movement was found to be insufficient when its importance was considered. So it may be increased; 4. When new buildings were to be constructed, books and furniture were purchased, the fifty percent of its expense may be met by the Government; 5. The land for the construction of new libraries may be purchased by the Government or the Government land may be given for that purpose; 6. Libraries should sent their application for grant through the All Travancore Library Association and the Libraries recommended by it may be awarded atleast rupees twenty five as grant. The rules regarding the library grant may be amended; 7. The Travancore Government Publications and the Travancore University publications may be freely sent to all libraries of the State.
57. *Ibid.,* pp. 71-78.
58. S.R. Ranganathan, *Golden Jubilee Souvenir of Sengupta Library - 1958,* (Mal.), Calicut, Sen Gupta Library, 1958, p. 1.
59. *Ibid.*
60. Akhila Thiruvithamcore Grandhasala Sanghom, No. 40, p. 77.

61. Kerala Grandhasala Sanghom Rajatha Jubilee Souvenir, No.27, pp. 30-31.
62. *Ibid.*
63. 1. A United Library Association may be established in every taluk; 2. to prepare a taluk-wise survey report of the libraries; 3. to open an adult education department along with libraries; 4. to make rules in the Travancore University for training library workers; 5. to publish a journal as the publication of the Sanghom; 6. to publish a library manual.
64. K.M. Lenin, "Randam Samelanam", "*Keralathile Grandhasala Prasthanam*", (Mal.), Trivandrum: Steps, 1982, p. 74.
65. *Ponnum Panam* – Acquisition of a property for a public purpose by giving the highest price available in that area.
66. File No. D. Dis. No. 2384/ 47/edn., 15 September 1947, Kerala Government Secretariat.
67. P. Ramanujan Nair, *The Library movement in Kerala : The need for reform and legislation,* Trivandrum : Tvm Writers Club, 1974, p. 16.
68. K. Damodaran and C. Narayan Pillai, *Keralathile Swathantriya Samaram,* (Mal.), Trivandrum : Department of Public Relation, Government of Kerala; 1957, p. 173.
69. *Grandhasala Sanghom Rajatha Jubilee Souvenir,* No. 27, pp. 31-32.
70. *Ibid.*
71. Letter No. 9003/ 111 of the D.P.I,., 21 December 1947, Trivandrum : D.P.I. Office.
72. *Report submitted by the Committee appointed to inspect the work done by the All Travancore Library Association,* No. 42, p. 1.
73. *Ibid.,* pp 3-4.
74. *Ibid.,* pp. 8-10.
75. Grandhasala Sanghom Rajatha Jubilee Souvenir, No. 27, p. 32.

5

United Travancore - Cochin Library Association

On 4 September 1947, Sree Chithira Tirunal, the Maharaja of Travancore, Proclaimed that adult franchise would be adopted, and the State had to be divided into several constituencies where political parties could contest. A Constitution Reform Committee was constituted and the election was conducted. The Travancore State Congress, the chief political organ of Travancore secured the majority of seats. It passed a resolution requesting the Maharaja to transfer political powers to the democratically elected ministers[1]. On 24 March 1948, the Maharaja agreed to the formation of an elected ministry and consequently the post of Dewanship was abolished. Accordingly, a ministry was formed under Pattom A. Thanu Pillai on the same day[2].

In the meantime, under the banner of Akhila Thiruvithamcore Grandhasala Sanghom, the Third Library Conference was held at North Parur on 15 and 16 July 1948. It was presided over by G. Ramachandran Nair, and Panampalli Govinda Menon who were the Ministers of Travancore and Cochin States respectively[3]. The following resolutions were passed in the meeting and they were sent to the Travancore State Government for taking further steps[4].

1. Library of the State may be divided into four grades, in which the first grade may get Rs. 600/- or more, while fourth grade may get at lead Rs. 120/- or more per year.
2. The copy of the *Grandhalokam* published by the Sanghom may be purchased by all Government Departments.
3. A Library Act may be passed soon.
4. Rural libraries of the State may be brought under the control of Grandhasala Sanghom.
5. The authority entrusted to School Inspectors to inspect the Grandhasalas (libraries) may be given to the Sanghom.
6. Rupees one lakh may be allotted for libraries in the next budget.
7. In order to carry out adult education programmes through the libraries a sum of Rs. 5000/- may be granted.

As a part of this meeting a seminar on "How adult education programmes can be expended through libraries" was also held[5]. From the Kottayam onwards certain steps had been taken in this regard but more active steps were taken after this meeting. The Sanghom had concrete ideas about the expansion of adult education programmes through libraries. In the meeting Parur T.K. Narayana Pillai was elected as President of the Sanghom and P.N. Panicker as the General Secretary[6]. During this year the number of affiliated libraries of the Sanghom increased to 512 in which Kerala University Library and Trivandrum Public Library were included[7].

The Prime Minister of Travancore, Pattom A. Thanu Pillai responded to the resolutions passed in the Parur Library Conference and increased the grant to libraries in his first budget itself.

But on 10 October 1948, Pattom A Thanu Pillai resigned his Prime Ministership due to internal problems in his State Congress Party and Parur T.K. Narayana Pillai, an eminent leader of the State Congress Party and the then President of the Sanghom was elected the Prime Minister of Travancore State[8].

In 1948 Akhila Thiruvithamcore Grandhasala Sanghom published a manual of libraries called "Grandhasala Manual." It contained a very learned article on library movements all over the world. Details on maintaining library records, qualities of a library, a model library law, and the Articles of Association and Memorandum of Association of the All Thiruvithamcore Grandhasala Sanghom were also included in the manual (See Appendix-E). A list of 1000 good books was also appended to the Manual which helped the book selection process of libraries[9]. It is considered to be the first authoritative book in Malayalam on library science. It was released by the State Education Director A.N. Thampi[10].

Another achievement of the Akhila Thiruvithamcore Grandhasala Sanghom was the publication of a monthly entitled *Grandhalokam*, the first issue of which came out on 20 July 1948. S. Guptan Nair, a vetaran Malayalam writer was its editor. This monthly contained book reviews, news on newly published books, short stories, poems, literary criticisms, library news and information to the affiliated libraries of the Sanghom. A list of books recommended by Book Selection Committee was also included in this journal. The Sanghom insisted on the affiliated libraries to purchase every issue of this journal[11].

Subsequently, a campaign of the Akhila Thiruvithmcore Grandhasala Sanghom for the spread of library movement in the State, harped on the following point:[12]

1. To propagate the concept of establishing a Central library in Trivandrum, a Taluk Reference Library in each Taluk, a library in each ward, and a library in every village where the population is not below two thousand.
2. To rejuvenate the libraries which had become inactive or defunct.
3. To from adult education centres in every library.
4. To reorganize the existing libraries into a new order.
5. To publish a journal periodically
6. To encourage translation of scientific books into the regional language.
7. To encourage works on national arts, literature, literary criticism and to hasten reading habits and to encourage writers to give birth to worthy literary works.
8. To take adequate steps for the distribution of valuable books to the readers.

At that time the Sanghom has also laid down certain conditions to the affiliated libraries and those seeking new membership. They were as follows[13]:

1. It will give recognition to only one library in each ward.
2. The library should have the books in Malayalam, Sanskrit, Hindi, Tamil and English languages.
3. All facilities for intellectual development must be available in the library.
4. Taluk Central Libraries may have their own buildings and landed property of fifty cents, for which Government assistance be provided.
5. The administration of libraries were to be placed under democratically elected committee and certain seats were to be reserved for women.

6. There should not be any division on the basis of religion or caste or other interests in the committee.
7. No public library shall be formed by a particular community or for their own purpose only.
8. In every rural library there were to be facilities for listening Radio Programmes, attending night classes and adult education programme and engaging in various types of recreational activities.
9. Each Taluk library should possess books worth, Rs. 50,000/- and rural libraries should posses book worth Rs. 20,000/-.
10. The libraries should have at least two newspapers, three weeklies and the Government Gazette.
11. Steps may be taken to purchase recently published books both in regional and national languages.
12. All important news should be exhibited in the library notice board.
13. The working hours of the library may be fixed by the Committee members of the library and the time schedule must be strictly adhered to.
14. The Central Library should function as a circulating library.
15. The influence of political parties in the library may be avoided.
16. There must be an annual meeting for the election of office bearers and regular meetings of the members of the committee for taking proper decisions.
17. The income of the library may be raised by conducting cultural entertainment programmes. The premises of the library should be beautified with gardens.

Meanwhile Aikya Taluk Grandhasala Sanghoms (United Taluk Library Association) were formed in the ten Taluks of Travancore, in each of which a President and one or more Secretaries were appointed[14]. These were constituted by the Sanghom to speed up the implementation of the various programmes of the all Travancore Library Association. This was intended to provide direct control of the Sanghom over affiliated libraries[15].

Before 1948 School Inspectors used to inspect the functioning of the libraries, and based on that grants were sanctioned. In 1948, a committee elected democratically was appointed to carry out the gradation[16] work which was a long standing demand of the All Thiruvithamcore Grandhasala Sanghom. The first Gradation Committee members were M.C. Narayana Pillai (Chairman), M. Thomas (Kerala University Librarian), and P.N. Panicker. It started to function from 19 June 1949 onwards. Its major recommendation was that the grants should be provided to the libraries, according to their quality[17]. The grants to be given to the libraries were as follows[18].

Table 3. Library Grant in 1948

Grade	*Rs. Per year*	*Number of libraries*
A	500/-	1
B	420/-	4
C	360/-	7
D	300/-	11
E	240/-	26
F	180/-	40
G	120/-	108
H	60/-	171

Apart from recommending some financial assistance to the libraries, the Gradation Committee could function at various levels for the development of library movement. On the visit of Gradation Committee, P.N. Panicker recapituates that they were cordially welcomed by the villagers. Many libraries had arranged public meetings on their visit. They used to conscientise the villagers on the importance of libraries. The Committee enabled the libraries to get their grants without difficulty[19]. S. Guptan Nair who travelled along with this Gradation Committee wrote: "It was not for mere gradation or grants that we travelled all the way. We took it as our duty to collect funds and lands for libraries, patch up differences among the library workers, unite workers and identify new energetic workers for the movements[20]." They requested the Government to appoint an officer to verify the proper utilization of the library grant, and then request was subsequently accepted[21]. These activities helped the Sanghom to grow rapidly.

The Travancore Education department reported to the Government that Akhila Thiruvithamcore Grandhasala Sanghom had affiliated more than 500 libraries as its members and organized Taluk Library Unions with a view to consolidating the efforts of the library movement. The Organisers under the Association had inaugurated adult education work in certain libraries. It was also seen that the Association had succeeded in compiling accurate library statistics[22]. The Government appreciated the laudable work done by the Association for the expansion and organisation of library movement in the State and was pleased to add that[23]:

1. All Travancore Library Association may be recognized by the Government.
2. All the libraries in this State be advised to get themselves affiliated to the Association: and
3. The monthly grant of Rs. 200/- be raised to Rs. 500 from the year 1948 A.D (See Appendix F).

Right from the time of its inception the Travancore Library Association tried to extend its activities to Cochin and Malabar areas. A high level Committee of the Sanghom consisting of P.N. Panicker, N. Kesava Pillai, W.O. Geroge, P. Madhavan Pillai and J. Kesavan met the Cochin Prime Minister, Ekkanda Warrier, his Cabinet colleagues A. Ayappan and Panampalli Govinda Menon, officials and men of letters of Cochin on 7 March 1949 and explained to them the work they had done in the field of library movement in Travancore. They also expressed their desire for extending the work of the Sanghom to Cochin area[24]. For this, a meeting was convened at Ernakulam Public Library on 11 March 1949, in which they discussed the affiliation of the libraries of Cochin with the All Travancore Library Association. The participants of the meeting were the Chief Ministers of Travancore and Cochin, namely Parur T.K. Narayana Pillai, Ekkanda Warrier, Ministers of States, leading workers of the All Travancore Library Association, members of Sahitya Parishath and the members of the legislatures of both states. Ministers of both the states wanted the affiliation of the libraries in the States into one organisation - All Travancore Library Association. In that meeting V.P. Menon, who came to Cochin for discussing the unification of Travancore and Cochin states, also participated, and stressed the need for the expansion of the library movement both in Travancore and Cochin[25].

A Joint Committee of Travancore-Cochin Library workers consisting of T.K. Krishna Menon (Chairman), R.K. Sastri, W.O.Geroge (Secretaries), and two other persons was formed to report within one month how to regulate the working of the libraries, and how to evolve a uniform pattern for them[26]. The first meeting of this Committee, held on 3 April 1949 at Ernakulam Sahitya Parishath Office, decided to include E. Raman Menon and Mathuravanam Krishna

Kurup, activists of the Malabar library movement, in to it. The Committee thus assumed an all Kerala nature[27]. This Committee recommended that the library movement might be extended throughout Kerala, and the library Association should give the lead in establishing libraries in each village[28]. Another Committee consisting of P.N. Panicker and P.V. Krishnan Nair, was formed for preparing a bye-law for the Thiruvithamcore-Cochin Grandhasala Sanghom. As per the law prepared by this Committee the Akhila Thiruvithamcore Grandhasala Sanghom turned into Aikya Tiruvithamcore - Cochin Grandhasala Sanhom (United Travancore-Cochin Library Association) in 1949[29].

Libraries of Cochin were divided under three heads during that time. The public libraries, major rural libraries and village libraries. The first two types were functioning in urban and semi-urban areas while the other in the rural areas. Office bearers of these libraries were elected. In order to retain continuity of policy in the village libraries, a local school teacher and a Panchayat member were nominated. This nomination did not in any way affect the popular representation, as these two always formed a minority among the seven members (of whom five were elected) of the Committee. In the public and major rural libraries, there were no nominations[30].

Though a library department was created by the Cochin Government inspection of libraries was being conducted by the staff of the Education and Panchayat Departments. Grants to public libraries varied from Rs. 100 to Rs. 1250 per annum and they could use this amount for the development of libraries. Rural libraries were receiving a grant of Rs. 50/- for the purchase of books and Rs. 25/- for running expenses per annum. They were also provided with furniture. During these years a sum of Rs. 50,000/- was spent for the libraries per annum[31]. Though the libraries in Cochin were fully under the control of the Government it could not make much progress. It was mainly owing to the lack of voluntary organisations like the Akhila Thiruvithamcore Grandhasala Sanghom. Those were officially controlled libraries and as such, a bureaucratic nature was evident in their style of functioning[32].

During the above period, there were 240 rural libraries in Cochin State. Each of these had some books and shelves purchased using Government grant. They had no building of their own and were functioning small rented rooms. The book distribution was meager, though there was a Library Director to look after libraries. However, Panampalli Govinda Menon, the Minister of the State, abolished the post of the Library Director, and the local committees began to support the libraries. He further ordered the rural libraries in Cochin to be affiliated to the All Travancore Library Association. This he did against the advice and opinion of the officials[33].

Meanwhile, Travancore and Cochin underwent substantial political changes. The Union Government took the decision to merge the local kingdoms to constitute unified states on 8 January 1949[34]. In Cochin, adult franchise and cabinet system had been adopted on 17 August 1946 itself[35]. On the basis of this, Travancore and Cochin States were united into "Travancore- Cochin State on 1 July 1949. Parur T. K. Narayana Pillai was elected the Chief Minister, and the King of Travancore Sree Chithira Tirunal was appointed as the Raja Pramukha of the new State.[36] These political changes, accelerated the library movements of both the states.

When the Aikya Thiruvithamcore-Cochin Grandhasala Sanghom was formed in 1949 it gave a boost to the working of the libraries. The number of books in the libraries increased and many libraries tried to construct their own building[37]. The second meeting of the United Travancore-cochin Library Committee was convened at the Ernakulam Sahitya Parishad Office on 2 September 1949, and it decided to extend the work of the Sanghom to Malabar area. It was also decided to hold a special meeting of the libraries when the Sahitya Parishad meeting was held at Neelaswaram in September 1949. In that meeting Prof. S. Guptan Nair and P. N. Panicker discussed the functioning of the Aikya Thiruvithamcore –Cochin Grandhasala Sanghom with the chief workers of Kerala Grandhalaya Sanghom, and urged the extension of the activities of the Sanghom to Malabar. The Raja of Neelaswaram donated Rs. 250/- to the Aikya Thiruvithamcore Grandhasala Sanghom as the recognition of its services[38].

Often the office bearers of Sahitya Pravarthaka Sahakarana Sanghom met the office bearers of the Aikya Thiruvithamcore Cochin Grandhasala Sanghom and requested to co-operate with them for selling their publications. On 31 July 1949 M. P. Paul, the Sahitya Pravarthaka Sahakarana Sanghom President and Karoor Neelakanta Pillai met P. N. Panicker in this regard[39].

The Sahitya Pravarthaka Sahakarana Sanghom was not only interested in selling its books through libraries, but also concerned very much with the growth of the library movement. The rural libraries of Kerala emboldened the Sahitya Pravarthaka Sahakarana Sanghom to go ahead with the publication of books. Most of their grant was spent for purchasing books from the Sahitya Pravarthaka Sahakarana Sanghom[40]. For many years since the formation of the S.P.C.S Karoor, D.C. Kizhakkemuri, C.K. Mani and Vettur Raman Nair served as office bearers. At the same time, they co-operated with the Aikya Thiruvithamcore-Cochin Grandhasala Sanghom in many way and kept live relations with it. Almost all members of the Sahitya Pravarthaka Sahakarana Sanghom were ardent library workers[41]. So the mutual co-operation between them was natural and advantageous to both.

During that time, the United Travancore-Cochin Library Association took keen interest in adult education programme. The progress achieved in the field of adult education had been slow but steady in the past, but the endeavour had been regional and unorganized. The establishment of Travancore University on 2 November 1937, and the introduction of compulsory primary education in 1945 opened a new era in Travancore[42]. The literacy rate of Travancore State was 47.17 percent in 1946-1947[43]. In order to eradicate illiteracy, the expansion of adult education programme had been recommended by the Education Reorganisation Committee consisted in 1943[44]. The report of the Committee recommended that the actual work of adult education should be left to the voluntary agencies[45]. The report further observed that in all forms and grades of education, library was one of the most important institutions. Thus adult education centres naturally developed close contact with the libraries of the State[46]. At that time, some of the adult education centres and libraries were maintained by the Travancore Village Unions which were formed under the Travancore Village Union Act of 1939 for rural development[47]. The system of awarding grant to the libraries was introduced in 1917 (1092 ME) with a view to encouraging adult education in the State[48]. Thus it had become the responsibility of every library to promote the adult education programme.

A meeting was held on 12 August 1949 (18 Karkidakam 1124 M.E) under the auspices of the All Travancore Cochin Library Association , at the office of the Trivandrum District Congress Committee to discuss the adult education programme of the State. The meeting was attended by the Chief Minister of Travancore-Cochin State Parur T.K.

Narayana Pillai, and his Ministers like Panampalli Govinda Menon, Ekkanda Warrier, T.M. Varghese, and District Congress President C. Kesavan. The Grandhasala Sanghom Office bearers like P.N. Panicker, N. Kesava Pillai, K.M. Augustin, K. Vasudevan and K. Thomas also participated in that meeting. They had decided to carry out adult education prgramme through libraries.[49]

An adult education training class organized by the Grandhasala Sanghom on 10 May 1950 at the University Hostel, Trivandrum, was inaugurated by the Travancore-Cochin Education Minister Panampalli Govinda Menon. He commented in his speech that the attempt of the Grandhasala Sanghom for the expansion of adult education programme was highly appreciable and all kinds of help could be expected from the Government for this venture[50]. He also added that it was for the first time that a training of this kinds was organized[51]. Rev. J.W. Rasalam was appointed the Principal of this training class. On 9 June 1950, the Chief Minister, Parur T.K. Velu Pillai, T.M. Varghese, the Speaker, Ministers like A.J. John, and N. Kunjuraman, Vice-Chancellor of the Kerala University V.K. Nandan Menon, and the Congress President, C. Kesavan, attended the Validictory function of the training programme. The Chief Minister observed in his speech, "now we are living in a democratic age when the freedom of the illiterate down-trodden people is insecure. So the great centres of culture like libraries have great importance and deserve much encouragement to these people"[52] . The Chief Minister declared that an Adult Education Board would be established soon for advising the Government in the matter, The training course was over on 10 June 1950 and the 54 trainees were sent to the Southern Travancore area for conducting studies on rural development programmes[53].

Soon an Adult Education Board was constituted and the Vice Chancellor of the University of Kerala was appointed the Chairman of the Board. The other members of the Board were Education Director, Education Secretary, C. Narayana Pillai, P.N. Panicker, A.P, Udhaya Bhanu, and Joseph Mundassery[54]. Besides, an Adult Education Research Training Centre was started at Trivandrum in February 1951[55]. Altogether, there were 150 adult education centres in the State in which 135 were libraries. More than 500 libraries sought permission to start new adult education centres[56]. At that time the UNESCO praised the adult education work of the Aikya Thiruvithamcore-Cochin Grandhasala Sanghom , and observed that "this kind of work unique of its kind[57]."

There were about 240 rural libraries (Grameena Libraries) in Travancore State during the region of Sree Chithira Thirunal Maharaja.These were functioning as appendages to Lower Primary Schools and the Head - Masters were in-charge of them. The Aikya Thiruvithamcore Cochin Grandhasala Sanghom requested the Government to merge the rural libraries with it. After a series of representations, half of the books of rural libraries were ordered to be given to the Sanghom[58].

Once again, the Aikya Thiruvithamcore-Cochin Grandhasala Sanghom approached the Government and finally all the books were released to them[59]. They further represented for the release of the furniture of rural libraries to the Sanghom. But the Education Department refused it, although later the Government ordered to give the Sanghom all the furniture in spite of the fact that Government owned property was releasing to a voluntary organisation[60].

The Sanghom, meanwhile, decided to hand over these rural libraries to the local people. P.N.Paniker writes: "the manner in which rural libraries of the Government were handed over to us has made me feel happy and satisfied. I myself went to all the schools for the purpose. I got agreements signed on stamp paper to the effect that the local people would run the libraries efficiently and usefully[61]."

No official of the school objected to this transfer of books and furniture. But the officials took some of the goods books from those libraries before the transfer and the remaining books were handed over to the Sanghom[62]. The Sanghom handed over these rural libraries only to the committees democratically formed in rural areas. These committess entered into agreements with Sanghom that they would collect an equal number of books within six months, and buildings would be constructed to house libraries[63]. Some of the libraries were directly under the control of the Village Uplift Committee and the Harijan Welfare Department. These libraries were also handed over the Sanghom. As in the case of the rural libraries, they were also transferred to the public[64].

The General Secretary of the Sanghom, P.N. Panicker, undertook an extensive tour to the libraries of Cochin area from I November to 8 March 1951. During that visit he gave valuable instructions to the library workers to make them more active and enthusiastic for the growth of library movement[65]. Meanwhile, some library workers of Cochin area were displeased with the unification of the Travancore-Cochin Grandhasalas, and they were even opposed to the unification of the two States. They feared that they would not get justice after the unification[66].

During that time Parur T.K. Narayana Pillai, was the President of the Aikya Thiruvithamcore-Cochin Grandhasla Sanghom (1948-53) and the Sanghom faced severe criticisms from different corners. The former Prime Minister of Travancore Pattom A. Thanu Pillai alleged that the libraries in the State were working as Centres of the Congress Party for securing vote in the elections[67]. Kaumudi, a leading

Malayalam weekly, wrote sarcastically that the *Grandhalokam* was a Government owned 'agricultural farm'. The writers of this journal were ardent supporters of the Travancore-Cochin government[68]. In spite of these allegations the Sanghom worked hard for the spread of the library movement.

The meeting of the office bearers of the Sanghom under Parur T.K. Narayana Pillai decided in 1950 to impose new regulations on the structure of the Aikya Thiruvithamcore–Cochin Grandhasala Sanghom[69].

(i) New office bearers of the Sanghom may be elected once in every three years;

(ii) Individual members, Uparakshadhikarikal (vice patrons) and three members elected from each Taluk constituted the general body of the Sanghom.

(iii) The office bearers of the Sanghom should consist of:

  (a) three members from each revenue division (total twelve members)

  (b) two Government nominees

  (c) one University nominee

  (d) two members nominated by the office bearers of the Sanghom.

  (e) Owing to political differences among the members of the Congress Party, T. K. Narayana Pillai resigned the Chief Ministership on 24 February 1951, and following that a new ministry was formed by C. Kesavan on 3 March 1951[70]. C. Kesavan had high appreciation for the service of the Grandhasala Sanghom. P. N. Panicker approached him seeking a piece of land for the purpose of the Sanghom office building on July 1951[71]. Eventhough the Chief Minister was favourably disposed towards his request, the officials expressed the view that when many of the Government offices were functioning in rented building the government could not entertain the request of the Sanghom. P.N. Panicker explained the importance of libraries and the need for an enlightened public opinion in strengthening the Government. Finally the Chief Minister issued an order to shift the Sanghom office to 'Tulasi Hill Bungalow' owned by Government[72]. All those who opposed in the beginning agreed to help the Sanghom in all possible ways very soon. The office was shifted to 'Tulasi Hill Bungalow' on 9 July 1951[73]. The personal interest of C. Kesavan was really an upswing to the activities of the Sanghom, which had not yet overcome the stage of infantile disorders.

At that time the Sanghom gave special instructions to the affiliated libraries for attracting children to the libraries. It aimed at developing an elite outlook in children. It further recommended to collect books useful to children and if possible to have a separate corner arranged in each library for them[74].

By the time, the Government ordered that all schools could be utilized for the functions of the Sanghom and its affiliated libraries. The Government also stipulated that membership fee or any other nominal charge should be levied from them[75]. As a matter of fact, the Government under C. Kesavan was really interested in doing all that was possible to promote the library movement.

In the First Five Year Plan (1951-56) due importance has been given to the promotion of the public libraries. The plan proposed the setting up of a National Central Library at New Delhi, backed by State Central Libraries, at nine State capitals with a network of Circulating Libraries in villages served through Deposit Stations and Mobile Vans[76] Under this scheme, in Kerala the district libraries of Quilon, Ernakulam, Kottayam and Trivandrum received Rs. 3000 each while the Taluk Libraries of Trichur, Muvattupuzha, Haripad and Nagercoil received Rs. 2000/- each as grant[77].

The non-political character of the libraries slightly changed during that period. The communist party of India became a major political force in Kerala, and it was keen on spreading its ideology. Gradually the libraries became the centrs of the party workers who were eager to read and discuss the communist ideology. *Malayala Manorama,* a daily wrote: "at present the libraries of the State are turned into communist centres and that the collections of the libraries are mainly communist literature which are immoral and irreligious[78]." another daily *Kerala Kaumudi* wrote that if the libraries of the State did not work in favour of the Congress Party it would be destroyed by them[79]. *Deepika,* yet another daily, commented that the libraries of the State were working for spreading communist ideology, and most of the literature available in these libraries were Russian literature which were actually spreading Communism in the name of progressive literature. The Government grant need not be spent for this purpose[80].

In this connection, it seems relevant to mention the observation made T.J. Nossiter. According to him, by 1947 almost every village in Kerala had its own library and reading rooms. The reading materials comprised mostly of newspapers, novels, copies of sacred texts, and famous Malayalam literature. The Communist Party used these prevailing circumstances and they recruited party members and sympathizers to supervisory positions in the village libraries[81]. Even then the readership consisted mainly of higher castes and communities. But the literature of the period hailed from the pen of the Progressive Writers Association in whose works social criticism was predominant. Kesava Dev, Thakazhi Sivasankara Pillai, K. Kumara Pillai, Vaikkom Mohammed Basheer and Joseph Mundassery and so on belonged to this group of writers[82].

In the Travancore-Cochin Assembly Election of 1952, the Congress party secured only 46 seats out of 108. But a Ministry was formed by the Congress under A.J. John, on 12 March 1952[83]. He ordered that the books with communist ideology were not to be purchased by any library in the State[84].

After the Tranvaore-Cochin unification twenty three new library Organisers had been appointed by a high level committee of the Sanghom, consisting of Kainikkara Kumara Pillai, A.P. Udayabhanu, and others[85]. Later, for the organizational work at the Taluk level, one library Organiser in each Taluk was appointed[86], and their number increased to 30 in 1951-52[87]. The General Secretary of the Sanghom complained to the Chief Minister about the activities of some of the library Organisers. In 1952 the Chief Minister advised him to remove those who were not fit for the work[88]. The financial difficulties might also have forced the Sanghom to relieve some dedicated library Orgnisers from the post[89]. When M.K. Sreedharan, one of the Organisers, was relieved from the post of Organiser, in April 1952, he wrote to the General Secretary of the Sanghom: "whenever my service is needed to the Sanghom or any other library of the State, I will be readily available[90]. It was this kind of dedicated work of the Organisers that made Sanghom a unique institution.

The Trivandrum District Gazette reported: "one of the leading cultural societies functioning with its Headquarters in Trivandrum is the Kerala Grandhasala Sanghom, the only organ of its kind in the State. It has succeeded in realizing the aim of establishing libraries even in the remote corners of the State, and in co-ordinating the activities of the various libraries to the benefit of the common people. It happened to democratise the administration of library, and to give the movement a popular appeal."[91]

In November 1955, the Sanghom instructed the affiliated libraries that if more than one library were necessary, a branch of the main library in that place may be established. It further instructed that the door to door delivery of books should done by the library workers in order to create reading habit among the public. A separate section for ladies was to be opened in the libraries where facilities should be made available to attract them to the programme of libraries[92]. Most of the affiliated libraries implemented these instructions of the Sanghom[93].

In 1953 Parur T.K. Narayana Pillai resigned from the post of President of the Sanghom. In his place, Panampalli Govinda Menon was elected as President[94]. He was also the Chief Minister of Travancore-cochin State, from 14 February 1955 to 23 March 1956.[95] During that period the total number of libraries affiliated to the Sanghom increased to 1657 in which 727 were newly formed and 833 were regenerated libraries[96]. To honour eminent personalities, libraries were named after them during that time[97]. Thus it is obvious that the formation of the Aikya Thiruvithamcore-Cochin Grandhasala Snaghom formed a landmark in the history of the library movement and general education. While its success centred round mainly the sense of dedication and determination of a galaxy of trained workers, the positive response of the governments too was a contributory factor, especially in overcoming the financial difficulties experienced by the Sanghom and the various libraries. At the same time the involvement of politically interested persons in the activities of the libraries naturally had impaired the progress of the movement at least to a certain extent. Still in view of the target visulated and the quantum of success registered, the Sanghom and its activities deserve encomiums from all sides.

Notes and References

1. P.S. Velayudhan, (ed.), *Kerala Charithram,* (Mal.) Vol.1, Ernakulam: Kerala History Association, 1973, p. 804.
2. C. Narayana Pillai, *Pattom muthal Panampalli vare,* (Mal.), Kottayam: D.C. books, 1976, pp. 5-58.
3. K.M. Lenin, "Moonnam Samelanam", *Keralathile Grandhasala Prasthanam,* (Mal.), Trivandrum: Steps, 1989, pp. 90-91.
4. *Ibid.*
5. *Ibid.*
6. Travancore Grandhasala Sanghom Meeting Minutes Books, 1947, Ambalapuzha : P.K. Memorial Library, p.12.
7. "Library Varthakal", Grandhalokam, Trivandrum : (Mal.)., vol. 1(2), 1948, pp. 101-102.
8. C. Narayana Pillai, No. 2, P. 89.9. Akhila Thiruvithamcore Grandhasala Sanghom, *Grandhasala Manual,* (Mal.), Trivandrum : Akhila Thiruvithamcore Grandhasala Sanghom, 1948.
10. *Annual Report of the Akhila Thiruvithamcore Grandhasala Sanghom,- 1948,* (Mal.), Trivandrum : Akhila Thiruvithamcore Grandhasala Sanghom, p.6.
11. *Grandhalokam,* License No. 592 dated 20 July 1948, Register.
12. Akhila Thiruvithamcore Grandhasala Sanghom, No. 9, pp. 77-78.
13. K.M. Lenin, "Prasthanathinte Kazhchapad", *Keralathile Grandhasala Prasthanam,* (Mal.), Trivandrum : Steps, 1982, pp. 86-88.

14. Annual Report of Akhila Thiruvithamcore Grandhasala Sanghom, 1947-48, (Mal.), Trivandrum : Akhila Thiruvithamcore Grandhasala Sanghom,, pp. 6-8.
15. 1. Vilavancode- K.N. Kunjukrishna Pillai (President), K. Nilakanta Pillai (Secretary); Neyyattinkara- A.P. Nair (President), J. Kesavan and R. Nanukuttan Nair (Secretaries); Trivandrum – Kalathil Velayudhan Nair (President), K. Kesavan Pillai (Secretary); Chirayinkil- G. Ravi Varma President); P. Ramakrishna Pillai, P.N. Gopalan Unnithan (Secretaries); Kottarakara- H. Esharan Pillai (President), K.G. Chellappan Pillai (Secretary); Alleppey C.N.. Nair (President), V.C. Panicker (Secretary), Kunnathur- Panangot Kesavan Unnithan (President), K. Kesavan Pillai (Secretary); Muvattupuzha - K.V. Chacko (President), N. Kesava Pillai, C.I. Chacko (Secretaries), Paravoor; K.R. Thampan (President), Ananthan Pillai (Secretary), Thodupuzha – K.A. Arumukham Pillai (President), M. Gopala Pillai (Secretary).
16. Gradation means libraries are divided into some grades on the basis of the document which possessed by each library and other facilities available in the libraries.
17. K. Sivadasan Pillai, (ed.), *Kerala Grandhasala Sanghom,* Trivandrum: Kerala Grandhasala Sanghom,, 1981. p. 8.
18. *Ibid.*
19. P.N. Panicker, "Grandhasala Prasthanathekurichu Cheru Vivaranum", *KANFED's 13th Anniversary Souvenir- 1990,* (Mal.) Trivandrum : Saksharathabhavan, 30 June 1990, pp. 16-17.
20. S. Guptan Nair, "Gradation Committeeyude Kude Randu Dhivasam", *Grandhalokam,* Trivandrum: (Mal.), Vol. 2 (9), 1950, p. 515.
21. P.N. Panicker No. 19, pp. 16-17.
22. File No. ROC. HO 5353/ 47 Edn., 12 July 1948, Trivandrum: Government Secretariat.
23. *Ibid.*

24. P.N. Panicker, (ed.), "Kochiyilekku" *Keralathile Grandhasala Prasthanam,* (Mal.), Trivandrum : Steps. 1982, pp. 106-107.
25. *Ibid.*
26. K. Sivadasan Pillai, No. 17, pp. 6-7.
27. P.N. Panicker, (ed.), 'Kochiyilekku', No. 24, pp. 106-107.
28. "Keralathile Grandhasala Prasthanam : Oru Gramathil Oru Grandhalayam", *Grandhalokam,* Trivandrum : (Mal.), Vol. 4 (1), 1952, pp. 93-94.
29. Pirappancode Murali, "Keralathile Grandhasala Prasthanam", *Grandhalokam,* Trivandrum : (Mal.), Special issue, September 1990, pp. 61-62.
30. State of Cochin, *Report of the Director of Libraries,* Cochin: Cochin Government Press, 1948, pp. 3-6.
31. *Ibid.*
32. P.N. Panicker, (ed.), "Kochiyile Grandhasalakal", (Mal.) Keralathile Grandhasala Prasthanam, Trivandrum : Steps, 1982, p.110.
33. K. Sivadasan Pillai, No. 17, p.7.
34. P.s. Velayudhan, (ed.), No. 1., p.805.
35. *Cochin Rajya Prajamandalam Charithra Rachana Committee,* (Mal.), Kottayam: Current Books, 1985, pp. 237-244.
36. *Ibid.*
37. K. Sivadasan Pillai, No. 17, p.7.
38. "Samastha Kerala Sahitya Parishathinte Meeting- Oru Report", *Grandhalokam,* Trivandrum : (Mal.), Vol. 1 (5-7), 1948, pp. 86-87.
39. Dairy of P.N. Panicker dated 31-6-1949.
40. K.M. Lenin, "S.P.C. Asumayulla Bandham", *Keralathile Grandhasala Prasthanam,* Trivandrum : Steps, 1982, p. 134.
41. D.C. Kizhakkemuri, "Randusanghangal", *Keralathile Grandhalaya Prasthanam,* (Mal.), Trivandrum: Steps, 1982, pp. 216-217.
42. *The Proceedings of the XXII All India Education Centre and the IV All India Adult Education Conference,* Trivandrum : government Press, 1947, p. x-vi.

43. *Travancore Administrative Report – 1122 M.E.* (1946-1947), Trivandrum : Government Press, 1947, p. 169.
44. English Records, File No. R.O.C. No. 1918/ 43 Edn., 24 November 1943, Trivandrum : Government Secretariat, Pro-vice Chancellor of Kerala University C.V. Chandrasekharan was appointed the President of the Education reform Committee in 1943.
45. *Report of the Travancore Education Reorganization Committee- May 1945,* Trivandrum : Government Press, 1946, p. 84.
46. *Ibid.*, p. 87.
47. *Travancore Administrative Report 1123 M.E.* 1947- 48, Trivandrum : Government Press, 1947, p. 175.
48. *Ibid.*
49. "Vayojana Vidyabhyasa Paripadi", *Grandhalokam,* Trivandrum : (Mal.), Vol.2 (6), 1950, p. 84.
50. "Vayojana Vidyabhyasa Parisheelanam", *Grandhalokam,* Trivandrum : (Mal.), Vol.2(9), 1950, p.56.
51. *Ibid.*
52. Vayojana Vidyabhyasa Classinte Samapana Sammelanam", *Grandhalokam,* Trivandrum. (Mal.), Vol.3 (7), 1951, p. 55.
53. "Vayojana Vidyabhyasa Parisheelana Class", *Grandhalokam,* Trivandrum: (Mal.), Vol.2 (1o), 1950, pp. 52-53.
54. *Ibid.*
55. *Ibid*
56. A Sreedhara Menon, (ed.), *Kerala District Gazetteers,* vol.1, Trivandrum District, Trivandrum , Government of Kerala, 1952, pp. 686-87.
57. "Vayojana Vidhyabhyasam", *Grandhalokam,* Trivandrum : (Mal.), Vol.3(8), 1951, p. 53.
58. "Grandhasala Varthakal", *Grandhalokam,* Trivandrum: (Mal.), Vol. 4 (1), 1952, p. 19.

59. "Kerala Grandhasala Sanghom", *Kerala Grandhasala Sanghom Rajatha Jubilee Souvenir,* (Mal.), Trivandrum: Kerala Grandhasala Sanghom, 1971, pp. 34-35.
60. *Ibid.*
61. P.N. Panicker, KANFED'S 8th Annual Souvenir, (Mal.), Trivandrum : Saksharatha Bhavan, 1985, p. 15.
62. *Ibid.*
63. Diary of P.N. Panicker dated 4-10-1951.
64. "Rural librarikal", Grandhalokam, Trivandrum : (Mal.) vol. 3 (1), 1951, pp. 52-53.
65. Diary of P.N. Panicker dated 3-11-1949 to 8-3-1951. The pages of the diary shows that he personally took interest to see Ministers and officials of cochin State and compelled them to affiliate all the libraries of the State into Travancore Grandhasala Sanghom.
66. *Ibid.,* dated 12-17-1950.
67. "Rashtriyaum Librarikalum", *Grandhalokam,* Trivandrum: (Mal.), Vol.2 (9), 1950, p. 1.
68. *Ibid.,* p. 2.
69. "Aikya Samsthana Grandhasala Sanghom", *Grandhalokam,* Trivandrum : (Mal.), Vol. 3 (2), 1951, p. 61.
70. *Hundred years of legislature bodies in Kerala 1888-1988, Centenary Souvenir,* Trivandrum: Kerala Legislature, 1990, pp. 678-683.
71. K.M. Lenin, "Swantham Asthanam", *Keralathile Grandhasala Prasthanam,* (Mal.), No. 5, pp. 165-169.
72. *Ibid.*
73. P.N. Panicker, No. 19, p.18.
74. "Kuttikalkku, librariyil Saukaryam", *Grandhalokam,* Trivandrum : (Mal.) Vol. 3 (8), 1951, pp. 5-6.
75. File No. D. Dis. No. 441/ 51 EHL dated 12-5-1951, Trivandrum : Government Secretariat.
76. P. Gopala Krishnan Nair, "Public Library Legislation in India: A National Perspective", *Public Library System in India,* Delhi: ESS Publication, 1990, pp. 24-25.

77. *Annual Report of Travancore Cochin Grandhasala Sanghom*–1951, (Mal.) Trivandrum : Aikya Thiruvithamcore- Cochin Grandhasala Sanghom, p.16.
78. Editorial, *Malayala Manorama* Kottayam , (Mal.) Daily, 22 May 1952.
79. Editorial, *Kerala Kaumudi*, Trivandrum, (Mal.), Daily 30, May 1952.
80. Editorial, *Deepika*, Kottayam, (Mal.), Daily, 30 May 1952.
81. T.J. Nossiter, *Communism in Kerala; A study in political adaptation*, Delhi: Oxford University Press, 1982, pp. 94-95.
82. *Ibid.*
83. C. Narayana Pillai, No.2, p. 238.
84. Editorial , *Grandhalokam*, Trivandrum, (Mal.), vol. 4,6& 7, 1952.
85. P.N. Panicker, (ed.), "Organisaranmmar", *Keralathile Grandhasala Prasthanam*, (Mal.), Trivandrum : Steps, 1982, p. 120.
86. K.M. Lenin, "Sanghathinte Khatana", *Keralathile Grandhasala Prasthanam*, (Mal.), Trivandrum : Steps, 1952, p. 172.
87. *The Kerala Public Libraries Bill – 1985*, Background materials, Trivandrum : The Secretariat of the Legislature, 1987, p. 14.
88. P.N. Panicker- Dairy dated 1-1-1951.
89. P.N. Panicker (ed.), No. 85, pp. 122-124.
90. P.N. Panicker- Dairy dated 20-5-1952.
91. A. Sreedhara Menon, *Kerala District Gazetteers, Trivandrum District*, Vol. 1, Trivandrum : 1952, p. 685.
92. "Library Pravarthakarude Shradhakku", *Grandhalokam*, Trivandrum : (Mal.), vol. 7 (11), 1955, p. 633.
93. All Thiruvithamcore – Cochin Grandhasala Sanghom, *Audit Report*, 1955-56, Trivandrum : Akhila Thiruvithamcore-Cochin Grandhasala Sanghom, p. 18.

94. "Sanghom Varthakal", *Grandhalokam,* Trivandrum, (Mal.) Vo. 5 (3), 1953, p. 16.
95. "Annual Report of Travancore-Cochin Grandhasala Sanghom 1953-54", *Grandhalokam,* Trivandrum: (Mal.), Vol. 6 (8), 1954, p. 46-47.
96. *Ibid.*
97. "Smaraka Vayanasalakal", Grandhalokam, Trivandrum : (Mal.), vol. 6 (1-2), 1954, p. 18.

6

Library Movement After The Formation of Kerala State

The State of Kerala was formed on 1 November 1956 by the integration of the major parts of the erstwhile State of Travancore, Cochin, Malabar Distrist and Kasargode Taluk of the South Kanara District of the Madras State following the promulgation of the State Reorganisation Act of Government of India[1]. The percentage of literacy in the State was 58.73 for males and 36.45 for females while the population was estimated to be 14,978,000 on 1 April 1957 and 15,230,000 on 1 April 1958, recording an increase of 252,000 during the years under report[2]. There was no other state in India where the density of population was as high as that of the State of Kerala[3].

The first democratic Government of Kerala State was formed by E.M.S Namboodiripad[4]. This was the first Communist ministry to come to power in any of the states in India. The Government had its own views and attitudes towards the library movement of the State, particularly the Grandhasala Sanghom.

In Malabar area, the work of the Kerala Grandhalaya Sanghom was not satisfactory for the expansion of the library movement when compared with the achievements of the United Travancore- Cochin Library Association[5].

Though activities like the holding of the North Kerala Library conference (1946), the arranging of Library Exhibitions (1945 & 1953), and the organising of training camp for library workers and so forth were conducted by the Kerala Grandhalaya Sanghom, it has been practically inactive since 1953[6]. In Malabar, the Madras Library Bill of 1948 had come

1.	District Central Library	-	1
2.	Branch Libraries	-	13
3.	Village Libraries	-	7
4.	Delivery Station	-	5
5.	Staff	-	65
6.	Total Books	-	63,000
7.	Annual Income of the Local Library Authority	-	Rs. 1,20,00

into effect. As a result of this Bill, a Local Library Authority had been formed in Malabar with Calicut as its headquarters in 1952[7]. The President and the Secretary of this Authority were nominated by the Government[8]. The status and nature of libraries coming under the Local Library Authority were as noted below[9].

Besides this, there were 128 aided libraries in Malabar which enjoyed a grant of Rs. 5370/- during 1956-57[10]. At that time there were 500 libraries in Malabar, which got no financial assistance[11]. Most of these libraries were mere reading rooms which possessed less than five hundred books. These libraries were attached to *Kala Samities* (Art centres). They formed drama clubs, wrote dramas, and staged them in different parts of the State. Some of these libraries made curtains for staging dramas and sold them. The income thus received was used for the development and maintenance of libraries[12]. The *Kala Samitis* of the people of Malabar comprised of the unorganized libraries on the once side, and independent specialised *Kala Samitis*, on the other[13].

As per the Madras Library Act of 1948, the Local Library Authority was entrusted with the collection of library cess. But the money was not used for the development of libraries. The amount was given to the Government as loans without any interest[14]. No effort was made to get the co-operation of the local public for setting up buildings for these libraries[15]. At that time, *Mathrubhoomi*, a leading Malayalam daily, pointed out that the style of functioning of the Local Library Authority was not conducive to the expansion of library movement in the State. So the libraries coming under Local Library Authority might be merged with the United Travancore Cochin Library Association, and a meeting of library workers of State could be held for the purpose[16].

Even before the formation of the Kerala State, the Aikya Thiruvithamcore Cochin Grandhasala Sanghom had its workers visited the libraries of Malabar, and discussed with the library workers on the expansion of United Travancore Cochin Library Association into Malabar[17]. The North Zone Library Conference convened at Calicut on 2 February 1957 made an earnest attempt for an All Kerala Grandhasala Sanghom (All Kerala Library Association)[18]. On 16 February 1957 the Thanoor Mobile Library merged with the Aikya Thiruvithamcore-Cochin Grandhasala Sanghom and it was the first Library from Malabar to accept membership in the Sanghom[19]. A working committee consisting of Panampalli Govinda Menon (President), K. Damodaran, M.P Manmadhan (Vice-President), P.N. Panicker (General Secretary), M.M. John (Treasurer), and A.P. Nambiar, K.K. Nair, A. Balagopal, and C.K. Mani (Members) was formed on 28 July 1958 by the Office Bearers of the Aikya Thiruvithamcore Cochin Grandhasala Sanghom. With the help of this working committee members, the Aikya Thiruvithamcore-Cochin Grandhasala Sanghom officially changed into Kerala Grandhasala Sanghom (K.G.S). On 15 September 1958, a governing body, with full representation of the library workers, all Taluks in Kerala, was formed[20]. Thus the long cherished desire of the Akhila Thiruvithamcore Grandhasala Sanghom was fulfilled, and it assumed an all Kerala character.

With a view to the efficient functioning of the library movement of the State, a Library Advisory Board was constituted on 10 August 1956. The Board consisted of 11 members of whom 5 were from Kerala Grandhasala Sanghom and the rest were Government nominees[21]. In 1959 a new Library Board, consisting of 15 members was constituted, in which the majority representation was given to library workers. Later, the Government decided to do away with the Board owing to the frequent conflict between the Library workers and the Board[22].

During the time of Panampalli Govinda Menon the right to distribute grants to libraries was handed-over to Panchayats[23]. The Panchayat Director wrote to the Government, "at present the distribution of grant is done through the United Travancore – Cochin Library Association, an autonomous body, after careful inspection of the libraries by Gradation Committee appointed for this purpose. This method of distribution of grants has been tried for the last five years, and found quite satisfactory, and it has been recognized as the most suitable and really useful way of distribution of grants, and there have been no complaints from any quarters. The existing system may be allowed to continue without any change in the interest of the library movement of the state"[24]. But, the Government issued an order which insisted that the distribution of library grant must be made through the Panchayats[25].

The public opinion rose against this move of the Government. *Malayala Manorama* stated that it was an unrefined order[26]. The other dailies of Malayalam like *Mathrubhoomi. Malayala Rajyam* and *Dinamani,* observed that the order might be withdrawn, and the earlier position maintained in the regard[27]. The first elected democrative Government of Kerala assumed its office on 5 April 1957[28]. This Government cancelled the order of distribution of library grants through Panchayats on 30 April 1957. The Government further ordered, "in future, library grants will be distributed through District Social Education Office and their subordinate officers. Pending the enactment of Kerala Libraries Act, the Local Library Authority will continue to be in-charge of the library movement in Malabar area. Travancore - Cochin Area District committee may be constituted by Government to take over the management of important libraries, village libraries will be placed under the control of Social Education Officers"[29].

The intention of the Government was to organize a separate department to look into social education, libraries, arts clubs, *Kathakali, Melas,* and so on. And it will distribute grants placed at their disposal by the State Govedrnment[30]. In the order, the role of the Aikya Thiruvithamcore-Cochin Grandhasala Sanghom has also been carefully commented to the tune that it played a definite role in the expansion of the library movement. Besides it was promised that the Sanghom would be given deserving representation in all library committees to be constituted by the Government[31].

The Government issued another order by which the full charge of the libraries of the State were given to the Director of Social Education. The right of fixing grant to libraries was also given to the Director of Social Education instead of the Gradation Committee constituted by the previous Government for the purpose.[32] The order curtailed the powers of the Sanghom, which it enjoyed in the previous years. Until then it was the sole agency of the libraries in the State, and that was appreciated and approved by all.

The dailies of Kerala expressed great concern over these orders. *Malayala Manorama* writes: "this order is to curtail the democratic nature of the Sanghom, and the ruling Communist Party is trying to increase their hold on the libraries in the State"[33]. Pothujanam, another important evening daily wrote: "the Communist Party has severe enemity towards Aikya Thiruvithamcore-Cochin Grandhasala Sanghom, and they are trying to change it as their spokesmen[34]". *Express,* remarked that the order of the Government is pitiable, and those who are talking about democracy are trying to destroy this democratic institution through foul means[35]. *Mathrubhoomi* appreciated the work the Sanghom, and viewed that the Local Library Authority and the new Act might be withdrawn; otherwise the fast growing library movement of the State might face severe setbacks[36]. By December 1957, the Government Ordered that the Library Advisory Board would utilize the service of the Kerala Grandhasala Sanghom and the quantum of grant for each library would be decided on the basis of the report available from the Kerala Granshasala Sanghom[37].

Meanwhile, an office for the Sanghom was opened at Trivandrum in the Public Library compound by Joseph Mundassery, the State Education Minister, on 18 August 1958[38]. According to him, the Gradation Committee was unnecessary, and the organizer of the libraries could often easily report the conditions of the libraries to the Sanghom, and on the basis of this report, the library grant could be fixed every year. Moreover, Kerala Grandhasala Sanghom was an unofficial organisation, and some sort of Government control was very necessary,[39] especially in view of the fact that it was the chief funding agency of the Sanghom.

The number of affiliated libraries to the Sanghom swelled to 2000 , and 45 Taluk Unions worked in the State for the speedy implementation of different programmes of Grandhasala Sanghom during that time. Two lakhs of people were members of the libraries, and the total collection of books was twenty one lakhs[40].

However most of the collections of the libraries were stories, poems, dramas, novels and detective stories. Most of the rural people preferred these detective stories. The lack of authoritative books, particularly science books, in these collections was a serious drawnback[41]. Some of these libraries were functioning as agencies to encourage the selling of low quality books of some publishers[42].

During that period certain libraries have started to function with Kala Samitis, Children's Club and Mahila Section (Ladies Section). Drama groups, dance classes, music troops and so on, were also organized by most of the libraries. The facilities for Sports Clubs were also provided by almost all the libraries[43].

In September-October 1955, a Seminar on the 'Role of Libraries in Social Education was organized by the Indian Adult Education Association in Delhi. As per the recommendations of the seminar an "Advisory Committee for Libraries" under the Chairmanship of K.P.Sinha was formed by the Ministry of Education, Government of India, to investigate into the situations of the state libraries in India[44].

The Committee visited the libraries of Kerala in January 1958. They pointed out the need for a scientific management of the libraries in the State, and the appointment of some qualified persons at the top levels of the Sanghom[45]. The State Education Minister Joseph Mundassery, reported to a Central Library Committee that the K.G.S of the State was working as a bogus institution[46]

The newspapers of Kerala severely criticized the policies and attitudes of the Government towards K.G.S . *Mathrubhoomi, Malayala Manorama, Janatha, Express, Deshabandhu, Kerala Kaumudi*, etc., wrote that the policies of Government were not favourable for the expansion of the library movement in the State. They appreciated the services of the K.G.S for the social and cultural development of Kerala[47]. Some political parties, especially, the main opposition party of the state, Indian National Congress, strongly condemned the attitude of the ruling Communist Party towards the Kerala Grandhasala Sanghom. The Kottayam District Congress Committee passed a resolution on the situation faced by the Kerala Grandhasala Sanghom[48]. The resolution sated: "The Congress party, and its members had the moral duty to restore the freedom, and democracy in the functioning of the Kerala Grandhasala Sanghom, and the libraries of the State"[49]. A notice published by the Kottayam Congress District Committee on 24 March 1958 stated that any attempt of the Communist, who were trying to capture both libraries and cultural centres, would be thwarted by the Congress[50].

During that time the Government, divided Malabar into three revenue district, namely, Calicut, Palghat and Cannanore. Consequently, three local library authorities, for these revenue districts were constituted in 1959. Each of the Local Library Authority had a District Central Library situated at the District Headquarters, and a branch under it[51].

The Chief Minister E.M.S Namboodiripad took interest to prepare a Library Bill, and the Education Minister, Joseph Mundassery, invited S.R. Ranganathan for this purpose. Accordingly, S.R. Ranganathan visited Kerala in April 1959 as a consultant for the development of a State Library System, and drafting a Library Bill[52]. Ranganathan, after consultation with Kerala Grandhasala Sanghom, and Balagopal, the Chairman of Local Library Authority in Kozhikode, visited some libraries in the State. He scrutinized the statistical data furnished by the Government and drafted a Library Bill, and worked out a library development plan. The plan consisted of general principles for the design of a public library system as part one. The second part dealt with Kerala the Public Library Bill, and the third part contained details of model rules. The plan stressed the need for an immediate recognition of Trivandrum Public Library as State Central Library, and the starting of Bachelor's Degree, and Certificate Course in Library Science[53].

In the Bill, there was provision for the State Library Authority, which has to function as the appex body in the managerial Authority. The Minister for Education to be an ex-officio member in the state library Authority, rural Library Authority, and duties and powers of each of them were included in the Bill. There was provision for the collection of library cess by local Authorities, and stipulation that the collected cess should be transferred to State Library Authorities within three months. Besides, there was provision for Government grant also[54].

The Government, after detailed study and discussion at various levels, decided to present the Bill in the Legislative Assembly. But before presenting the Bill in the Legislative Assembly a series of agitations were organized by the Opposition Parties and communal groups against the Communist government. A Conference of all communal organisations was held at Changanacherry on 1 May 1959, and a Liberation Council or *Vimochana Samara Samithi* was constituted under the leadership of Mannathu Padmanabhan who was the leader of Nair Community[55]. A joint convention of the leaders of Congress Party, the Praja

Socialist Party, Muslim League, the Nair Service Society, and the Church Council were held at Ernakulam on 11 June 1959, and the final decision was taken to start the 'liberation struggle' from 13 June 1959, following the state-wide strike on 20 June 1959[56]. In the struggle, many institutions, including the K.G.S also indirectly participated[57]. Their target was to topple the Communist ministry. At last, the Central Government interfered, and the Communist Ministry of Kerala was dismissed on 31 July 1959[58].

Before the dismisal of the Government, a new Order for the Gradation of libraries was published; thereby the different Grades of libraries were decided as per the following standards presented in the Table[59] (Table 4).

A new Ministry which assumed power on 22 February 1960 headed by Pattom A Thanu Pillai, who belonged to the Praja Socialist Party (PSP),[60] followed the gradation policy of the previous Government. He was in favour of S.R. Ranganathan's Library Bill. But the Kerala Grandhasala Sanghom was against it, and, instead, it held that when the Bill became law it should get majority representation in the State Library Authority and Local library Authority[61]. The Taluk Unions of the libraries passed resolutions against the draft bill, and demanded that statutory powers might be given to the Kerala Grandhasala Sanghom. It may be allowed to continue to function as the pivot of the library movement in the State. They also added that Ranganathan prepared the draft bill on the model of Madras Library Act without considering the prevailing situations of the libraries in the State[62].

The office bearers of the Sanghom met at Ernakulam under the Chairmanship of K.A. Damodara Menon, the President of the Sanghom, (1961-62) on 20 October 1960 and requested for some substantial changes in the draft bill of Ranganathan. A new Library Bill prepared by

Panampalli Govinda Menon, the former President of the Sanghom, (1953-60) was sent to the Government for its consideration[63].

According to S.R. Ranganathan, the work of the people of Kerala for the expansion of library movement was highly appreciable. He wrote that in every village, library was functioning as a community centre attached to recreation clubs, sports clubs, *kalasamithies* and so on. The library workers in Kerala consisted mostly of dedicated social workers. But a state central library and a library law were the need of the hour[64].

Ranganthan's Library Bill was discussed widely by the people of the Kerala. E. Raman Menon, the President of the Kerala Grandhalaya Sanghom welcomed the Bill, and argued that undue importance should not be given to the K.G.S. which was a voultary organisation[65]. C. Narayana Pillai, freedom fighter and journalist, expressed the opinion that in the event of this Library Bill being implemented, after thirty years there should be a central library, and district libraries, a few libraries in places where the population was less than one lakh. After thirty years the present village libraries, cease to function as the cultural centre of each village. He also requested the Government not to take over these institutions[66].

Malayala Manorama wrote that some basic changes might be made in the bill in order to give the K.G.S an important place in the development of the library movement in the State and it might be allowed to function as before[67]. *Mathrubhoomi* pointed out that while making a library legislation all the aspects of this problem should be considered , and proper place should be given to the Library Association of the State[68].

The number of libraries affiliated to the Sanghom increased to 2848 and the membership of these libraries

Table 4. Basis of Grades of Libraries

Sl.No.	*Grade of Libraries*	*No.of books possessed*	*No.of news papers (M)*	*(E)*	*No.of Magazines*	*Equipments (Necessary items)*	*Distribution of books per month*
1	2	3	4		5	6	7
1	H	600-800	3	-	5	Yes	100
2.	H1	750-800	3	-	5	"	100
3.	G	800-1200	3	-	7	"	175
4	G1	1000-1200	3	-	7	"	175
5	F	1200-2200	5	-	7	"	266
6	F1	1800-2200	5	-	7	"	300
7	E	2000-3200	5	-	7	"	333
8	E1	2700-3200	5	-	7	"	392
9	D	3200-4500	5	2	10	"	450
10	D1	4000-4500	5	2	12	"	500
11	C	4500-6000	5	2	12	"	550
12	C1	5300-6000	5	2	12	"	558
13	B	5300-6000	5	2	15	"	625
14	B1	6000-7000	5	2	15	"	754
15	A	6750-7500	5	2	15	"	883
16	A1	Above 10000	5	2	25	"	1250

(Contd....)

(Contd. Table 4.)

Library users per year	*Building rented/ owned*	*Expenditure of books and periodicals per year*	*Salary of Library staff*	*Income from library*	*Year of functioning*	*Grant from Govt.*
8	9	10	11	12	13	14
1000	Rented Owned	Rs.60	No.	Rs.60	1 Yr.	100
1000	"	60	"	60	"	120
2000	"	120	"	120	"	140
2000	"	120	"	120	"	170
3000	"	180	"	180	"	200
3000	"	180	"	180	"	225
4100	"	240	"	240	5	250
4100	"	300	"	240	5	300
5000	"	300	"	300	10	350
5000	"	360	"	300	10	375
8000	"	360	"	360	10	400
8000	"	360	"	360	10	450
10000	"	420	420	420	10	500
10000	"	420	420	500	10	550
15000	"	500	500	500	10	600
20000	"	800	800	800	10	1000

was 298,376 during 1959-60. Among these libraries 146 were in towns, and the remaining situated in the villages of Kerala. Ninety per cent of these libraries had buildings of their own and did not get any financial assistance from the Government[69]. These libraries had fullfledged sections for women and children. Every year, about two hundred new libraries emerged under the patronage of the K.G.S. The total number of collections in these libraries were 341352[70]. The reason for this speedy growth of the library movement in the State was its democratic framework, and the co-operation of the public[71].

The post of Organising Inspectors was completely abolished by the K.G.S in 1960. Since the formation of the K.G.S. these inspectors have been working hard for the growth of the library movement. At first, their number was four, and in 1950, it increased thirty[72]. During the time of P.S. Rao, Advisor of Kerala State (1956-57), they got salaries and Dearness Allowances equal to the Government employees, and it continued up to 1960. However the K.G.S. felt that their function was not satisfactory. Meanwhile the instructors organized a union and submitted a representation to the Sanghom. It contained, among other things, monetary demands too. The financial position of the Sanghom was too weak to consider it sympathetically. This was another reason to abolish their post[73]. Two Malayalam dailies, mouth piece of the Communist Party of India, i.e., *Janayugam* and *Deshabhimani,* severely criticized this step of the Sanghom. They delineated the decision as undemocratic[74].

As in the case of the previous Congress Government (Ministry of A.J. John), Pattom Government also interfered with the selection of books in the libraries. P.T. Chacko, the Home Minister, ordered the libraries of the State not to purchase "Nishagandhi", a leading Malayalam novel of veteran novelist S.K. Pottakad,[75] who secured the Jnanapeetham (1980), the greatest literary award of India. The Minister felt that the book dealt with too much of sex and as such it was misfit to be kept in the libraries of the State[76].

The Government grant was the main source of income to the libraries affiliated to the Sanghom. During the time of Pattom Thanupillai many complaints were raised against the distribution of library grant. In order to fix the grant to the libraries, a Gradation Committee was constituted on 17 June 1960 and in each district a district committee was constituted on 15 June 1960[77]. But most of the libraries recommended by this Gradation Committee could not get grants due to the super checking of recommendations by the State Education Department. Since 20 September 1956, the library grants have been distributed through District Education Offices[78].

All Malayalam dailies criticized the double verification process of the Government. They wrote that the only reputed socio-cultural institution in Kerala was the K.G.S and its service to the society was considerable. So, no Government could by-pass the K.G.S. A liberal library policy was the need of the hour, and all possible facilities should be at the disposal of the K.G.S. for a better library set up in the State[79].

When Pattom A Thanu Pillai, Chief Minister of Kerala, was appointed as the Governor of Punjab, a new Ministry under R. Sankar assumed charge on 26 September 1962[80]. According to R. Sankar, the library movement was the only movement that could contribute much to the socio-cultural development of the State. He admitted that the Government was not rendering much help to it. Since 1962, he had been the President of the K.G.S[81] He sanctioned building grants to libraries. Along with this order two models of library building were published, and stipulated that if any one constructed this type of libraries it would be entitled to get Rs. 2080/- (1/3 of the total expenses) as building and equipments grant. Prior consent of the Government for the construction of these libraries was needed[82]. As a result of this, many libraries constructed their own buildings by making use of this aid. In 1969, 1920 libraries has constructed new buildings, and some of them raised funds from the public by conducting cultural programmes[83].

The Mysore Public Library Act came to the scene in 1964, with more equitable distribution of library fund than what had been provided in the earlier Madras Act. To incorporate similar changes with the Bill, S.R. Ranganathan requested the Kerala Government to provide some more financial data[84]. Before necessary changes in the Bill could be effected in the light of the data, R. Sankar resigned from power on 10 September 1964 due to the internal problems that brew up in the State unit of the Congress Party[85]. In that year P.S. George was elected the new president of the Sanghom who continued in this post till 1970.

In 1965, the Sanghom submitted a report to the Government regarding the functions of the Kerala Grandhasala Sanghom and its financial position. It stated that the grant to libraries was decided ten years back, and it should be revised in accordance with the hike in the prices of books and other unforeseen expenditure. The government made certain changes to the rules regarding the grade of libraries, but the grant to libraries was not raised[86]. On 26 May 1965 the leading Malayalam newspapers wrote editorials on the importance of the K.G.S, and called the attention of the Government to the matter. *Mathrubhoomi* stressed the need for giving more powers to the K.G.S[87]. Likewise, *Malayala Manorama* stated that the complete administration of libraries might be given to the

Sanghom which was the sole agency of the library movement of the State[88].

Table 5. The New Grades and Grants of Libraries

1966-97		*1967-68*	
Grade	*Grant Rs.*	*Grade*	*Grant Rs*
A1	1000	A	1200
A	600		
B1	550	B	700
B	500		
C1	450	C	550
C	400		
D1	375	D	450
D	350		
E1	300	E	325
E	250		
F1	225	F	275
F	200		
G1	170	G	200
G	140		
H1	120	H	150
H	100		

The total number of libraries affiliated to the Sanghom increased to 3881 in 1965-1966, when some districts of Kerala had distributing library system. The distributing library system was conducted by the Government as a part of the Five year Plan of the Central Government[89]. The K.G.S started state-wide literacy campaign during this period.

The K.G.S focusing on the need for eradicating illiteracy requested the public to take membership in their nearest libraries[90]. At that time 'Sunday Standard' the weekend edition of the Indian Express commented that library movement in Kerala was going ahead with different novel programmes and the people should give all possible help[91].

With the increase in the collections in the libraries, the number of trash literature also increased during this time. Most of the Malayalam writers were of opinion that since libraries were the cultural centres, the spread of pot-bellied literature should be controlled. Otherwise, it would adversely affect the quality of readers and their taste in literature[92]. The K.G.S also invited the attention of the library workers to this pollution in the literary front[93].

During 1967-68, the grades and grant of libraries were revised by the state Government. The existing number of grades were reduced and the grant to books and furniture were increased. The different grades of libraries existed before 1966-67 and the new grades and grants are given in the Table[94] (Table No.5).

The Communist Party of India (C.P.I) underwent a vertical split into two groups in 1964. The break away group formed a new political party called Communist Party of India Marxist [C.P.I (M)] in the same year. However, these two political parties came together in the Assembly Election of 1967 and secured majority. They formed a coalition Government under E.M.S Namboodiripad, the leader of the C.P.I (M) on 6 March 1967[95]. During the tenure of this ministry another public library bill was piloted by the Government. It was actually the draft bill prepared by S.R. Ranganathan in 1960, with slight modifications. It attempted to give due representation to the K.G.S. in the State Library Authority[96]. But the K.G.S. was not at all pleased because the Government Act did not recognize the necessity for the continued working of the K.G.S. the Sanghom pointed out the set back experienced in Cochin area where the library system was under the Government control. It also laid stress on and the non-functioning of libraries in Malabar, where the public libraries were under the Local Library authorities[97]. But before anything could be done, the Government of E.M.S. Namboodiripad resigned on 14 October 1969 due to the internal problems among the coalition partners[98].

After the formation of the Kerala State, a sweeping land reform policies and educational reforms- were brought about, which caused fundamental changes in the society of Kerala. One of the radical provisions of the Agrarian Relations Act of 1958 was the prohibition of eviction[99]. However many provisions of this Act were struck down by the Supreme Court. Hence a new legislation, called the Land Reform Act of 1964, was passed which favoured the Land Lords[100]. But the coalition Ministry which came to power in 1967 passed the Kerala stay of Eviction Proceeding Act of 1967 staying evictions of all types[101]. The amendment to the Land Reforms Act enacted in 1969 conferred security to all categories of tenants in Kerala materializing the maxim 'land to the tiller[102]. It was a radical economic measure which provided succour to the tenants and peasants.

Likewise on 1 June 1959, a new educational policy came into existence. As per this, the Government support and control over the schools was important. It also visualised direct payment to the private school teachers like the Government school teachers[103]. Owing to political pressure, the Governments were forced to sanction new schools. As a result of this, the number of schools increased (see table 6) and almost all children in the state got an opportunity to go to schools[104]. The literacy rate in Kerala began to rise[105] (see table 7). The Government expenditure on education also increased. But the amount spent for the development of libraries was very meagre when compared to the amount spent for the educational development in the State[106] (see table 8).

Table 6. Literacy Rate from 1901 - 1981 (in percentage)

Year	*India*	*Kerala*
1901	3.35	11.14
1911	5.92	13.31
1921	7.16	19.02
1931	9.50	21.34
1941	16.10	Not available
1951	16.67	40.47
1961	24.02	56.85
1971	29.45	60.40
1981	36.30	70.42

By the 1970's the K.G.S had developed into one of the important cultural centres of Kerala. On 8 November 1970, in connection with the Silver Jubilee Celebrations of the Sanghom, it conducted a cultural procession starting from Kasargode, the northern part of the State, to Trivandrum, the capital of the State. In the course of the long procession two slogans were raised, "read and grow", and "think and act"[107]. The slogans attracted the public, and they welcomed the processionists. The officials and ministers came out to the public road and welcomed the procession.

It was a new experiment in Kerala which was later followed by other organisations to spread their ideas[108].

It showed the rest of the country that the people belonging to different faiths and creeds, and political affiliations could be united into one unit by a socio-cultural organization like the K.G.S. It also stated that, of all the varied programmes which the Sanghom successfully carried out, the one which attracted them most was the literacy march which touched every nook and corner. According to them, this march gave the people an air of cultural heritage. The march reached Trivandrum on 20 December 1970. It enabled the Sanghom to impress upon the masses with its contributions during the past twenty five years. All the dailies of the State came forward commending on the meritorious service rendered by it. The *Kerala Kaumudi* wrote that the K.G.S had attained wonderful achievements, and there was no other voluntary organisation on par with it.

Table 7 Number of Schools from 1961 – 81

Schools	*1960-61*	*1980-81*
Lower primary schools (L.P.S)	6,705	8,013
Upper primary schools (U.P.S)	1,932	2,732
High Schools (H.S)	895	1,680
Total	9,532	12,425
Teachers	108,867	164,000
Students	1,690,400	5,650,798

Table 8. Amount Spent for Libraries and Educational Institutions

Year	*Grant in aid libraries (Rs)*	*Education Expenditure (Rs)*	*Government*
1945-46	4,000	81,12,670	Travancore
1946-57	4,000	1,07,95,270	"
1947-48	10,695	1,21,56,798	"
1948-49	44,060	1,53,59,497	"
1949-50	78,000	1,50,64,413	Travancore-Cochin
1950-51	90,886	2,64,20,400	"
1951-52	83,340	27,60,000	"
1952-53	1,45,485	3,20,25,800	"
1953-54	1,45,485	3,81,08,000	"
1954-55	1,70,415	3,8071,000	"
1955-56	2,40,410	7,11,39,800	"
1956-57	2,55,930	2,88,25,600	"
1957-58	3,10,655	9,58,40,400	Kerala Government
1958-59	3,25,400	13,74,39,460	"
1959-60	4,04,340	13,66,61,000	"
1960-61	4,53,230	13,37,26,566	"
1961-62	4,27,790	18,54,83,722	"
1962-63	4,76,125	19,14,14,000	"
1963-64	4,93,760	20,19,46,000	"
1964-65	5,14,870	28,07,80,000	"
1965-66	5,51,030	28,37,43.000	"
1966-67	5,43,750	37,34,60,000	"
1967-68	11,18,615	41,47,85,000	"
1968-69	9,13,610	43,63,98,000	"
1969-70	7,22,135	54,28,98,000	"

(Contd.)

(Contd. Table 8)

Year	*Grant in aid libraries (Rs)*	*Education Expenditure (Rs)*	*Government*
1970-71	10,39,475	60,12,37,000	"
1971-72	12,50,000	66,14,87,000	"
1972-73	13,00,000	71,04,72,000	"
1973-74	13,40,000	82,34,58,000	"
1974-75	14,00,000	1,03,17,00.00	"
1975-76	14,00,000	1,28,97,00,000	"
1976-77	30,00,000	1,41,62,88,100	"

Sanghom was blessed with thousands of dedicated social workers. The paper requested the urgent enactment of a law for the conduct of the libraries[109].

Malayala Manorama and *Mathrubhoomi* wrote that the cultural leadership of the state had reached the hands of the K.G.S and it was a decisive cultural force in the State. In their opinion, the ability of the Sanghom to mobilize human power was accepted by earlier administrators who came forward with liberal grants. The papers pleaded for a considerable increase in the grant given to the Sanghom[110]. *Mathrubhoomi* remarked that the libraries have developed due to the untiring efforts of dedicated workers in the rural areas. The libraries were considered as the nucleus of the rural community, where the facilities for reading were provided. The library movement in Kerala had secured a formidable place owing to the sense of dedication and intensity of action of the true library workers[111].

The other Malayalam dailies like *Chandrika, Deepika, Deshabhimani, Express, Janayugam, Kerala Bhooshanam* and *Malayala Rajyam* too wrote about the achievements of the Kerala Grandhasala Sanghom, They also praised the work of P.N. Panicker and described him as the 'life and soul' of the library movement in Kerala [112].

After the cultural procession and jubilee festival of 1970, the Sanghom diverted its attention to new ventures. Among these, literacy programme was an important one. Eventhough the adult education programme had been promoted after the formation of the Sanghom, an exclusive programme of eradication of illiteracy had commended only in 1971. In order to eradicate illiteracy completely from the State a comprehensive plan for functional literacy was chalked out and submitted to the Central Government by the Sanghom in 1970[113]. It proposed to open seven thousand literacy centres in the State to complete the programme. The ministry, however, directed the Sanghom to launch pilot projects in two development blocks ie., Athiyannoor and Malapuram. Both these places were backward areas of Kerala. For the purpose, about one lakh rupees was sanctioned. Ten centres, from each of these two very underdeveloped blocks were selected and teachers were given training. From among fishermen and agricultural labourers, forty persons in the age group of eighteen and thirty were selected for the experiment. They were taught reading and writing as well as the techniques of their profession[114].

The Athiyannoor centre and the Malappuram centre were opened in December 1971 and January 1972 respectively[115]. The library workers and social workers were given training in order to conduct classes in these centres. Most of these centres were attached to the libraries. A literacy procession was conducted in Novemebr 14 and 15 of 1971 at Athiyannoor block in order to attract the illiterate to these centres[116]. In Athiyannoor, the inhabitants were mostly fishermen and coolies. During the literacy procession they raised certain slogans which were capable to attract fishermen and coolies. The slogans meant:[117]

"Sea faring brothers
Don't you want to learn"
Toiling brothers
Don't you want to learn ?
Go to the literacy centre
And learn the alphabet"

When the procession was in progress the local people and children joined the procession and shouted the following slogan[118]:

"We will fight against illiteracy,
It is our slogan
We will learn and we will grow
It is our slogan".

It was the first time that such a literacy procession for attracting illiterates and neoliterates to literacy centres was conducted in the State[119]. The editorial of Sanghom's official journal, Grandhalokam observed on the procession that if one wanted to understand the pulse of the local people, one should go to them[120].

These experimental literacy centres attracted a large number of illiterate people who attended the classes after 7 P.M every day. These centres were primarily for literacy classes but they discussed general science and social problems also. Literacy centres for ladies were opened separately. In Maruthor, a place in Athiyannoor Block, Trivandrum, there was one such important centre, where 82 ladies studied[121]. Neoliterate used these centres as a place for continuing education. The Grandhasala Sanghom prepared certain books for this neoliterates and in 1972 it started a weekly called *Sakshara Keralam*. The liberacy programme of these centres continued for six months[122].

During that time some libraries were started in different parts of the state especially for the *Harijans* (the downtrodden section of the society), for their socio-cultural developments. They were conducted by the State Government. In 1970, seventy two Harijana Libraries were transferred to the K.G.S and the Sanghom gave affiliations to these libraries[123].

In 1970 and 1971 two library bills were introduced in the Kerala Legislative Assembly. The first bill was called The Kerala Grandhasala Bill 1970 and it was presented by K.G. Kunjukrishna Pillai, M.L.A. In that Bill, the library workers and Grandhasala Sanghom Officers were given due representation in the State Library Union. The administrative strata of the libraries of the State were the Panchayat Library Union, Block Union, District Union and State Library Union respectively[124]. But this private Bill did not get through the assembly. A new library bill was moved by the Government in 1971.

The new bill, called 'the Kerala Public Libraries Bill of 1971 was presented in the Assembly by the Minister for Education C.H. Mohammed Koya (1970-71)[125]. The salient feature of this bill were[126]:

1. Provisions for one State Library Authority for the whole State and District Library Authority for each revenue district.
2. Provision for a Director of Libraries with prescribed qualifications who shall be the Secretary to the State Library Authority.
3. Library Cess to be levied at not more than ten per cent.
4. Provision for grant not less than the total of library cess collected.
5. Rule for the absorption of 4000 public libraries of the State into the new system.

Justice V.R. Krishna Iyer, a Supreme Court Judge and a Member of the Indian Law Commission observed that while preparing a library bill for the State, the democratic character has to be maintained as in the case of the K.G.S[127]. *Mathrubhoomi*, severely criticized the bill and pointed out the following defects[128].

1. There is no provision for establishing a public library system in the state.
2. No place is given to library professionals in the Library Authority.
3. The provision of the library cess is not satisfactory; an amount for continuing education may be included in the budget.

The other Malayalam dailies like *Malayala Manorama*, *Kerala Kaumudi*, *Deshabhimani* and *Express* stressed the urgency for a library law in the State[129]. But this bill was also not considered by the Kerala Legislative Assembly. Justice Krishna Iyer had drafted a new library bill at the request of the K.G.S. The title given to the draft was 'The Kerala Grandhasala Sanghom Bill' instead of 'The Kerala Public Library Bill'. The title asserted that K.G.S was the pivot of the library movement in the State. But the Government rejected this bill too. On 18 June 1973, a *Dharna* (protest meeting) was organized by the library workers in front of the Government Secretariat for implementing a library bill. The then Education Minister Chakkeri Ahamedkutty (1973-77) assured the Sanghom workers that their demands would be considered at the earliest[130].

Subsequently, 'The Kerala Public Libraries Bill of 1971' was reintroduced by him, and the Assembly referred the bill to the Select Committee[131]. The Select Committee held various sittings in different parts of Kerala, and collected evidence from the public. At that time, most of the library workers expressed the view that the K.G.S has been mainly responsible for the development of the library movement in the State, particularly in the rural areas. It was a representative body, democratically elected from among the affiliated libraries, and they felt that they could adequately supervise, and co-ordinate the activities of libraries. The Bill provided provisions for giving representation to the K.G.S on the various library authorities[132].

The Annual Library Conference of the K.G.S was held at Trivandrum on 21 March 1976 and passed a resolution in favour of this Bill. It requested the Government to pass the Bill in the ensuing session of the Assembly[133]. But the request remained unfulfilled owing to the dissolution of the legislature.

Table 9. Refixed Grades and Grants

Grade	*Issue of books*	*Number of Newspapers (Malayalam)*	*Number of Newspapers (English)*	*Period- -icals*	*Grants (Rs)*
A	12000	4	1	15	1800
B	8000	4	1	12	1000
C	6000	4	1	10	850
D	5000	4	0	8	600
E	4000	4	0	8	500
F	3000	4	0	6	375

At that time a new Gradation Committee was constituted on 21 February 1976 by the Government which refixed the grades of libraries and grants as given in the Table[134] (Table 9) .

Thus ever since the formation of the Kerala State many efforts were made by various Governments for library legislation. During this period the Sanghom had widened its functional activities by introducing many novel programmes. In fact the K.G.S had become a focus of public opinion whenever the Government tried to touch the affairs of its.

Notes and References

1. *Kerala State Administrative Report- 1957-58,* Trivandrum : Government Press, 1958, p.1.
2. *Ibid.,* pp. 1-2.
3. *Ibid.*
4. *Hundred years of legislature bodies in Kerala 1888-1988,* Centenary Souvenir, Trivandrum : Kerala Legislature, 1990, p. 673.
5. K.P. Kesava Menon, *Presidential address of North Malabar Library Conferences,* (Mal.), Calicut, Spector Press, 1957, p. 2.
6. N. Vasudevan, Chairman, *Report of Local Library Authority,* (Mal.), Calicut: L.L.A , 1985, pp. 1-2.
7. K.A. Issac, "Keralathile Grandhasala Prasthanam: Kerala *Grandhasala Sanghom Rajatha Jubilee Souvenir,* (Mal.), Trivandrum : Kerala Grandhasala Sanghom, 1971, p. 105.
8. Pirappancode Murali, "Keralathile Grandhasala Prasthanam": *Grandhalokam,* Trivandrum, (Mal.), Special Issue, September, 1990, p. 54.
9. K. P. Kesava Menon, No. 5, p. 2.
10. *Ibid.*
11. *The Kerala Public Library Bill, 1985: Background Material,* Trivandrum: the Secretariat of the Legislature, 1987, p.13.
12. "Malabarile Grandhasalakal", *Grandhalokam,* Trivandrum, (Mal.), Vol. 9 (6), 1957, p. 332.

13. S. Guptan Nair, "Vayanasalakalum Ethara Samskarika Pravarthanaum", *Grandhalokam,* Trivandrum, (Mal.), Vol. 9 (7), 1957, p. 403.
14. "Malabarile Grandhasalakal", *Mathrubhoomi,* Calicut, (Mal.), Daily, 15 June 1956.
15. P. Ramanujan Nair, *The library Movement in Kerala: The need for reform and legislation,* Trivandrum : Tvm writers club, 1974. p. 22.
16. "Malabarile librarikal", *Mathrubhoomi,* Calicut, (Mal.), Daily, 16 August 1956.
17. The Diary of P.N. Panicker, dated 24-05-1956.
18. K.M. Lenin, *Keralathile Grandhasala Prasthanam,* Trivandrum: Steps, 1982, p. 171.
19. Pirappancode Murali, No. 8, p. 61.
20. *Ibid.*, pp. 61-62.
21. "Kerala Governmentum Library Prasthanavum", *Kerala Kaumudi,* Trivandrum, Daily, 7 April 1958.
22. Pirappancode Murali, No.8, p.63.
23. "Panchayath Librarikal," *Grandhalokam,* Trivandrum, (Mal.), Vol. 8(1), 1956, p. 635.
24. File No. E1/81/55 dated 15-3-1956 by the Director of Panchayats, Trivandrum : Government Secretariat.
25. *Ibid.*
26. "Library Grant", *Malayala Manorama,* Kottayam, (Mal.), Daily, 21 October 1956.
27. (a) "Librarykalkulla Grant", *Mathrubhoomi,* Calicut, (Mal.), Daily 8 October 1956.

(b) "Grandhasala Sangathe Paripozhippikkanam", *Malayala Rajyam,* Quilon, Daily, 5 October 1956.

(c) "Panchayath Grant", *Dinamani,* Quilon, (Mal.), Daily, 8 August 1956.

28. *Hundred years of legislature bodies in Kerala, 1888- 1988,* No. 4, p. 673.
29. File No. Ed (D) 3-6110/ 57 EDHD dated 30-4-1957, Trivandrum : Government Secretariat.

30. *Ibid.*
31. *Ibid.*
32. File No. ED (D) 4-6110/57, G.O. dated 30-4-1957, ED (D)/ E.H.D, Trivandrum : Government Secretariat.
33. Editorial, *Malayala Manorama,* Kottayam, (Mal.), Daily, 5 July 1957.
34. Editorial, *Pothujanam,* Trivandrum, (Mal.), Daily, 8 May 1957.
35. Editorial, *Express,* Trichur, (Mal.), Daily, 19 May 1957.
36. Editorial, *Mathrubhoomi,* Calicut, (Mal.), Daily, 9 May 1957.
37. English
38. "Puthiya Sanghom Office", *Grandhalokam,* Trivandrum: (Mal.), Vol. 9 (9), 1957, p. 590.
39. Joseph Mundassery, *Kozhinja Elakal: Athmakadha,* (Mal.), Kottayam: D.C. Book, 1978, pp. 340-341.
40. Kerala Grandhasala Sanghathinte Varshika Report", *Grandhalokam,* Trivandrum: (Mal.) Vol. 9 (9), 1957, p. 604.
41. K.M. George, "Salgrandha Vyavasayam", *Grandhalokam,* Trivandrum, (Mal.), Vol. 9 (11), 1957, p. 681.
42. Joseph Mundassery, No. 39. pp. 340-41.
43. "Grandhasalayum Samskarika Stapanaum", *Grandhalokam,* Trivandrum, (Mal.), Vol. 10 (11), 1958, pp. 667-68.
44. Government of India, *Report of Advisory Committee for Libraries,* (Delhi: Ministry of Education, 1959, p. 117.
45. "Central Library Committee", *Grandhalokam,* Trivandrum, (Mal.), Vol. 10 (2) , 1958, p. 66.
46. C. Narayana Pillai, "Grandhasala Bharanam Government Eattedukkaruthu", *Grandhalokam,* Trivandrum, (Mal.), Vol. 12 (7), 1960, p. 390.
47. a. Editorial, *Mathrubhoomi,* Calicut, (Mal.), Daily, 6 July 1958.

    b. Editorial, *Deshabhandu,* Kottayam, (Mal.), Daily,3 August 1958.

c. Editorial, *Janatha,* Ernakulam, (Mal.) Daily, 23 August 1958.

d. Editorial, *Express,* Trichur, (Mal.), Daily 31, August, 1958.

e. Editorial, *Kerala Kaumudi,* Trivandrum, (Mal.), Daily, 5 September 1958.

f. Editorial, *Malayala Manorama,* Kottayam, (Mal.), Daily, 5 September 1958.

48. Resolution introduced by K.M. Chumar, D.C.C. President in the D.C.C meeting held at Kottayam, (Mal.), supported by Antony Joseph, Palai: Prakash Press, 3 February 1958, p.1.

49. *Ibid.*

50. *Samskarika Swathandriyam Samrakshikkan Urachuninnu Poruduka,* (Mal.), Notice published by Kottayam D.C.C., Palai: Prakash Press, 24 March 1958, pp. 1-2.

51. A. Balagopal, Chairman, *Calicut Local Library Authority,* (Mal.), Calicut : L.L.A, 1974, pp. 1-2.

52. G. Devarajan, "Public Library Billile Prashnangal", *Mathrubhoomi,* Calicut, (Mal.), Daily, 5 April 1985.

53. S.R. Ranganathan, *Kerala Public Library Bill - 1960,* Trivandrum : Kerala Legislative Assembly, 1960.

54. *Ibid.*

55. N. Josechandran, (ed.), *Dynamics of State Politics* – Kerala, Delhi: Sterling Publishers, 1986, pp. 137-39.

56. Ibid.

57. "Kerala Grandhasala Sanghathe Mojippichilla", *Kerala Kaumudi,* Trivandrum, (Mal.) Daily, 4 January 1961.

58. T.J. Nossiter, *Communism in Kerala :* A study in Political Adaptation, Delhi: Oxford University Press, 1982, p. 147.

59. "Library Grantinulla Rule Library Boardum Governmentum Angeekarichu", *Grandhalokam,* Trivandrum, (Mal.), Vol. 11 (11), 1959, p. 571.

60. *Hundred years of legislature bodies in Kerala* 1888- 1988, No. 4, p. 673.

61. P. Gopala Krishnan Nair, "Public Library Legislation in India", *Public Library System in India,* New Delhi: ESS ESS Publication, 1980, p.45.
62. "Library Karadu Bill- Janadhipathiya Virudhavum Thanmmulam Asweekariyavum", *Grandhalokam,* Trivandrum, (Mal.), Vol. 12 (9), 1960, pp. 561-62.
63. "Library Karadu Billil Maulika mattangal anivariyam", *Grandhalokam,* Trivandrum, (Mal.), Vol.12(11), 1960, pp. 620-23.
64. S.R. Ranganathan, "Keralathile Library Prasthanathode chila nirdesangal", *Mathrubhoomi,* Calicut, (Mal.), Daily, 14 August 1960.
65. E. Ramana Menon, "Kerala Library Niyamum", *Grandhalokam,* Trivandrum, (Mal.), Vol.12 (7), 1960, p.364.
66. C. Narayana Pillai, "S.R. Ranganathante Report", *Grandhalokam,* Trivandrum, (Mal.), Vol. 12(8), 1960, p. 464.
67. "Library Bill", *Malayala Manorama,* Kottayam, (Mal.), Daily, 26 October 1960.
68. "Library Niyamanirmanam, *Mathrubhoomi,* Calicut, (Mal.), Daily, 27 October 1960.
69. "Library Billum vikasanapadhadiyum", *Grandhalokam,* Trivandrum, (Mal.), Vol. 13 (1), 1961. pp. 711-12.
70. *Kerala State Administrative Report- 1959,* Trivandrum: government Press, 1961, p. 98.
71. Machad T. Neelakantan, "Library Bill Nadappilakumbol Orkenda Chila Adisthana Thathuvangal", *Grandhalokam,* Trivandrum, (Mal.), Vol. 13 (1), 1961, p. 712.
72. "Organisaranmare pirichuvittu", *Grandhalokam,* Trivandrum, (Mal.), vol. 12 (12), 1960, p. 635.
73. *Ibid.*
74. "Kerala Grandhasala Sanghathinte Pokku", *Janayugam,* Quilon, (Mal.), Daily, 26 April 1960 and "Grandhasala Sanghathile Udhyogasthanmmar", *Deshabhimani,* Calicut, (Mal.), Daily, 26 November 1960.

75. Editorial, *Grandhalokam,* Trivandrum, (Mal.), Vol. 14 (2), 1962.
76. *Ibid.*
77. "Library Niyama Nirmanum", *Mathrubhoomi,* Calicut, (Mal.), Daily, 27 October 1962.
78. "Grandhasala Sanghathinethire", *Malayala Manorama,* Kottayam, (Mal.), Daily, 15 June 1962.
79. (a) "Librarykalkulla Grant", *Pothujanam,* Trivandrum, (Mal.), Daily, 7 June 1962.

    (b) "Library Grantinte Kuzhappam", *Malayala Manorama,* Kottayam, (Mal.), Daily, 16 June 1962.

    (c) "Library grant", *Deepika,* Kottayam (Mal.), Daily, 16 June 1962.

    (d) "Library grant", *Mathrubhoomi,* Calicut, (Mal.), Daily, 19 June 1962.

    (e) "Grandhasala Sanghom Prathisandhi Khattathil", *Deshabandhu,* Kottayam, (Mal.), Daily, 19 June 1962.

    (f) "Grant Nalkiyathre", *Keralabhooshanam,* Kottayam, (Mal.), Daily, 20 June 1962.

    (g) "Grandhasalakalum Governmentum", *Deshabhimani,* Calicut, (Mal.), Daily, 23 June 1962.

    (h) "Urangunna Pattikal Urangate", *Kerala Kaumudi,* Trivandrum, (Mal.), Daily 27 July 1962.

    (i) "Grandhasala Kuzhappam Veendum" *Chandrika,* Calicut, (Mal.), Daily, 22 June 1962.

    (j) "Grandhasala Prasthanam Samarathinte Margathil", *Janayugam,* Quilon, (Mal.), Daily 28 June 1960.
80. *Hundred years of legislative bodies in Kerala,* 1888- 1988, No.4, p. 673.
81. "R. Sankarinte Prasangangal", *Grandhalokam,* Trivandrum, (Mal.), Vol. 15 (8), 1963, pp. 416-417.
82. File No. G.O. (MS.) No. 429/ Edn. D25/ 7-61 and G.O. (MS) No. 48 (Edn. Dated 25-1-1963, Trivandrum : Government Secretariat.

83. Dr. K. Sivadasan Pillai , "Vayikuka Valaruka", *Kerala Grandhasala Sanghom Rajatha Jubilee Souvenir,* (Mal.), Trivandrum: Kerala Grandhasala Sanghom, 1971, p. 26.
84. S. Gopalakrishnan Nair, No. 61, p. 46.
85. *Hundred years of legislature bodies in Kerala (1888-1988).* No. 4 pp. 673-74.
86. P. Udhayabhanu, "Gradation Committeeyum Vivathangalum", *Keralathile Grandhasala Prasthanam,* (Mal.), Trivandrum: Steps, 1982, p. 194-95.
87. Editorial , *Mathrubhoomi,* Calicut, (Mal.), Daily, 26 May 1965.
88. Editorial, *Malayala Manorama,* Kottayam, (Mal.), Daily, 21 May 1965.
89. "Distributing library", *Grandhalokam,* Trivandrum, (Mal.), Vol. 18(6), 1966, p. 56.
90. "Librarykalum Saksharatha Paripadiyum", *Grandhalokam,* Trivandrum, (Mal.), Vol. 18 (6), 1966, pp. 15-21.
91. "Libraries of the country", *Indian Express,* Sunday Standard, (Madurai), 5 March 1961.
92. "Ashleela Sahithyam Nirodikkum", *Grandhalokam,* Trivandrum, (Mal.), Vol. 18 (12), 1966, pp. 7-8.
93. *Ibid.*
94. P. Udayabhanu, No. 86, pp. 194- 95.
95. *Hundred years of Legislature Bodies in Kerala (1888- 1988),* No. 4, p. 637.
96. P. Gopalakrishnan Nair, No. 61, p. 40.
97. *Ibid.*
98. *Hundred years of Legislature Bodies in Kerala (1888-1988),* No.4, p.673.
99. K.C. Sankaranarayanan and P. Karunakaran, *Kerala Economy,* (Delhi : Oxford, I.B.H., 1985), p.77.
100. M.A. Oomen, *A Study on land reforms in Kerala,* (New Delhi: IBH Publishing Co., 1975), p.16.
101. *Ibid.*
102. *Ibid.*

103. Dr. John Vallamattom, "Keralathile Vidhyabhiyasam Kazhinja Muppathu Varshangalil". (Mal.), *Keralathinte Moonu Dashakangal,* (Trivandrum : Language Institute, Government of Kerala, 1982), p.98.
104. *Ibid.*
105. P. Govinda Pillai, "Keralathile Vidhyabhyasam : Abhivridhiyum Apachayavum". *Keralathinte Moonu Dasakangal,* (Mal.), (Trivandrum : Language Institute, Government of Kerala, 1982), p.110.
106. Government of Kerala, *Economic Review 1981,* (Trivandrum: State Government of Kerala, 1982), p.2 and Government of Travancore, *Travancore - Cochin and Kerala's Budget Estimate* from 1945-1977, Trivandrum : Government of Travancore, Travancore Cochin and Kerala.
107. "Kerala Grandhasala Sanghom". *Kerala Grandhasala Sanghom Rajatha Jubilee Souvenir,* No.83, p.44.
108. K. Savadasan Pillai, *Kerala Grandhasala Sanghom,* (Trivandrum : Kerala Grandhasala Sanghom, 1981), p.38.
109. "Albuthakaramaya Nettangal", *Kerala Kaumudi,* Trivandrum, (Mal.), Daily, 30 December 1970.
110. "Samskarika Nethruthwam". *Malayala Manorama,* Kottayam, (Mal.), Daily, 27 December 1970.
111. "Gananeeya Shakti". *Mathrubhoomi,* Calicut, (Mal.), Daily, 27 December 1970.
112. (a) "Niswartha sevanam", *Chandrika,* Calicut, (Mal.), Daily, 30 December 1980.

     (b) "Janakeeya Sarvakalasala", *Deepika,* Kottyam, (Mal.) Daily, 27 December 1970.

     (c) "Bahujanangalude Prasthnam", *Deshabhimani,* Calicut, (Mal.), Daily ,31 December 1970.

     (d) "Keralathinte chaithanniyam", *Express,* Trichur, (Mal.), Daily, 25 December 1970.

     (e) "Saucharinee depashikeva", *Janayugam,* Quilon, (Mal.), Daily, 28 December 1970.

(f)"Abhimanakaramaya charithram", *Keralabhooshanam*, Kottayam, (Mal.), Daily, 29 December 1970.

(g) "Janadhipathyam", *Malayala Rajyam*, Quilon, (Mal.), Daily, 30 December 1970.

113. P.T. Bhaskara Panicker, "Grandhasala Sanghaum Saskharatha Paripadiyum". *Keralahtile Grandhasala Prasthanam*, (Mal.), Trivandrum : Steps, 1982, p. 255.
114. P. Ramanujam Nair, "Strong library movement in Kerala". *Trivandrum Public Library Platinum Jubilee Souvenir*, Trivandrum : Government of Kerala, 1974, p. 114.
115. P.T. Bhaskara Panicker, No.113, p. 238.
116. *Ibid.*, pp. 235-36.
117. *Ibid.*, p. 236.
118. *Ibid.*, p. 237.
119. "Saksharatha Paripadi". *Grandhalokam*, Trivandrum, (Mal.), Vol.28(8), 1976, p. 30.
120. "Literacy Jatha". *Grandhalokam*, Trivandrum, (Mal.), Vol.23(12), 1971, p. 8.
121. P.T. Bhaskara Panicker, No.113, p. 240.
122. *Annual Reports of Grandhasala Sanghom 1971-72*, (Mal.), (Trivandrum : K.G.S., 1972), p. 6.
123. P. Udhayabhanu, "Sanghathinte Sarghatmaka Paripadikal:. *Keralathile Grandhasala Prasthanam*, Trivandrum : Steps, 1982, p. 27.
124. *Kerala Grandhasala Bill - 1970*, Trivandrum : Kerala Legislative Assembly, 1970.
125. *The Kerala Public Libraries Bill - 1971*, Trivandrum : Kerala Legislative Assembly, 1971.
126. *Ibid.*
127. Justice V.R. Krishna Iyer, "Library Movementum Niyamaum", *Grandhalokam*, (Trivandrum), (Mal.), vol.25(2), 1973, p. 56.
128. "Puthiya Library Bill". *Mathrubhoomi*, Calicut (Mal.), Daily, 22 September 1972.

129. *Malayala Manorama, Kerala Kaumudi, Deshabhimani* and *Express*, dated February 24, 20, 16 and 19 of 1973.
130. P.T. Bhaskara Panicker, "Grandhasala Billinuvendy". *Keralathile Grandhasala Prasthanam,* (Mal.), Trivandrum : Steps, 1982, pp. 244-250.
131. *The Kerala Public Library Bill, 1971*, Vol.II, Proceedings of the meeting of the Select Committee held on August 8, 9, 16, 19 and 21, 1974 and September 26, 1974 at Cannoore, Calicut, Trivandrum, Palghat, Ernakulam and Memorandum received from various individuals and organizations, Trivandrum : Government of Kerala, 1975, p.1
132. *Ibid.,* pp.114-116.
133. "Library Bill". *Grandhalokam,* Trivandrum, (Mal), Vol.28(4), 1976, p.47.
134. Gradation Committee, File No.G.O. Rt.No.375/76/ H.Edn. dated 21.2.1976, Trivandrum : Government Secretariat.

7

Take Over of The Kerala Grandhasala Sanghom

After the fall of the Ministry of E.M.S. Namboodiripad, the C.P.I took the leadership for the formation of a non C.P.I (M) coalition ministry. The Party's choice of Chief-ministership fell on C. Achuthamenon, who was a member of the Rajya Sabha when the coalition ministry of Namboodiripad fell. In November 1969 C. Achuthamenon was sworn in as the Chief Minister with the support of the Congress Party[1]. A few months later the Congress Party itself underwent a split and the Party under the leadership of Indria Gandhi became acceptable to the C.P.I[2].

The smooth and popular working of the Achutha Menon's Cabinet was disturbed by the threat of defection in the ranks of the P.S.P (Praja Socialist Party) which was one of the coalition partners. Soon the Cabinet met and decided to recommend the dissolution of the legislature and a mid-term poll. Before the midterm poll, the Congress Party under Indira Gandhi joined Achutha Menon's band wagon and together they won an absolute majority in the election to the Kerala Legislative Assembly in 1970. The C.P.I (M) sat in the opposition and watched the performance with considerable animosity[3].

Achutha Menon embarked upon an ambitious legislative programme during this period. Private forests were nationalised, and land reform act was amended. For the first time, the working conditions and other benefits of the farm labourers protected by legislation[4].

And then the national emergency was declared on 25 June 1975[5]. But, for Achutha Menon, who was completing his five years tenure it was an indirect order to continue in power without a fresh election. The C.P.I did not oppose the emergency[6].

It was in amidst this political tempest that the Government decided to lay hand on the K.G.S. During that time the strength of the public libraries in the state was full-fledged.

By 1976-77 there were more than 4,000 libraries including one State Central Library (Trivandrum Public Library), District Libraries (including the libraries run by the Local Authorities in the Malabar area), 100 Branch and Rural Libraries of the Local Library Authority in Malabar, 4183 affiliated libraries of K.G.S., scattered throughout the state, in its villages, Panchayats, Taluks and Districts and about 1000 libraries of smaller size which were in the process of development so as to be able to get government grant[7]. Eventhough the number of libraries was quite impressive the number and the quality of books possessed by them were not satisfactory. It may be pointed out that only 116 libraries in Kerala had more than 8000 books. Libraries that had a stock in between 5000 and 8000 books were only 313[8].

In 1977 there were over one crore books, worth around Rs. 175 lakhs in these public libraries (the average cost of each book is Rs. 1.75, which reveals the low quality of the books) with a paid membership of more than seven lakhs but a large number utilized the library facilities free of charge. Of the 7 lakh members, a good number was quite ineffective. Many small libraries had inflated number in membership just to get higher grade[9].

Among these libraries about 2500 were run in their own buildings; 2800 had children's and women's sections, as well as cultural and sports wings; and 1715 had their own radio sets for the benefit of their clientele[10].

There were about 1000 libraries affiliated to the Kerala Grandhasala Sanghom from the Malabar area. Of this, 800 got government grant, 9 libraries had a stock of more than 8000 books; 25 had in between 8000 and 5000 books These 1000 libraries altogether had a stock about of 10 lakhs books[11].

It was obvious that the K.G.S was not in a position to look after the interest of the District Libraries, and other big libraries for it had to look after the larger interest of numerous village libraries managed by the voluntary workers. A Central Libraries Association of Kerala was formed in 1975 by the District Libraries. The Association made representations to the Government for improving the conditions of District Libraries. It demanded, among other things, the enhancement of annual library grant, building grant and their proper channelisation and the timely payment . It also requested the early enactment of a proper and effective library legislation and the establishment of a scientific, and well-organised library for a more fruitful library service in the State[12].

The Kerala Government had established a few distributing libraries attached to the District Libraries even without having a library legislation. Nine mobile units were working for the distribution of books to taluk, panchayat and village level libraries in the year 1975-76, but their working came to a standstill soon. It was regrettable to note that the Government had not taken any step to recognize and revitalise the services of the Distributing Libraries[13]. This was the picture of the libraries in the state during that time.

The K.G.S., by now, had grown into a very big cultural, social and educational organisation in the State. There were thousands of dedicated social workers as volunteers behind the Sanghom and its affiliated libraries. This cordination enhanced the success of the Sanghom. From the Government of Travancore the Sanghom received a grant of Rs. 200/- in 1947 and by it had grown to the stature of receiving an amount of Rs. 2,31,834 as grant during 1977-78 . The Sanghom received an annual recurring grant from the Government towards its establishmental and organizational expenses which include expenses for the organisation of new libraries, the inspection of affiliated libraries, for conducting discussions, meetings and seminars, and for the publication of articles, pamphlets, list of books and so on[14]. Even though the Sanghom was not a statutory body, the State Government was actually meeting the recurring expenditure of the Sanghom. This was quite a unique feature because in no other state in India a library association had enjoyed such government support and assistance as was being received by the Sanghom.

The Sanghom was purely a democratic body, and it consisted of affiliated unit libraries (at the base), taluk unions, district committees, government councils, and an executive committee (at the top), all formed by the chain of elections right from the general bodies of the unit libraries.

Thayat Sankaran, a C.P.I (M) intellectual has been the President of the Sanghom since 1973. He was the editor of *Grandhalokam* also[15]. The relationship between the President and the General Secretary P.N. Panicker was cordial and co-operative. The President issued a notice to the public on 15 July 1975 inorder to raise money, which was to be handed over to the Secretary as mark of his service to the library movement in the state. The notice praised the service rendered by P.N. Panicker in the field of library movement and cultural life of Kerala. The President went to the extent of saying that he hadn't seen such a social worker as Panicker in the cultural life of Kerala[16].

But before long the relationship between the two got strained due to the political differences. The President was a staunch Marxist, and some of the office bearers stood with him. He began to question the activities of the Secretary, which was rather uncommon[17]. The Secretary who was endowed with long experience, was quite displeased with the situation. During that time Thayat Sankaran wrote an article in a leading Malayalam weekly, *Kalakaumudi* in which he severely criticized P.N. Panicker[18].

Meanwhile, in May 1976 the notifications for election to libraries, Taluk Unions, District Committees and office bearers of the Sanghom were issued. The election schedule as given below[19]:

1. Each library affiliated to the Sanghom may elect two representative to each Taluk Union, between September 1 and 25, 1976.
2. A District Committee member may be elected by the Taluk Union on or before 25 October 1976.
3. Three members may be elected as the representatives to Bharana Samiti of the Sanghom on or before November 13, 1976 by Each District Committee.
4. Two persons shall be elected by the life members of the K.G.S. and one person may be elected by the employees of the K.G.S to the *Bharana Samithi* on or before November 30.
5. The eleven executive members of the K.G.S for the next three years may be elected by the governing body

which consists of two Government nominees, a representative of the Kerala University and the other elected members, mentioned above.

By that time Emergency was declared and most of the opposition leaders of Kerala especially the C.P.I (M) leaders, were arrested and imprisoned[20]. The Emergency triggered political tension in the state. The election to the libraries was conducted at this juncture to form the new *Bharana Samiti* of the Sanghom, After the announcement of elections, differences among library workers gathered momentum in some pats of the state, especially in Cannoore district. In this election, representatives of major political parties of Kerala contested. The unnecessary interference of political parties in this election led to irrational conflicts, and finally the final destruction of some libraries of the state by antisocial elements[21]. The following libraries were destroyed in the clashes, and the Sanghom President requested the Government to provide financial help for restoring the earlier position of these libariries[22].

1. Aripuram Public Library (Cannoor).
2. Mudoor Library (Cannoor).
3. E.S.J.M Library, Kanddakyakam (Cannoor).
4. Kunnathu Library (Cannoor).
5. Joji Library (Cannoor).
6. Peringalassery Labrary (Cannoor).
7. A.K.G. Library (Cannoor).
8. Kalippankulangara Sanmarga darshini Library, (Trivandrum).

On 20 May 1976, the K.G.S appointed a committee consisting of Thayat Sankaran, P.N. Panicker, Thengamam Balakrishnan (M.L.A) and P. Narayana Kurup (M.L.A) to enquire into the unhealthy developments in these libraries.

The members of the enquiry committee were threatened, and tried to manhandle by some miscreants while they were discharging their duties[23]. Political interference was responsible for this hurly-burly.

On 3 August 1976, a Memorandum signed by twelve office bearers of the K.G.S was submitted to C. Achutha Menon, the then Chief Minister, in which many charges were levelled against the functioning of the K.G.S. They were[24]:

1. For the last thirty years it was working without any political affiliation to any party in the State. But in the last election to the office bearers of the Sanghom, the C.P.I (M) members secured majority and they used these cultural institutions as their party office. They were giving membership only to those who pursued their line of political thinking. They were not ready to handover their office to the newly elected office bearers of the libraries. This led to clashes in different parts of the State, especially in Cannaoore district. It was not fit to the functioning of the library movement in the State.

2. The present office bearers and working committee members were not interested to impart the different programmes of the Sanghom like literacy campaign.

3. They were trying to interfere with the functioning of the office of the K.G.S especially of the General Secretary , who has been working as the Chief Executive of the Sanghom since its formation. The President asked the employees of the office not to abide by the orders of the Secretary. He sought the help of the office bearers and working committee members of this purpose.

4. The present President of the Sanghom, Thayat Sanakaran had no time to work for the library movement of the State, because he was working in Brannen College, Cannaoore.

5. The President and his associates were corrupt and they were alleged of nepotism. To a clerical post, he appointed his relative without conducting a test or interview. Also, he appointed a sub-editor to the *Grandhalokam* which was unnecessary.

6. The official publication of the K.G.S. the *Grandhalokam* criticizes Government policies. It raised obstacles on the way of the implementation of the policies of the Government. If the twenty point programme had been given publicity through the libraries, it would have boosted the image of the Government.

7. Those who criticized the policies of the Government were arrested and put behind the bars. Those workers of the Sanghom who were talking in favour of the Government and its policies being criticized by these elements.

8. After the publication of the new election schedule, the President and the members of the C.P.I (M) were openly trying top capture the libraries. But when their attempts failed in some places they resorted to clashes and confrontations.

In this background, the functioning of the K.G.S was not smooth. The employees of the Sanghom were paid by the Government, and the books were purchased mostly with the grant of the Government. So the Government could not remain either helpless or lukewarm in the squabbles of the Sanghom [25].

On the submission of the Memorandum, Thengamam Balakrishnan, the then Vice President of the Sanghom, recollects that they had foreseen a split in the K.G.S and it was to avoid this possibility that they had submitted such a memorandum[26].

The General Secretary of the Sanghom writes: "For the first time in the history of the Sanghom, it failed to complete the elections as per schedule due to the clashes among the library workers in different libraries and also due to the complaints received about the election process. Though, to some extent, the election at the Taluk level was completed, a number of complaints were received from different corners about the election malpractice, and in prima facie it was found that they were not totally baseless. This was mainly due to the narrow views of political parties with vested interests. Finally it was decided to put off all the elections in the libraries until a peaceful atmosphere was created"[27].

Veekshanam a pro-Congress party daily, wrote that the clashes occurred in different libraries for the Taluk Union elections were due to the political interference in the libraries of the State by the C.P.I (M). The Taluk Union elections were not even completed due to this conflict. If this crisis was not solved, the Government should interfere in the affairs of the Sanghom, and take control of it[28].

During the time of Emergency (June 25, 1975 to March 27, 1977), the functioning of the opposition parties, especially C.P.I (M), became very difficult. They used the libraries as their media for their political activities and it was this trend that led to large scale politicization of the K.G.S and the libraries which caused the present malady[29].

A notice was issued to counter the arguments in the memorandum by the fraction of office bearers of the

Sanghom, who alleged that the crisis was not due to the political interference, but because of the doubt raised by the President and some of the Members about the financial matters of the Sanghom. It was alleged in the notice that they requested the Secretary to summoning the office bearers of the Sanghom to discuss matters. They alleged that the General Secretary was not keen on summoning the meeting but was trying to prorogue the office bearers of the Sanghom, and to form a Government controlled Board, instead of elected members. The notice appealed to all library workers to press the General Secretary to summon a meeting of the office bearers of the Sanghom and re-instate the democratic nature of the libraries and the Sanghom[30].

The General Secretary claimed that the financial allegations against him were baseless and he asked those who levelled charges against him to check Account Book of the K.G.S. He also added that the then office bearers created additional posts and sanctioned new allowances, which really led to the financial crisis in the Sanghom[31]. To overcome these financial difficulties, two financial programmes of the Sanghom, viz., "Special Grandhasala Fund of 1973-74" and the "Two lakhs Fund of Grandhasala Sanghom", were arranged by the Sanghom. The collection of the Funds was started immediately but the account of these were not cleared, even then.

Deshabhimani, a pro-C.P.I. (M), daily also accused financial irregularities against the General Secretary and requested him to summon the *Bharana Samiti* meeting for clarification of the Sanghom accounts[32]. In the meantime, Thayat Sankaran, who was the honourary editor of the *Grandhalokam*, was disallowed to continue in the post by the General Secretary. He, then, approached the Munsiff court in Trivandrum against the publication of *Grandhalokam.* But the Court verdict was against him and it pointed out that the Journal had to be published in on behalf of the name of the General Secretary[33]. Hence Thayat Sankaran had no right to challenge the publication.

At that time the accounts of the Sanghom were audited and the auditors reported that the "Kerala Grandhasala Sanghom receipt and payment accounts for the period from 4 April 1974 to 17 December 1975, the scheme of assistance for running Adult Literacy Centres are examined and found correct as disclosed by books of accounts and records produced before us"[34]. In 1979, all the accounts of the Sanghom were also audited by Accountant General and no discrepancy had been reported in financial matters[35].

P.N. Panicker recollects: "all the elections of the Sanghom were almost unanimous. A sense of unity was there in Taluk, District and at the State level. But the interference of unconstitutional external forces created bitterness in seventeen taluk Unions last year (1976). This was, perhaps, my first bitter experience in life in my long association with the orgasnisation. The greatness of K.G.S was that, it could accommodate all types of people. The attempt of a group of people who wanted to undo it, had created chaos in the last year. The Sanghom was on the brink of a break down. I approached C. Achutha Menon, the then Chief Minister, with a few other workers of the Sanghom and had long discussions with him about the situation"[36] .

At this juncture, the Government interfered with the affairs of the Sanghom. An ordinance was issued to that effect by the Governor N.N. Wanchu on 16 May, 1977 which said "an ordinance to provide for taking over, in the public interest of the management of the undertaking of the Kerala Grandhasala Sanghom, with a view to ensuring the proper work to Sanghom and for matters connected herewith or incidental thereto"[37]. The official record of the Government of Kerala stated that certain specific events compelled the

Government to take over the administration of the K.G.S[38]. The opposition parties pooh-pooched the ordinance and demanded restoration of democracy in the Sanghom and its affiliated libraries[39].

As per this ordinance, the entire administration of the K.G.S was vested with a Board of Control, consisting of the State Education Minister (Chariman), P.N. Panicker (full time Member Secretary), Chithran Namboodiripad, P.T. Bhaskara Panicker, N.V. Krishna Warrier, A.N.P. Ummerkutty, A.D. Krishnan Assan, and Balagopal (Chairman of the Local Library Authority, Calicut). Thereafter, the post of the other elected office-bearers of the Sanghom in various levels were considered to be null and void[40]. Chakkeeri Ahammedkutty, the then Education Minister, who was also in charge of the Library affairs remarked that, the K.G.S and the libraries attached to it had become venues of strong political currents. The order to avoid further complications in that field and also to maintain the earlier position of the Sanghom the Government interfered and took over the control of the Sanghom[41].

It was obvious that the President and the Secretary were on the path of war. Since these two important office bearers were in confrontation, government interference, naturally became unavoidable. But the election process of the Sanghom should not have been stopped. Once the election process has started it should not have been interrupted before the final results came out. Had it happened, there would have been no need for establishing a Board of Control to look after the affairs of the Sanghom and its affiliated libraries. The Government failed to do so, and even after years they could not have democracy restored in the Sanghom. It was a great set back to the activities of the Sanghom.

Notes and References

1. *Hundred years of legislature bodies in Kerala (1888-1988), Centenary Souvenir,* Trivandrum : Kerala legislature, 1990, pp.683-687.
2. "Two faces of Achuthamenon", Indian *Express, Express Weekend,* Cochin, 21 April 1990.
3. *Ibid.*
4. *Ibid.*
5. Vimal Kaul, *India Since Independence : Chronology of Events-1947-1977,* Vol. 2, Delhi : Sagar Publications, 1978. p. 644.
6. "Two faces of Achuthamenon", No. 2.
7. P.A. John and V.K.G Nair, "Public library movement in Kerala", *Souvenir of the XXV All India Library Conference held at Trivandrum in May 14-18, 1979,* Trivandrum, Geo Printers, 1979, pp.161-67.
8. *Ibid.*
9. K. Sivadasan Pillai, "*Librarikal Ennale, Innu, Nale*", (Mal.), Paper presented in the Kottayam District Seminar of the K.G.S February, 1975, p. 4.
10. *Annual Report of the K.G.S- 1976-77,* (Mal.), Trivandrum: K.G.S. 1978, p. 34.
11. *Administrative Report of the Education Department – 1976-77,* Trivandrum: Government of Kerala, 1978, pp. 80-84.
12. P.A. John and V.K.G Nair, No.7, pp. 161-67.
13. *Ibid.*
14. Annual Report of the K.G.S, (Mal.), Trivandrum : K.G.S., 1977, pp. 8-10.
15. *Ibid.*
16. *Thayat Sankaran, Notice,* (Mal.), issued on 5 July 1975.
17. Pirappancode Murali, "Keralathile Grandhasala Prasthanam", *Grandhalokam,* Trivandrum: (Mal.), Special issue, September, 1990, p. 64.
18. *"Oru Samuhiya Pravarthakante oru divasam",* (Mal.), Kalakaumudi, Trivandrum, Vol.46, 16 June 1976, pp. 18-20.

19. *Kerala Grandhasala Sanghom election notification* – 1976, Trivandrum: K.G.S 1976.
20. "Emergency declared", *Indian Express,* Madurai, 26 June 1975.
21. Editorial, *Grandhalokam,*. Trivandrum, (Mal.) Vol. 28(6), 1976, p. 1.
22. *Ibid.*
23. *Ibid.*
24. Copy of the memorandum (Mal.) submitted to the Chief Minister C. Achuthamenon on 7 March 1976, Trivandrum.
25. The members who signed the Memorandum were, C.N. Balakrishnan, Working Committee Member & Trichur District President; P.C. Abdul Rahiman, Working Committee Member, Ernakulam District Secretary; M.C. Chacko, office bearer, Kottayam Taluk Union President; C.G. Vasudevan Nair, Kottayam District Committee President; N.M. George, Office bearer, Kunnathunadu Taluk Library Union President; K.K. Ebrahim, Office bearer, Secretary, Muvattupuzha Taluk Union; K. Kuttikrishnan, Office bearer, Secretary, Chavakkad Taluk Union; Karavaloor Sivasankara Pillai, Office bearer, Punalur; K.C. Chacko, Idukki; K.R. Balakrishnan Nair, Office bearer, Adoor; K. Narayanakurup (M.L.A) and Thengamam Balakrishnan, (M.L.A) the Vice President of the Sanghom.
26. Interview with Thengamam Balakrishnan at Saksharata Bhavan, Santhamangalam, Trivandrum on 8 October 1990.
27. P.N. Panicker, "Grandhasala Sanghom Election", *Grandhalokam,* Trivandrum, (Mal.), Vol. 28(12), 1976, pp. 3-4.
28. "Kerala Grandhasala Sanghom", *Veekshanam,* Ernakulam, (Mal.), Daily, 4 December 1976.
29. Interview with P.N. Panicker on 19 July 1990 at KANFED, Trivandrum

30. *Kerala Grandhasala Sanghathile Prathisandhi Enthukondu?* (Mal.), A notice issued by the signaturies on 27 December 1976 from Trivandrum, R. Achuthan Nair, Vice President, K.G.S.; I.V. Das, Joint Secretary; K.C. Chacko, Working Committee Member; P. Chellappan Pillai, Office bearer of Snaghom; Pookadi Moidu, Office bearer; C. Achuthan, Office bearer; M.C. Krishnan Unni, Office bearer, V. Muthu, Office bearer, K.R. Cherian, Office bearer and Palakishu Narayanan, Office bearer.
31. P.N. Panicker, "Kuruppukal", *Grandhalokam* , (Mal.), Vol. 29 (5), 1977, pp. 2-9.
32. *Deshabhimani,* "Grandhasala Sanghathile Prathisandhi", Calicut, (Mal.), Daily, 24 January 1977.
33. P.N. Panicker "Kuruppukal", *Grandhalokam,* Trivandrum, (Mal.), Vol. 29(2), 1977, pp. 4-6.
34. "Aadittarammarude Report", Grandhalokam, Trivandrum, (Mal.), Special Suppliment, vol. 29 (2), 1977, pp. 2-7.
35. *Copy of the Accountant Generals Report of 1977-78,* Trivandrum: A.G.S. Office.
36. P.N. Panicker, "Grandhasala Sanghathekkurichu Padikanam", (Mal.), *KANFED's 8th Annual Souvenir – 1985, Trivandrum: Saksharatha Bhavan, 1985,* pp. 19-20.
37. *Kerala Gazette,* (Extra Ordinary) Vol. XXII. No. 169, 16 March 1977, Trivandrum.
38. *Administrative Report of the Education Department 1976-77,* Trivandrum : Government press, 1978, pp. 80-81.
39. An interview with P. Govinda Pillai and I.V. Das at Trivandrum and Calicut on 27 Sept. 1990 and 28 August 1990, respectively. They are the veteran C.P.I. (M) ideologist and strong leaders of the library movement of the State and "Grandhasala Sanghathinethire Pokunna Pookil Bharanakkarude Kathiyere', *Deshabhimani*, Calicut, (Mal.), 19 March 1977.

40. *Ordinance No. 5 of 1977,* 16 March 1977, Trivandrum : Government Secretariat.
41. Interview with Chakkeeri Ahammed Kutty, the Education Minister, 2 March 1973 to 25 March 1977, at his residence at Vengara, Malappuram, on 15-12-1990.

8

The Structural Framework and Functional Details

All the libraries affiliated to the K.G.S functioned on the basis of a common law. The administration of the libraries was being conducted by a democratically elected Executive Committee. The number of members of this Executive Committee ranges between five and eleven. In this committee, a teacher and a member of the local bodies may also be included. The committee would elect the President, the Secretary, and the Treasurer. The tenure of this committee is three years; after that the members could contest again as the committee member of the library. The library shall be opened on all days and the time of functioning was from 8 a.m. to 11 a.m and 4 p.m to 7 p.m. The holidays for libraries may not exceed more than twelve days in a year. The membership of the library was opened to all people of the locality without any discrimination. A membership fee, as well as a small amount as annual fee was collected from members[1]. The following were the powers of the Library Executive Committee[2].

1. To admit new members;
2. To remove defaulters;

3. To take actions against the members who cause loss to the libraries;
4. To meet and conduct the expenses and activities of library as per library budget;
5. To conduct classes in education, arrange- elocution competitions, dramas and other art festivals for the overall development of the people;
6. To decide the purchase of books and periodicals; and,
7. To organize other activities which are beneficial to the development of libraries.

The President of the Committee would preside over the meetings, and the Secretary would keep all accounts of the libraries. The meeting of the committee members shall be summoned atleast once a month and the quorum of the committee is sixty percent of the total committee members. The library records like Membership Register, Book Accession Register, Periodical Register, Cash Book, Visitor's Diary, and Acquisition Register were maintained by every library[3].

Once in every year the annual meeting of the library members was held in every library, and the previous years' audit was conducted. The quorum of the meetings was twenty five percent of the total members[4]. During the annual meetings, libraries organised various cultural programmes, especially, dramas. The members of the libraries as well as local people acted in these dramas. The role of libraries in promoting amateur and professional dramas had been phenomenal. For instance the Sree Chithira Thirunal Library, Vanchiyoor, Trivandrum and Deshaposhini Library, Calicut made it a point to stage a new drama every year in connection with their annual meetings[5]. Some of the prominent play wrights of Malayalam like, E.V. Krishna Pillai, Kainikkara Kumara Pillai, G. Sankara Pillai, M.G. Kesava Pillai, K.T. Mohammed,

P.C. Appukkuttan Nair, Thikkodian, M.R. Raghava Warrier, N.P. Chellappan Nair and T.N. Gopinathan Nair wrote dramas for these two libraries[6].

T.N. Gopinathan Nair, recollects that he became a dramatist through the dramas which he wrote for Sree Chithira Thirunal Library[7]. The themes of the dramas were usually historical and social. It exposed the real life of the society. The dramas against social evil and injustice influenced the public, and helped to improve the intellectual and cultural attitudes of the people. It also helped the participants to develop their dramatic skill and career. Thikkodian, another famous playwright, admits his indebtedness to the Deshaposhini Library of Calicut to establish himself in the field of drama[8].

Likewise, in Malabar most of the libraries had Kalasamitis (Arts Centres) and Sahitya Samitis (Literary Centres) which staged dramas and arranged other cultural activities along with the annual meetings of the libraries[9]. Some of the libraries conducted dramas for collecting funds for the development of libraries. In 1964, Kottayam Public Library conducted a drama festival, and collected one lakh rupees for the development of the library. It also raised Rs.130000/- by selling lotary tickets, and used it for the development of the library[10]. Now it is one of the leading libraries in Kerala.

Many educated women were attracted to the field of acting owing to the interest of libraries in dramas. Annachandy, Rugmini Amma, Omana Kunjamma and Indira Pothuval were a few of them[11]. They acted in dramas staged by the Sree Chithira Thirunal Library, Trivandrum, and they introduced many new techniques in the amateur and professional dramas of the State. The new experiments endowed the dramas with a new outlook, and charm, and the benefits of these were shared by the successors in the field[12].

For each taluk there was a Taluk Library Union, each library in the taluk can send two representatives to the Taluk Union, and the representatives of all the libraries in the taluk constitute the general body of the Taluk Union. The general body elects a working committee of nine members. The Taluk Union has a President, a vice-President, a Secretary, and a Joint- Secretary. The administration of the Taluk Union was vested with the working committee. The term of office of a Taluk Union was three years. The source of revenue for the Taluk Union was thirty-six percent of the subscriptions paid by the individual libraries of the Sanghom. In addition, it also received a monthly grant from the centre for organizational work. The Taluk Library Union kept a close surveillance over the working of each library in its jurisdiction, and ensured that the libraries maintained records and generally observed the rules laid down by the Sanghom. It also helped in the establishment of libraries by local initiative, and the strengthening of the existing libraries in the taluk[13].

There was District Library Committee consisting of:

1. the representatives of the Taluk Unions in the district on the basis of one representative per Taluk;
2. three members of the *Bharana Samiti* from the district; and
3. two persons nominated by the *Bharana Samiti* of the Sanghom from a panel of five members proposed by the elected members of the committee.

The District Library Committee co-ordinated the activities of the Taluk Library Union, and convened district level library conferences and seminars. It also rendered assistance to Taluk Unions for their smooth functioning and for the development of the libraries in the districts. It received from the Sanghom twenty percent of the subscriptions paid by libraries and also ad-hoc grants for the conduct of conferences and seminars[14].

The General Body of each Taluk Union, while electing members for its working committee, also elected representatives for the General Body of the Sanghom on the basis of one member for every ten libraries in a taluk. It was stipulated that there should be not less than three, and not more than seven members for each taluk. The representatives so elected along with the life members (those who have donated not less than Rs.100/-) and Vice-Patrons (those who have donated not less than Rs.250/-) constituted the General Body of the Sanghom[15].

The General Body elects members of the *Bharana Samiti* of the Sanghom on the basis of three members for each revenue district. Two members were elected by General Body among the life members and Vice-Patrons of the General Body. These elected representatives nominate six persons from among renowned educationsists, literary men, lawyers, social workers, etc. There were also two members of the *Bharana Samiti* nominated by representatives of libraries. The controlling role of library workers in the affairs of the Sanghom was evident from this[16].

The *Bharana Samiti* elects a President, two Vice-Presidents, a General Secretary, two Joint Secretaries, and a Treasurer, who along with four other elected members constituted the working committee. The *Bharana Samiti* was the chief executive and policy making body of the Sanghom. The working committee concerned itself with the administrative matters within the framework of the policy laid down by the Bharana Samiti[17].

The Sanghom had a Secretariat which was headed by the General Secretary who was assisted by an Administrative Assistant, a Superintendent, and Accountant and other staff. The Government sanctioned annual grants for the maintenance of the office and for organizational work. The other sources of revenue of the Sanghom were the subscriptions from the affiliated libraries, sale proceeds of publications and donations from institutions and individuals[18].

The structural frame of the Sanghom manifested itself in its functional pattern also. Most of the libraries of the State were the products and publicity medium of the national movement. The slogans of national movement like boycott of foreign clothes, upliftment of the Harijans, eradication of untouchability, and spreading of Hindi language were the other activities undertaken by the libraries[19]. These libraries helped political workers to improve their standard of political knowledge by reading the books and periodicals available in these libraries. T.K. Ramakrishnan, a leading leftist politician of Kerala, admits that he started his political career as a library worker[20].

The hundreds of libraries scattered in different parts of the State stood for creating social harmony among the people of different groups and sects. Each library was a centre for social activity in every village. These libraries served as focul points in the society which helped to solve many social problems. It was a link between different cultures of the society[21]. The members of the libraries belonged to different strata of the society possessing different cultural traits. It resulted in the interaction among various groups[22]. The libraries, thus turned out to be an agency for social education and linking among various segments of people.

One important duty of the K.G.S was to provide good literature to the public through its affiliated libraries. Since its formation it has a very effective Book Selection Committee consisting of eminent literary men of the State. The affiliated libraries of the Sanghom purchased majority of their books from the recommended list. Through these books the public developed a fairly good taste for better literature[23]. The members of the library got the rare opportunity for reading worthy books of the world literature by paying a small amount as subscription. According to Parur T.K. Narayana Pillai, the libraries of the State have played an important role in developing literacy achievements of the nation[24].

The Sanghom has won the confidence of the general public. It aimed at making every library in the rural and urban areas as centres of different activities. The Sanghom planned to provide for nursery education to children. The Government, the Bharat Sevak Swamaja, the Child Welfare Council, and some Voluntary agencies were running nursery schools in the state. They were not however, sufficient to meet the ever-increasing needs of the people. The growing children need special attention during their formative stages. Hence, the Sanghom decided to start nursery classes attached to 100 libraries in 1970[25]. Their number increased every year, and more libraries came forward to start nursery classes. The service of the Sanghom in this field has been fully recognized and appreciated by all people. Some of the libraries have a separate section for children. In 1975, 820 libraries had children's section. A special issue of *Grandhalokam* monthly was published during 1979 commemorating the International Children's Year[26].

An award called "Jayasankar Award" has been instituted by the Grandhasala Sanghom for children below the age of fourteen, who have read the maximum number of books in a year and have taken note of them. From among the applicants, the best reader of the year is selected by a selection committee. This prize was instituted during 1971, using an endowement instituted by Sri. K.N. Damodaran Nair[27].

When the Sanghom celebrated its Silver Jubilee in 1970, it was felt that the number of readers have not increased in proportion with the increase in the number of libraries. The Sanghom wanted to find out the reason for this strange phenomenon . So the Sanghom organised sample surveys in different parts of the state. It was revealed that even in the capital city of Trivandrum, there were certain wards having more than 80 percent illiteracy[28]. This helped the authorities open their eyes and think of trying to eradicate illiteracy from the state. One of the primary aims of the Sanghom had been the spreading of literacy among the rural folks, and making steady progress in this regard since 1950. The census figures of 1970 showed that nearly forty percent of the total population of 2.12 crores in the State remained illiterate. Even after setting aside the younger age groups, the adult illiterates numbers about forty lakhs[29].

The Sanghom submitted a proposal to the Government of India to start 7000 literacy centres in Kerala with 3500 libraries as the nucleus. The Government of India sanctioned a pilot project in 1971 to start twenty literacy classes. These were started in the Athiyannoor Block (Trivandrum district) in the south and Malappuram Block (Malappuram district) in the North, each having ten centres. Literacy *Jathas* were organised as a prelude to starting these centres[30].

The project was completed in six months, but the evaluation showed that the literacy level attained was not upto the expectation. The experts from the Ministry of Education, Government of India, and UNESCO agreed with the Sanghom and suggested an overhauling of the project. Hence it was decided to extend the duration of the project to ten months with atleast three hundred instructional hours. It was also suggested to have primers to ensure the literacy component. Different schemes like agriculture, fisheries, animal husbandry, dairying, book binding and the like were planned, to implement the scheme efficitively[31].

During the next year, twenty more centres were sanctioned to the Sanghom. These were also organised in the same areas as in the first project. The evaluation carried out towards the end of the ten months period showed considerable improvement in the outcomes, when compared with those of the first project. Another set of twenty centres, ten exclusively for women, and ten for men, were sanctioned for the Sanghom as the second project. In July 1974, twenty more centres were sanctioned for the Sanghom[32].

For the implementation of the functional literacy programme the Sanghom prepared a scheme and constituted an Expert Committee consisting of doyens hailing from various disciplines and backgrounds[33].

The committee was expanded later, nominating more members. It prepared primers separately for workers, women, slum dwellers, and so on. In addition to common primers, Hand books, Guide books, literacy charts, etc., were also prepared by the expert committee (See Appendix – H). A fortnightly *Sakshara Keralam* was published by the Sanghom from 1972 for the neoliterates, and was sent free of cost, by post, to them. In addition to this, workshops were organised for the production of books for neoliterates.[34]

The literature helped the neoliterates to save themselves from illiteracy and ignorance. This was made possible by their association with libraries and books. Sufficient books written in simple style on useful subjects by good and experienced authors were a must to theses readers. The scheme was intended to make available such books to the neoliterates besides other publications. As an experimental measure, the scheme was started in some of the libraries including Harijan Welfare libraries during 1979-1980[35].

The UNESCO have awarded one of the honourable mentions of 'Nadesh K. Krupskaya Prize' for 1975 to the K.G.S., for its service in the field of adult education. This was actually a moral booster for the Sanghom to strengthen its activities into new fields. In a letter from the Government of India to the State Secretary for Education communicating the award, it was mentioned thus; "This is indeed an honour bestowed not only on the Sanghom but on the adult education efforts of the country. On behalf of the Government of India, I would like to covey an appreciation of the services rendered by the Sanghom. We hope the association will continue its pioneering work with the zeal"[36] .

A three-day workshop on curriculam preperation was organized by the Sanghom in collabaration with the Indian Adult Education Association at Kanakakunnu Palace, Trivandrum in March 1977[37].

The literacy programmes, already in existence are being continued even after the take over of the Sanghom by the Government, in 1977. The two hundred women's centers already sanctioned to the Sanghom were organized during 1978-79. The *Sakshara Keralam* weekely for neoliterates which was discontinued in May 1977 was revived with effect from January 1980. The publication of neoliterate books has also been taken up again with financial support from the Government[38].

Every year '8 September' is being celeberated all over the world in memory of the 1965 Teheran Conference which evolved the concept of functional literacy in place of adult education. The Sanghom and its libraries have been celebrating this day every year since 1970 by organizing seminars, conferences, public meetings, and conducting essay and elocution competitions for the school and college students, and social workers separately[39].

The rural libraries also, in turn, celeberate the day in a befitting manner highlighting the urgent need for eradicating illiteracy from the State. Some libraries organized exhibitions and arranged cultural programmes in order to motivate adult illiterates, and to create awareness among the literate elite[40].

In addition to issuing books to those who come to the library, some of the affiliated libraries of the Sanghom had a system of taking books to the doorsteps of the readers. Ananda Pradayani Library at Alleppey has continued this system for the past several years. Even today books are distributed to two hundred families in the town and suburbs in this manner. The founder of the library, V.G.Panicker himself was seen taking books to customers[41]. The common method of distribution was as follows. Books were carried in a box attached to a bicycle to the street corners. People assembled on hearing the bell and the books were then distributed. On a later day fixed by the volunteers, the books will be returned by the customers and, if necessary exchanged. This scheme was first introduced in the Koothuparambu Block at Cannaoore district in 1973[42].

When this was found to be successful, it was extended to four more districts, namely, Trivandrum, Quilon, Trichur, and Calicut covering hundred villages. This programme was first implemented in 61 libraries at 61 Taluks and 12300 families were beneficiaries of this programme every year[43]. This scheme helped the housewives of Kerala to develop a reading habit and establish acquitance with worthy books.

In order to propogate the reading habit of good books among the members of the family, a scheme called 'Family Reading' was introduced by the Sanghom, in 1971. In this, all the members of the family assembled at a convenient time in the house, and one of them will read a book, while others listened to it. In each home gatherings, books having some message alone will be read. This scheme was expected to improve the reading habits of people. Reports of such home reading sessions were regularly received by the Sanghom from people belonging to different walks of life[44].

Along with the spread of literacy, the reading habit of the people of Kerala increased tremendously. It helped the growth of the publication of books in the state. The total number of books published in Kerala between 1941 and 1980 is as follows[45].

Table 10. Number of Books published between 1941 and 1980

	YEAR			
Subjects of Books	*1941-50*	*1951-60*	*1961-70*	*1971-80*
Literary Books	2013	4606	4565	4406
Educational Books	1154	2856	2749	2817
Total	3167	7462	7314	7224

Table given above indicates that the number of books published in between 1941-50 was more than double that published in 1951-60. One important factor for this increase might be the work done by the United Tracancore-Cochin Library Association, and to some extent the work done by Malabar Local Library Authority for the expansion of the library movement[46]. The K.G.S and its affiliated libraries were also responsible for the growth and development of publishers and writers of Kerala. It could find out market for their books. It was one of the reasons for the healthy existence of publishers and it indirectly sustained the writers of Kerala[47].

The growth of literacy, increase in the publication of books and periodicals and the easy availability of literature through the libraries moulded the reading habit of the people. Some commercially motivated publishers of books and periodicals of Kerala misused this reading habit[48]. They published low quality novels and stories through which they exploited the weak sentiments of the people[49]. A leading Malayalam Magazine *Kalakaumudi* wrote that the cheap weeklies called *Painkili magazines* spread *Painkili Sahithyam* (trash literature). Most of these magazines are being published from Kottayam and their names begin with the Malayalam Alphabet 'Ma' and so they are called 'Ma' publications. It is very difficult to get a novel by paying rupees ten but by paying rupees ten, seventy novels can be read in every week[50]. Cheap novels are serialized through such periodicals. The growing commercialism is reflected in these magazines which attempt to present stereo-type romances and detective stories instead of the real life of the society[51].

Apart from books, the K.G.S has played an important role in developing the habit of newspaper reading. Almost all the libraries have more than three newspapers. In some libraries, the literate would read the newspaper loudly and the illiterates who gathered in the library premises would listen to it. It is normal process especially in some of the libraries in north Kerala[52].

The number of newspaper readers is the highest in Kerala in comparison with other states of India. The fifty-five percent of the people of Kerala is newspaper readers[53]. According to Sakkariya, a well know Malayalam writer, the thoughts of the people of Kerala is designed by the newspapers. Their self-perception is done through this media. They are the prey and product' of newspapers. The newspapers decide what a Malayalee should think; perhaps a Malayalee is the first person in the whole World who has been intellectually doomed by his high rate of literacy[54].

Since the formation of Kerala Grandhasala Sanghom it had taken interest to start separate section for ladies. In 1975, 179 libraries had separate sections for ladies. It also celebrated international women's year in 1975 with different special programmes for women in accordance with the direction of the UNO. The Sanghom had submitted a proposal to the Government of India for starting 1000 women library centres for eradicating illiteracy among women[55]. This programme had attracted the attention of the house wives of Kerala and educationally backward women who had established a rapport with libraries. The membership of ladies in the libraries have considerably increased due to the above programme.

The Central Social Welfare Board had a scheme to educate women of the age group between 18 to 20 years to pass S.S.L.C in the course of two years. Preference was given to the under privileged sectors of the society who had studied at least upto the fifth standard and have not appeared for the S.S.L.C examination. Thirty women from a group, and majority of them were provided with free boarding and lodging. Those who came from their houses were given pocket allowance. Once such project was allotted to the Sanghom during 1975-76. Along with the academic subjects, cutting and tailoring, book binding, basket making, and so on were also taught[56]. The programme was a success but during the time of Board of Control the Sanghom failed to continue such programme.

Agriculture, the backbone of Kerala economy, has been given due importance by the K.G.S. With the collaboration of the State Institute of Languages and the Farm Information Bureau, the Sanghom started a pilot project to organise agricultural book corners in selected libraries in 1974[57]. Books on agriculture were supplied to popularize agriculture in the village and to improve agricultural methods. The scheme was being extended to more libraries. Such book corners existed in 1246 libraries during 1977-78, and the membership had risen to 2000 in 1980. The State Institute of Languages had produced standard books on various aspects of agriculture. Book worth Rs.300/- were supplied to libraries receiving only one third of its price, ie., Rs. 100/-. The other two parts were shared by the Institute and the Farm Information Bureau. The area where these books were kept was noted as 'Farm Book Corner'. Discussions, group seminars, film shows and so forth one farming were also arranged in these libraries[58].

In the number of libraries scientific books were stored, exhibited and distributed for reading. Books produced by the *Sasthra Sahitya Parishad* and popular science, and books published by different agencies were included in this special corner[59]. This was expected to spread scientific literacy among the villagers.

In different parts of the state, twenty one libraries had organised Jail Library Service effectively during 1976-77. Books which might improve the character of the inmates of the jails were mainly distributed through them[60]. This scheme was extended. In 1985, jail libraries were opened by the Sanghom in important jails of Kerala and now they have the same status of the affiliated libraries.

This was a peculiar service rendered by the K.G.S., unique in many respects. Likewise, in the Nooranand Leprosy Centre a library has been in existence since 1960. This library has 11000 books and 34 periodicals. There were two sections in the library of the leprosy hospital where men and women had separate library facilities. There was a library meant for the T.B. Patients also, at Pulayanarkotta Hospital in Trivandrum[61]. Similiary, connected with the factories like Titanium (Trivandrum) and the FACT (Alwaye), libraries have been organised for the benefit of the workers. Also, a scheme had been prepared to start libraries in hospitals for the benefit of patients[62]. The Sanghom provided all timely help and facilities to these libraries.

The Sanghom has a scheme to supply dictionaries, lexicons and reference books at concessional rates to the deserving libraries. The Kerala University, State Institute of Languages, State Institute of Encyclopedia, and such other institutions collaborate in this scheme. The government gazette was also supplied at concessional rates to libraries receiving grant-in-aid from the Government[63].

District and taluk level seminars were organised by the Sanghom every year. These aim at reviewing the working of libraries and explaining distribution system. In the beginning, no financial support was given to organise such seminars but recently financial help is being given for this purpose at the Taluk, District and State levels[64].

The libraries in Kerala celebrate along with libraries in other parts of the country, the National Library Week every year. Book exhibitions were organised on these occasions. Likewise the birthdays of local, national and international leaders like, Kumaranasan, Gandhi and Lenin were celebrated by the libraries of the State[65]. During these occasions, people got opportunities to understand the ideas and lives of these great men.

The K.G.S paved the way for the formation of similar organisations in the State. *Kerala Sastra Sahitya Parishad* (1968) , is a leading voluntary organisation in Kerala and India. It is the offshoot of the work done by P.T. Bhaskara Panicker at Ottappalam in 1957[66]. He was one of the leading personalities of the library movement and he was the President of the K.G.S from 1970 to 1973. The K.G.S and *Kerala Sastra Sahitya Parishad* are complementary to each other. These organisations worked together to conduct different public programmes through libraries. Often science classes were conducted in different libraries of the State by the Parishad[67]. The aim of the Parishad is to cultivate scientific knowledge and scientific awareness among ordinary men in order to equip them to live in the modern society. It is also one of the aims of the K.G.S.

For spreading national integration, Hindi classes have been conducted by the Sanghom through the libraries of the State since 1961[68]. Selected Hindi books were purchased and a portion of *Grandhalokam* was used for Hindi language and literature. In 1961, the Government of India gave an aid of Rs. 30,660 for libraries for encouraging Hindi sections in the libraries of the State[69].

One of the important drawback of the libraries of the State was that in most of the rural libraries, books were not scientifically arranged and they were not functioning scientifically. This was mainly due to lack of qualified library persons in these libraries. Most of the librarians were not qualified, but they were persons voluntarily serving the libraries. Taking this fact into consideration, the Sanghom had given adequate training to library organisers, since 1948[70]. A three-month training course for library workers was commenced by the Sanghom in 1958[71]. Likewise, workshop on librarianship and hundreds of lectures of library scientists were arranged by the Sanghom in different libraries. Moreover, the Sanghom compelled the Kerala University to commence a Bachelor's Degree Course in library science, and the University opened a Library Science Department in 1961[72]. Even then, the situation has remained the same in most of the rural libraries.

The K.G.S. also supported the Government for the speedy implementation of the latter's different programmes. For instance, when the *Vana Maholsava* (forest festival) was conducted by the Government of India in 1950, the Sanghom gave instructions to the affiliated libraries to celebrate the festival by planting trees in the premises of libraries and also in dry land. Most of the libraries celebrated the festival and cautioned the people against deforestation[73]. Likewise, for the spread of certain other Government programmes like National Savings Scheme (1973)[74] and the Twenty-point programme (1975-77)[75] the Sanghom extended it helping hand by activating and motivating[76]. The Sanghom, through its libraries, sold application forms of Public Service Commission, and other Government forms which were highly helpful to the public[77].

The libraries also rendered services for slum clearings, market cleanings, road repairs, house construction, thatching of huts, flood relief works, war helps and so forth. According to Prof. Malkom Adisesha Aiya, a famous educationst of India, through there was no public law prevalent in the state of Kerala, the conditions of public libraries in the State were better than elsewhere in India[78].

Thus it is obvious that the K.G.S has made liaison with the social and economic life of the people of the state, though it was previously introduced for the promotion of literacy and education. This socio-economic commitment of the K.G.S is a unique feature and it is quite natural that the activities of the Sanghom are keenly watched by the general public as well as the people at the helm of affairs in the Government.

Notes and References

1. "Mathruka Niyamavali", *Grandhalokam*, Trivandrum, (Mal.), Vol. 3 (8) 1950, pp. 14-19.
2. *Ibid* .
3. *Ibid.*
4. *Ibid.*
5. Deshaposhini library was established in 1938.
6. "Deshaposhiniyude Nataka Rajaithakkal", *Deshaposhini Suvarnna Jubilee Souvenir,* (Mal.), Calicut: Deshaposhini Library, 1988, p. 88
7. T.N. Gopinathan Nair, "Valarunna Grandhasalayum Valarthachanum", *Sree Chithira Thirunal Library Upahara Grandham,* (Mal.), Trivandrum: Sree Chithira Thirunal Library, 1976, pp. 46-47.
8. Thikkodian, "Arangu Kanatha Nadan", *Mathrubhoomi Weekly,* Calicut, (Mal.), Vol. 68(27), 15 September 1990, pp. 35-36.
9. "Keralathile Nataka Kalasamithikal", *Janapadham,* Trivandrum, (Mal.), Vol. 22 (2), 1991, pp. 25-27.

10. The Kerala Public Library Bill, 1971, Vol. II., *Proceedings of the meetings of the select committee held in 1974 in different places and memorandum received from various individuals and organisations,* Trivandrum : Government Secretariat, 1975, p. 83.
11. T.N. Gopinathan Nair, "Marthanda Varma Muthal Samasamam vare", *Sree Chithira Thirunal Golden Jubilee Souvenir,* (Mal.), Trivandrum: Sree Chithira Thirunal Library, 1966, p. 18.
12. *Ibid.*
13. *The Kerala Public Library Bill, 1985; Background Materials,* Trivandrum : the Secretariat of the Kerala legislature, 1987, p. 14.
14. *The Kerala Public Library Bill,* 1985, No. 13, pp. 14-15.
15. *Ibid.*
16. "Kuttu Nibanthanakal", *Grandhasala Manual,* (Mal.), Trivandrum: Grandhasala Sanghom, 1948, p. 185.
17. *Ibid.*
18. *The Kerala Public Library Bill,* No. 13, p. 15.
19. Manalil G. Narayana Pillai, *Grandhasala Prasthanaum Saksharathayum,* (Mal), Paper presented in the 45 Library Conference held at Ernakulam, 16 September , pp. 2-3.
20. Speech delivered by T.K. Ramakrishnan in connection with the Annual Library Conference held at Ernakulam on 14 September 1990.
21. C.K. Mani, "Erupathu Varsham", *Kottayam Public Library Souvenir,* (Mal), Kottayam: Kottayam Public Library, 1967, p. 25.
22. *Report of Advisory Committee for Library,* New Delhi: Government of India, 1954, p. 65.
23. Parur T.K, Narayana Pillai, "Sahitya Prashanathil Grandhasalakalkulla Sthanam", *Grandhalokam,* Trivandrum, (Mal.), Vol.3 (8), 1951, pp. 9-10.
24. *Ibid.*

25. P.N. Panicker, (ed.), *Keralthile Grandhasala Prasthanam,* Trivandrum: Steps, 1982, p. 265.
26. *Annual Report of the K.G.S. 1975-1976,* (Mal.), Trivandrum: K.G.S, 1977, p. 34.
27. *Annual Report of the K.G.S. 1971-72,* (Mal.), Trivandrum: K.G.S. 1973, pp. 4-8.
28. K. Sivadasan Pillai, *Kerala Grandhasala S*anghom, Trivandrum: Kerala Grandhasala Sanghom, 1981, pp. 12-13.
29. *Ibid.*
30. P.T. Bhaskara Panicker, "Grandhasala Sanghaum Saksharatha Paripadiyum", *Kerlathile Grandhasala Prasthanam,* (Mal.), Trivandrum : Steps, 1982, pp. 235-240.
31. K. Sivadasan Pillai, No. 28, pp. 14-15.
32. *Ibid.*
33. 1. A.G. Menon, Professor of Extension, Agricultural College, Vellayanil; 2. A. Sankara Pillai, Dean of Adult Education, Calicut University; 3. K. Madhavankutty, Principal, Medical College, Trivandrum; 4. N. Balakrishnan Nair, Professor of Marine Biology, University of Kerala; 5. K.P.George , Assistant Director of Fisheries; 6. K. Sivadasan Pillai, Department of Education, University of Kerala; 7. R. Gopalakrishnan Nair, Farm Information Bureau; 8. K.G. Balakrishnan Pillai, Trained in Adult Literacy from Literacy House, Lucknow; 9. Justus Lazaras, State Vocational Guidance Officer; 10. N.V. Krishna Warrier, Director, State Institute of Languages, Kerala; 11. M. Viswanathan, Director, Mithranikethan; 12. G.K. Ravindranath, Evaluation Officer, State Institute of Education; 13. Leela Devi, Counseller, State Institute of Education; 14. P.T. Bhaskara Panicker, (1970-73), President, Kerala Grandhasala Sanghom; 15. P.N. Panicker, General Secretary, Kerala Grandhasala Sanghom, Trivandrum.
34. K. Sivadasan Pillai, No. 28, pp. 16-18.

35. *Ibid.*, p. 19.
36. Letter No. D.O.F. 1229/ 75, HE-1 (NF FE.1 dated 20-10-1975), by Government of India, Delhi: Central Secretariat.
37. K. Sivadasan Pillai, No. 28, p. 19.
38. *Ibid.*, p. 24.
39. *Annual Report of the K.G.S. 1970-71*, (Mal.), Trivandrum: K.G.S. , 1972, pp. 5-6.
40. K. Sivadasan Pillai, No. 28, p. 24.
41. *Ibid.*, p. 25.
42. *Annual Report of the K.G.S. 1978- 79*, (Mal.), Trivandrum: K.G.S. 1980, pp. 4-5.
43. *Annual Report of the K.G.S. 1980-81*, (Mal.), Trivandrum: K.G.S. 1982, pp. 8-9.
44. K. Sivadasan Pillai, No. 28, p. 27.
45. K.N. Gopi, "Pusthakarangam", *Kazhinja Moonnu Sathabdhangal*, (Mal.), Trivandrum: Kerala State Language Institute, 1988, p. 87.
46. Ibid., p. 80.
47. K.M. Mathew, "Mahathaya Nettangalude Kal Nootandu", *Kerala Grandhasala Sanghom Rajatha Jubilee Souvenir*, (Mal.), Trivandrum : Kerala Grandhasala Sanghom, 1971, p. 82.
48. "Pankiliyude Dhukham", *Kalakaumudi*, Trivandrum: (Mal.), weekly 7, June 1987, p. 12.
49. *Ibid.*
50. "Vilkan 12 Laksham Vayikkan 69 Laksham", *Kalakaumudi*, Trivandrum, (Mal.), 8 July 1990, pp. 10-13.
51. Sreemanthini Nirajuna, "Negotiating Totalities, Towards an analysis of popular Nagazine fiction", *Social Scientists*, New Delhi: Vol. 16 (8), 1988, p. 16.
52. T.K. Sadanandan, "Thirinju Nookumbol", *Chowa Thozhilali Yuvajana Vayanasala and Grandhalayam, Suvarna Jubilee Souvenir*, (Mal.), Kannoor, Chowa Thozhilai Yuvajana Vayanasala and Grandhalayam, 1986, p. 12.

53. "Pathra Vayanakkar Kuduthal Keralathil", *Current Book Bulletin*, Kottayam, (Mal.), Vol. 10 (94), 1990, p. 19.
54. "Durgathiyde Manashasthram", *India Today,* (Mal.), Madras, Vol.1 (17), 1990.
55. *Annual Report of the K.G.S. 1975- 76,* (Mal.), Trivandrum: K.G.S., 1977, pp. 3-6.
56. K. Sivasanan Pillai, No. 28, p. 25.
57. *Annual Report of the K.G.S. 1974, 75,* (Mal.), Trivandrum: K.G.S. 1975, p. 7
58. P. Udayabhanu, "Sanghathinte Saragathmake Paripadikal", *Keralathile Grandhasala Prasthanam,* (Mal.), Trivandrum: Steps, 1982..
59. K. Sivadanan Pillia, No.28, p.27.
60. *Ibid.*, pp. 27-31.
61. File No. G.O. M.S. 41/ 86/ Home dated 28-02-1986, Trivandrum: Government Secretariat.
62. K. Sivadasan Pillai, No. 28, p. 31.
63. *Ibid.*, p. 33.
64. *Annual Report of the K.G.S. 1973-74,* (Mal.), Trivandrum: K.G.S. 1975, pp. 5-7.
65. *Ibid.*
66. *Janakeeya Shasthram,* (Mal.), Trivandrum: Kerala Shasthra Sahithya Parishath, 1988, p.5.
67. C.G. Vasudevan Nair, "Shasthra Sahithya Parishathum Librarikalum", *Grandhalokam,* Trivandrum, (Mal.), Vol.1(1), 1977, pp. 29-36.
68. P. Udayabhanu, "Sangathinte Sargathmake Paripadikal", *Keralathile Grandhasala Prasthanam,* (Mal.), Trivandrum: Steps, 1982, p. 268.
69. *Ibid.*
70. "Akhila Thiruvithamcore Grandhasala Sanghom Varshika Report", *Grandhalokam,* Trivandrum, (Mal.), Vol.1, 1948, p. 133.

71. K.A. Isac, "Keralathile Grandhasala Prasthanam", *Kerala Grandhasala Sanghom Rajatha Jubilee Souvenir*, (Mal.), Trivandrum : Grandhasala Sanghom, 1971, p. 7.
72. The University of Kerala, *Handbook*, 1977-78, Trivandrum: Kerala University, 1977, p. 120.
73. "Vanamaholsavam", *Grandhalokam*, Trivandrum, (Mal.), Vol. 3 (1), 1951, p. 53.
74. It is one of the Saving Schemes introduced by Central Government for developing saving habit among the public.
75. The economic programme of the Government of India consisted of 21 programmes for promoting the economic conditions of the country.
76. "Desheeya Sampadya Padhathiyum Librariyum", *Grandhalokam*, Trivandrum, (Mal.), Vol. 25 (3), 1973, p. 8.
77. K. Sadasivan Pillai, No. 28, p. 37.
78. "Kerala Grandhasalakku Abhinandanam", *Sakshara Keralam*, Trivandrum, (Mal.), Vol.5 (33), 1976, p. 3.

9

The Present Status of The Kerala Grandhasala Sanghom

From 1977, when the Government took over the management of the K.G.S a Board of Control nominated by the Government consisting of eight non-official and three official members have been in charge of administration. Out of the eight non-official members, one is a full time member, who governs the routine works of the Sanghom. The official members are the Minister for Education (Chairman), Higher Education Secretary (Member Secretary) and Secretary of the Finance Department[1].

After the imposition of Government control over the K.G.S nine different ministries have been formed[2]. The ministries constituted their own Control Boards to look after the affairs of the K.G.S. During these periods, the main complaints of the library workers were that the library grant was not distributed properly. The grant arrears upto 1985-86, had been disbursed during 1988-89 only. Similarly, the grant for 1985-86, had been disbursed during 1989-90[3].

Further, many attempts were made for making a library law. In 1977, a draft bill called 'The Kerala Public

Library Bill 1977' was presented in the Assembly by U.A. Beeran, the then Minister for Education, and it was referred to the Select Committee. The Select Committee collected evidence and a report on the Bill was presented. But the legislature could not consider it facourably following its dissolution[4].

In the Bill, there was a provision for a State Library Authority (S.L.A) in which, the Minister for Education was the ex-officio chairman. Besides this, in the S.L.A., there were provisions for the nomination of one person each from the Heads of the University Departments and representatives of the Grandhasala Union, Sahitya Academy, Sangeetha Nataka Academy, and the Lalithakala Academy. The S.L.A was also to maintain a fund from the grant provided by the State or the Central Government, and the contributions or gifts made to the S.L.A. Another major provision in the Bill was the dissolution of the K.G.S and the transfer of its assets and liabilities to the State Grandhasala Union[5].

In the same year, another library bill was drafted by the joint effort of Kerala Library Association, Indian Library Association, and Central Libraries Association of Kerala, largely based on the consensus arrived at the library seminar held at Trivandrum on 25 July 1977[6]. According to them, 'the Kerala Public Library Bill of 1977' does not take into consideration the special features of the state, and its library movement and this necessitated a new bill[7].

The special feature of the Bill was the provisions for the inclusion of library science experts and the *Bharana Samiti* of the members of the K.G.S in the S.L.A. The establishment of the District and Taluk Central Libraries and the proposal for a library cess at the rate of two paise for each cent of land were the other important provisions of the Bill. But it was also not accepted by the Government[8].

The next attempt in this regard was made in 1985. The new bill called "The Kerala Public Libraries Bill, 1985" insisted that there was no need for two level organisations, one as a statutory body and the other the K.G.S. In the Bill there was also a provision for the dissolution of the K.G.S. As per the Bill the State Library Authority was to be the state library board with Education Minister as ex-officio-chairman . Moreover it was for the first time in the history of the state public library bill that the District collector was made the ex-officio-chairman of the District library Board[9]. But the bill could not be enacted due to the strong opposition from the public.

During the reign of the Left Democratic Front government (26 March, 1987- 22 June 1991) a new Library Bill called 'the Kerala Public Library (Kerala Grandhasala Sanghom) Act, 1989' was presented in the Kerala Legislative Assembly by the Education Minister K. Chandrasekhar on 25 January 1989. The discussion on the Bill commenced in the Assembly on 3 February 1989 which continued upto 23 February 1989 when it was unanimously passed by the legislature with sixty amendments. The Bill has got the President's assent on 16 May 1989[10]. Thus Kerala became the seventh state which has got a library legislation[11].

The Bill is different from the other Bills presented by the previous Governments. It is an experienced step to handover the administration of the libraries to the library users without any interference of the local bodies. The salient features of this Act are as follows[12]:

1. The State Library Council (S.L.C) is the highest body charged with the responsibility of advising the Government on Library matters, and supervising and directing all matters connected with the library service

in the State. It is a body corporate consisting of one member from each Taluk elected by the general body of the District Library Council. Below the S.L.C there is District Library Council and Taluk Library unions to look after the library matters in the district and the Taluk level respectively.

2. An executive committee, consisting of twenty five members, is to be constituted with five officials from among the members of the State Library Council.

3. In the Act the President, the Vice- President, the Secretary and the Joint Secretary are elected from among the Executive Committee members.

4. The term of office of the members other than the ex-officio members are fixed as three years and members of the State Library Council shall not be eligible for re-election or re-nomination for more than two terms consecutively.

5. The Secretary of the State Library Council shall be the Chief Executive authority of the S.L.C

6. Under the Act, below state library council there are District Library Council (D.L.C) and Taluk Library Union (T.L.U) to look after the library affairs of districts and taluks respectively.

7. The office bears of the D.L.C and T.L.U are elected representatives who originally belong to the membership of the individual libraries.

8. The term of office bearers of the D.L.C and T.L.U are the same as the S.L.C.

9. Provisions are made in the Act to have representation of the Scheduled Caste and Scheduled Tribe and women who would be nominated by the Government to the S.L.C., D.L.C. and T.L.U.

10. Provisions are made for mobilizing a state – library fund, collected from sources like the grants given by the state or the central government, contributions and gifts, provident fund, superannuation fund, welfare fund, and other funds of the K.G.S .

11. A library cess of five paise from the building tax or property tax shall be levied by the S.L.C.

12. Each D.L.C is to prepare a District Library Development plan for establishing and co-ordinating and spreading library service within the district . The plan sent through the president of the S.L.C may be approved with or without amendments by the Government and every sanctioned plan has to be implemented by the D.L.C concerned.

13. As per section 38 of the Act, the K.G.S will be deemed to have merged with the Kerala State Library Council.

Though there was general acceptance of the Act, these were critics too who pointed out some major defects in the Bill. For instance, it was pointed out that Library professionals were generally disappointed, for, the Act did not provide much scope for any radical change in the library set up in the State[13]. Professional's involvement in the policy making and decision making process would be significant[14]. Out of the three bodies, viz., the S.L.C., the D.L.C and the T.L.U only in the S.L.C ., there was provision for nomination of a librarian by its members. Similarly, there was no representation from Panchayats, Municipalities, and Municipal Corporations[15].

According to another critic, all the library bills except the present one, prepared hitherto had the Education Minister as the ex-officio Chairman of the S.L.C. But in this Bill of office bearers of the S.L.C., the D.L.C and T.L.U are to be democratically elected. Such a provision was unique, and was not to be seen in any other Library Act of the country[16]. Inspite of these marginal criticism, both for and against the Act, it was implemented in 1989. As per the new Act election was held in different stages and finally an elected body headed by Kadammanitta Ramakrishnan and I.V. Das as President and Secretary of the State Library Council took over the leadership of the great movement on 27 April 1994.

Notes and References

1. *Kerala Grandhasala Sanghathinte Bharana Report - 1985-86,* (Mal.), Trivandrum: government of Kerala, 1990, p.1.
2. Government of Kerala, *Library Movement in Kerala, Trivandrum,* Public Relations Department, 1990, p.3. At present the ninth Ministry headed by Mr. K. Karunakaran is in power.
3. K. Sunilkumar, "Library Legislation in Kerala- A Survey", *Kerala Public Library System in India,* New Delhi: ESS ESS Publications, 1980, pp. 47-48.
4. *Ibid.*
5. *The Kerala Public Library Bill, 1977,* The Seventh Kerala Legisaltive Assembly, Trivandrum: Kerala Legislative Assembly, 1977.
6. K. Sunil Kumar, No. 3
7. *Ibid.*
8. *Kerala Public Library Bill of 1985, Trivandrum:* Kerala Legislative Assembly, 1985, pp. 4-26.

9. Manayath Chandran, "Kerala Grandhasala Sanghom Act: Background and special features", Public Library System in India, New Delhi: ESS ESS Publication, 1980, p. 52.

10. *Ibid.*

11. Alexander Abraham, "Public Library Legislation in India", *Public Library System in India,* New Delhi: ESS ESS Publication, 1980, p.10.

12. Kerala Gazette extraordinary, Vol. XXXIV, No. 452, Trivandrum : Governmetn of Kerala, 18 May 1989, pp. 6-27.

13. M.N. Ramakrishnan, *Kerala Public Libraries (K.G.S) Act 1989, An over view,* Paper presented in one- day seminar on September 25, 1989 at VJT Hall in Trivandrum sponsored by Kerala University, pp. 4-5.

14. *Ibid.*

15. *Ibid.*

16. Manayath Chandran, "*Kerala Grandhasala Niyamum, Pachathlavum*", (Mal.), Paper presented in a one-day seminar on 25 September 1989 at V.J.T Hall in Trivandrum sponsored by Kerala University, pp. 5-6.

10

Opinionnaire Survey

So far, the report has presented the details of the library movement in the State, the present state of affairs has also been highlighted using the following procedures.

In order to study the socio-cultural relations of the libraries with the society, an opinionnaire survey has been conducted. The details of the nature and development of the Opinionnaire Survery are given below:

As a tool used in Survey Research, Opinionnaire Survey is a device for securing facts about the current conditions and to make enquiries about attitudes and opinions.

The term opinionnaire refers to a systematic compilation of opinions that are submitted to a sample from which information is derived[1]. The researcher's contentions depend on the responses of people, regarding their beliefs and feelings. Through the use of questions or by getting people's expressed relations to statements, the degree of their agreement or disagreement on certain aspects is obtained.

The Opinionnaire Survey developed for the present study consists of fifty five relevant items coming under eleven categories as listed below:

(a) Political activities of the libraries
(b) Relations with the Communist parties
(c) Social renovation
(d) Economic condition of the libraries
(e) Educational role of libraries
(f) Libraries in the scientific front
(g) Libraries and the promotion of literature
(h) Libraries role in the cultural and sports fields
(i) Relations with the K.G.S
(j) Achievements of the society through the libraries
(k) Suggestions of the public for the improvement of the libraries (See Appendix-I for the details of the Opinionnaire Survey).

In order to get fifty five items, for the final scale, a total of two hundred and twenty items have been prepared for the draft role, having twenty items in each category. The opinionnaire survey then administered to an initial sample of 60 public library readers, for checking the appropriateness of the items. The final items have been selected on the basis of two criteria: (1) Difficulty level of the items (the proportion of library readers marking the keyed-response) (2) Index of items discrimination (the ability of the item to differentiate high scorers from low scorers). The items which have high discriminative index and average difficulty power above are selected[2]. As there were five or more items found suitable to be selected in each of the eleven categories, it was decided to select five items from each category out of the twenty items.

The responses of the subjects have been elicited in one of the three categories, viz., 'Yes', 'Undecided' and 'No' (Y, U, N), for each item. For a positive item, a scroe of 3,2 or 1 is given, corresponding to 'Yes', 'Undecided', and 'No'. For a negative item, the scoring process is reversed.

Administration of Opinionnaire Survey on a Sample and Collection of Data

For getting individual responses, the final tool (Opinionnaire Survey) containing the selected 55 items, was administered to a sample of individuals. The group of subjects selected from a population for the purpose of obtaining information about the population is called a sample[3]. For the purpose of generalization of results as in the case of the present study, it is necessary that the sample be selected by a process involving randomness. Here, 'Random Sample' means that each of the elements of the population has an equal probability of being included. In other words, the selection of any element is independent of the selection of any other element[4].

The sample for the present study has been selected in the following manner: copies of 1000 opinionnaire survey have been distributed among library readers in different parts of the state. The investigator personally met majority of them, and the rest have been contacted by his friends who were fellow researchers. It may be noted that several individuals have no response to the opinionnaire. Out of those who responded, 300 response sheets have been included for the study. They belonged to different strata of the society. They are different in age, locality, sex, occupation, educational backgrounds, and earning of incomes.

The responses of the subjects (library readers) were analysed and classified on the basis of sex, area of residence, age group, educational level, occupation and income level. The total score under each category was taken, and they were statistically analysed.

A measured value based upon sample data is called statistic[5]. It is one of the devices by which men try to understand the generality of life. The principal aim of the method is to summaries data, which by their very bulk are difficult to comprehend and which, therefore, need to be analysed by appropriate methods before they can be understood or made to supply useful information[6].

Discussion and Analysis of the Data

The data gathered from the respondents constitute the use of 'Opinionnaire Survey' the basis for the analysis. It may be remembered here that in statistical inference, there are many choices of techniques, when the focus is on a single variable at a time univariate analysis is required. Proportion and percentage come under univariate analysis[7]. The term 'proportion' is used here to mean the percentage of respondents giving the desired response for each of the items[8].

Table 11. Category A : Political Activities of Libraries

In	*Y*	*P*	*R*	*N*	*P*	*R*	*U*	*P*	*R*	*T*
1	127	42.3	3	141	47.0	3	32	10.7	5	300
2	144	48.0	2	118	39.3	4	38	12.7	4	300
3	163	54.3	1	89	29.7	5	48	16.0	1	300
4	108	36.0	4	150	50.0	2	42	14.0	3	300
5	45	15.0	5	209	69.7	1	46	15.3	2	300

The first item of the opinionnaire survey is as follow: "This library discusses political subjects which have contemporary importance". The data obtained from the 300 respondents (library readers) show that 127 (42.3%) respondents are agreeing with this view. At the same time 141 (47%) respondents disagreed with this opinion, while 32 (10.7%) persons took a neutral view. The details relating to the percentage of the respondents answering 'Yes', 'No' and 'undecided' to the various items of the 'opinionnaire survey' are given in the following tables.

The first five statements of the opinionnare belong to 'A' category which deal with the political activities of the members of the libraries in the library premises. The data show that 163 respondents marked 'Yes' against the item number three of the opinionnaire survey, i.e., "this library helps a great deal to bring about an understanding of the political conditions of the country." This shows that 163 (54.3%) of the respondents agreeing with this view. There are 89 (29.7%) respondents disagreeing with this view. The remaining 48 (16%) respondents did not share any of this views, who formed the "undecided" group. Contrary to the above statement, item number five (the same category) ie "the meeting of political parties are convened in this library" is favourably responded to by only 45 (15%) of the respondents. This shows that a big majority of the respondents is of the opinion that meetings of political parties are not convened in their library.

Table 12. Category B : Relation with Communist Parties

IN	*Y*	*P*	*R*	*N*	*P*	*R*	*U*	*P*	*R*	*T*
6	143	47.7	1	107	35.7	5	50	16.6	4	300
7	85	28.3	5	155	51.7	1	60	20.0	3	300
8	107	35.7	2	147	49.0	3	46	15.3	5	300
9	101	33.7	3	116	38.7	4	83	27.6	1	300
10	86	28.7	4	151	50.3	2	63	21.0	2	300

Category 'B' of the Opinionnaire Survey is concerned with the libraries relation to communist parties using five different items. One of these items (IN. No.6) reads as follows: "This library contains several publications based on communist ideology". The data show that 143 (47.7%) of the respondents are agreeing with this opinion. For the other items in this category, a lesser percentage of the respondents are agreeing with this.

Table 13. Category C : Social Renovation

IN	*Y*	*P*	*R*	*N*	*P*	*R*	*U*	*P*	*R*	*T*
11	198	66.0	1	47	15.7	5	55	18.3	4	300
12	109	36.3	5	133	44.3	1	58	19.4	3	300
13	188	62.7	2	66	22.0	4	46	15.3	5	300
14	151	50.3	3	86	28.7	3	63	21.0	2	300
15	115	38.4	4	113	37.7	2	72	24.0	1	300

Items dealing with 'social renovation' owing to libraries are concerned with the 'C' category of this Opinionnaire Survey (Items 13 to 18). The opinions of the items number eleven, the thirteen of the survey are as follows: "this library helps to promote unity among various groups of people" and "it contributed much to the social changes in the area around". The data show that 198 (66%) and 188 (62.6%) respondents respectively are agreeing with this. It indicates that above 60% of the respondents are agreeing the opinion that the library is promoting the unity among various sections of the society and it contributes much for solid changes.

Table 14. Category D : Economic Condition of the Libraries

IN	*Y*	*P*	*R*	*N*	*P*	*R*	*U*	*P*	*R*	*T*
16	173	57.7	3	82	27.3	5	45	15.0	1	300
17	172	57.3	4	102	34.0	1	26	8.7	5	300
18	175	58.3	2	90	30.0	3	35	11.7	4	300
19	163	54.3	5	101	33.7	2	36	12.0	2	300
20	184	61.3	1	82	27.3	4	34	11.3	3	300

The items sixteen to twenty in the 'D' category deal with the libraries economic conditions. Of these, item number twenty states: "Owing to financial difficulties, the library could not be made spacious". There are 184 (61.3%) respondents who support this view, and it indicates that some more financial assistance is needed for providing more accommodation to library readers and to keep documents of the libraries.

Table 15. Category E : Educational role of Libraries

IN	*Y*	*P*	*R*	*N*	*P*	*R*	*U*	*P*	*R*	*T*
21	169	56.3	4	87	29.0	2	44	14.7	2	300
22	176	58.7	2	74	24.6	4	50	16.7	1	300
23	134	44.7	5	129	43.0	1	37	12.3	4	300
24	231	77.0	1	44	14.7	5	25	8.3	5	300
25	173	57.7	3	85	28.3	3	42	14.0	3	300

The educational role of the libraries is dealt with in the category 'E' of the survey. The item number twenty four of this survey, i.e., "news papers and current publications of this library encourage the people in the vicinity to improve their knowledge" is agreed by 231 (77%) respondents, while only 44 (14.7%) did not agree. Here also, a vast majority of the respondents are in favour of the given opinion.

Table 16. Category F : Libraries in the Scientific Fronts

IN	*Y*	*P*	*R*	*N*	*P*	*R*	*U*	*P*	*R*	*T*
26	143	47.7	1	110	36.6	5	47	15.7	4	300
27	115	38.4	3	118	39.3	4	67	22.3	1	300
28	116	38.7	2	122	40.6	3	62	20.7	2	300
29	67	22.3	5	192	64.0	1	41	13.7	5	300
30	112	37.4	4	127	42.3	2	61	20.3	3	300

In category 'F', the libraries role for scientific development is referred to. For item number twenty six of the survey , ie., "there are lots of scientific publications in this library", 143 (47.7%) respondents are in favour and 110 (36.6%) against.

Table 17. Category G : Libraries and the Promotion of Literature

IN	*Y*	*P*	*R*	*N*	*P*	*R*	*U*	*P*	*R*	*T*
31	212	70.7	1	62	20.6	5	26	8.7	5	300
32	121	40.3	5	145	48.3	1	34	11.4	4	300
33	155	51.7	3	75	25.0	4	70	23.3	1	300
34	136	45.3	4	110	36.7	2	54	18.0	2	300
35	176	58.7	2	78	26.0	3	46	15.3	3	300

The literary role of the libraries is dealt with in the 'G' category. In this category, item 31, that is the library reader is not subjected to mental frustration by reading trash literature (Painkili Sahityam) available in the library, is agreed by 212 respondents (70.7%) . This indicates that the reading of low quality literary works do not cause any mental frustrations among the readers.

Table 18. Category H : Libraries role in the cultural and Sports fields

IN	*Y*	*P*	*R*	*N*	*P*	*R*	*U*	*P*	*R*	*T*
36	218	72.7	1	43	14.3	5	39	13.0	3	300
37	159	53.0	2	108	36.0	3	33	11.0	5	300
38	108	36.0	4	132	44.0	2	60	20.0	2	300
39	158	52.7	3	106	35.3	4	36	12.0	4	300
40	87	29.0	5	151	50.3	1	62	20.7	1	300

The 'H' category of this survey concern with the role of the libraries in the field of arts and sports. "This library is a cultural centre of the area" is the thirty-sixth item of the Opinionnaire survey. There are 218 (72.7%) respondents agreeing with this opinion. It is clear that majority of them consider the library as a cultural centre of their area.

Table 19. Category I : Relation with K.G.S

IN	*Y*	*P*	*R*	*N*	*P*	*R*	*U*	*P*	*R*	*T*
41	280	93.3	1	20	6.7	5	—	—	5	300
42	125	41.7	4	101	33.6	1	74	24.7	3	300
43	209	69.7	2	48	16.0	4	43	14.3	4	300
44	162	54.0	3	50	16.7	3	88	29.3	2	300
45	111	37.0	5	86	28.7	2	103	34.3	1	300

The relation between the K.G.S and its affiliated libraries is explored by the 'I' category of the survey. The item number fortyone and fortythree, ie., "this library is a member of K.G.S". and "membership to this library is increasing every year" are the opinions coming under this category. The data show that there are 280 (93.3%) and 209 (69.7%) respondents respectively favouring this opinions. It means that almost all of the respondents are the readers of the affiliated libraries of the K.G.S and the number of readers in this library is on the increase in every year.

The category 'J' discusses the achievements of the society through the libraries. The item 46 and 47 of the survey are as follows: "Because I am a member of this library, my reading habit is improving and "I am able to acquaint myself with men of letters and their works through this library."

The category 'J' discusses the achievements of the society through the libraries. The item 46 and 47 of the survey are as follows: "Because I am a members of this library, my reading habit is improving and "I am able to acquaint myself with men of letters and their works through this library."

Table 20. Category J : Achievements of the Society through the Libraries

IN	Y	P	R	N	P	R	U	P	R	T
46	220	73.3	2	42	14.0	4	38	12.7	4	300
47	229	76.3	1	39	13.0	5	32	10.7	5	300
48	119	39.7	4	102	34.0	2	79	26.3	1	300
49	87	29.0	5	137	45.7	1	76	25.3	2	300
50	138	46.0	3	91	30.3	3	71	23.7	3	300

The data show 220 (73.3%) and 229 (76.3%) respondents agree with this opinion. It highlights the fact that library helps its members to increase their reading habit and to establish a rapport with men of letters.

Table 21. Category K : Suggestions of the Public for the Development of the Libraries

IN	Y	P	R	N	P	R	U	P	R	T
51	224	81.3	4	34	11.3	2	22	7.4	4	300
52	252	84.0	2	20	6.7	4	28	9.3	2	300
53	229	76.3	5	46	15.3	1	25	8.4	3	300
54	250	83.3	3	20	6.7	5	30	10.0	1	300
55	264	88.0	1	20	6.7	3	16	5.3	5	300

The items 51 to 55 (K category) contain some suggestions of the respondents for improving the present conditions of the libraries. The suggestions of the survey which are relevant for majority of libraries are the following:

1. "Politics of individuals should not be interfere with the functioning of the libraries.
2. For the development of the library the fund should be raised.
3. The library should have a Radio and a Television
4. The individual effort and efficiency of the members of the library should be utilized for the constructive works of the government.
5. Every year the K.G.S should conduct competitions in sports and arts."
6. The data show that 224 (81.3%), 252 (84%), 229 (76.3%), 250 (83.3%) and 264 (88%) of the respondents agree with this opinions.

Among the 55 items of the survey a lion share of the respondents agree with the last five opinions in the survey. It shows that the five suggestions are agreeable to the readers for improving the present conditions of the libraries.

The following analysis of the survey further shows that the opinions of the categories viz., K, E, D, I, J, G and C agreed with by above 50% of the respondents. These categories mainly discuss the role of the library in educational (category "E") Social (Category "C") and literary (Category "G") fields. The other categories, viz., 'D' and 'I' deal with the economic conditions of the library, and the role of the K.G.S for the development of the library. The 'J' and 'K' categories concern with the contributions made by the libraries in that area and the respondents forward new ideas for the improvements of the present conditions of the library.

Table 22. Category Analysis

C	*Yp*	*R*	*Np*	*R*	*Up*	*R*
A	39	9	47	1	14	8
B	35	11	45	2	20	3
C	51	7	30	6	19	4
D	58	3	30	7	12	10
E	59	2	28	8	13	9
F	37	10	45	3	18	5
G	53	6	31	5	16	6
H	49	8	36	4	15	7
I	54	4	23	10	23	1
J	53	5	27	9	20	2
K	83	1	9	11	8	11

(C = Category, Yp = Percentage of 'Yes' answer, R = Rank, Np = Percentage of 'No' answer, Up = Percentage of undecided answers).

The other opinions of the four categories of the survey, viz., H,A,F and B are agreed with by 49%, 39%, 37% and 35% of the respondents respectively. Among the respondents 36%, 47% and 45% are disagree with the given opinions of the category. The data shows that there are meagre differences between these two groups regarding their opinions.

The analysis of the Opinionnaire surveys, in short, shows that the public libraries of the state play important role in many ways. Thus these institutions are doing valuable services in the process of change and development in the society.

References

1. John W. Best, *Research in education*, New Delhi: Prentice Hall Pvt. Ltd., 1982, p. 179.

2. Anne Auastasi, *Psychological Testing,* 6th edition, New York: Mac Millon, 1988, p. 202.
3. Nan-Liew, *Foundation of Social research,* New York : Mc Graw Hill, 1976, pp. 144-167.
4. Mark Abrahanson, *Social research methods,* Englewood: U.S.A. Prentice Hall INC, 1983, p. 219.
5. John w. Best, No. 1.
6 Helen M. Walker and Joseph Leve, *Elementary Statistical Methods,* Calcutta : Oxford, IBH Publishing Co., 1976, p. 224.
7. Nan- Liew, No. 3, p. 74.
8. Helen M. Walker and Joseph Leve, No. 6, p. 244.

[illegible] *Anthropological* [illegible] [illegible] 1949, p. [illegible]

[illegible]

11
Conclusion

The state of Kerala has been unique in many a field. In the field of education and social development the state has achieved the highest position among the Indian states. The torch of learning had been carried from the ancient period and libraries had a pivotal role in this unbroken evolutionary process.

The libraries of Kerala have an impressive historical antiquity. They were in existence even before the Christian era. During that time libraries were neither institutions of mass education nor of social activities. Most of them were of private nature to which entry was restricted. Besides, the habit of reading and preserving books were found only among the educated upper class in those days. During that time education was the monopoly of the ruling class. The arrival of European powers and the development of Malayalam language effected far reaching changes in the Society of Kerala. The Europeans who later on dominated Kerala had brought with them an ideology and literature embodying the aspirations of the common man. They shared these aspirations and ideals with the natives of Kerala. They introduced western educational system and printing technology. The enlightened rules of the state actively supported and supplemented these attempts. It was the British paramountcy in Trvancore that was responsible for the setting up of the first Public Library in India. The rise of literacy rate and the availability of printed books created an atmosphere for starting new public libraries in the State. The educated people, social reformers and political leaders came out to encourage the setting up of public libraries. Thus by the beginning of the twentieth century many libraries began to spring up in almost all parts of the state. Before that, they had been basically urban institutions, set up in palaces, noblemen's homes, religious institutions. In the then socio- political atmosphere, it could not make its way into the villages.

At that time the state was politically divided into three parts, viz., Travancore, Cochin and Malabar, of which the first two were ruled by local kings who provided grant-in-aid to the public libraries, as an encouragement for their development. But the political involvement of these public libraries was disfavoured by the rulers who warned against political activities of the library workers. The library workers of Travancore and Cochin convened conferences of the library workers and formed certain organizations as a central agency of the libraries for creating public awareness about the public libraries and to attract the government towards this movement. But these organizations were short-lived. However they gave wide publicity to this movement which made easy the work of the library organizations formed later.

Malabar, the northern part of Kerala, was then under the British rule, who were not keen on giving encouragement to the public libraries formed by the local people. The political scene of Malabar was more critical than the local kingdoms of Travancore and Cochin. The people of Malabar had actively participated in the freedom struggle, and they formed a number of public libraries as part of their political activity. The library workers and politicians were the same persons in this area and were viewed with suspecion by the government. Therefore, the libraries of Malabar had not recived any kind of financial assistance from the government. In short, the public libraries of Malabar were not mere centres of reading and learning but effective centres of political activity. The public library workers of that area were strong political activists - unlike their counterparts in Travancore and Cochin.

On the eve of Independence, the public library movement gathered momentum and two active library organisations were formed in the northern and southern parts of the state. The library movement of the southern part was backed and patronized by the rulers and the intelligentsia, while in the north, it was a part of freedom struggle. Though the Kerala Grandhalaya Sanghom had begun to organize different activities, after Independence it became inactive without doing anything significant for the development of the public library movement. But the formation of the *Akhila Thiruvithamcore Grandhasala Sanghom* was a milestone in the history of the library movement in the state. It gave effective leadership for the movement and even now the Sanghom is the pivot around which the movement revolves.

The *Akhila Thiruvithamcore Grandhasala Sanghom* extended its activities from Trvancore to Cochin and later to Malabar in 1956 and assumed a new name- The Kerala Grandhasala Sanghom, (K.G.S) under the initiation of the K.G.S a large number of new public libraries sprang up throughout the state and the public libraries which remained defunct were resuscitated. The democratic governments of Kerala evinced keen interest in this movement and they rendered more financial assistance than that was given by the pre-independent government. Still, the financial assistance was inadequate to cater the various needs and developmental activities of the Sanghom and its affiliated libraries. One of the interesting features in the state is the government is spending around thirty percent of income for education, but only a fraction of one percent is spent for the development of the public libraries. The K.G.S and the elite public have been pleading against this inadequate government allotment made for the public libraries. But the per capita expenditure of public libraries is Rs. 0.44 which, is even below the national average (Rs. 0.46). The Opinionnaire Survey points out that, owing to the lack of funds, the libraries have failed to purchase necessary materials not could it attend to the maintenance works properly. Moreover, inadequate furniture, dust wrapped and scattered books, point to the sad plight of the libraries in the State. So, the libraries need more financial assistance, to overcome all this difficulties.

As a result of consistent pressure exerted by the Sanghom the Government has raised the annual grant to the public libraries every year. The libraries could also raise funds by organizing cultural performances, selling lotteries and collecting voluntary donations. In spite of all these, the amount at hand is far below the actual requirements of the libraries. It may be remembered that in the developed countries the amount utilized for education and for libraries could be found to be the same. In the modern society, the public libraries occupy an important place and for strengthening this institution more financial assistance is needed. Unless the state government comes out in a big way to finance public libraries, the latter cannot function properly, and meet the requirements of the general public.

Most of the public libraries have a very meagre budget with which they can hardly manage their day-to-day affairs. In this background, it is but natural that these libraries cannot procure new publications. If the libraries are not equipped with modern publications, they will fail to satisfy the needs of the members who fall back on them for the latest developments and progress in various disciplines or subjects all over the world.

The library movement in the state served as a microcosm for the successive-socio-cultural tutelage in the country. The K.G.S is the core of cultural life in Kerala. The Sanghom has got deep rooted organizational structure in each village in the State. The public libraries of the state were not mere places where the members could use the documents for reference or borrow books on payment of fee. They may be better called cultural centres of the community as has been perceived in the Opinionnaire Survey also. Cultural entertainment programmes, functional literacy programmes and sports and games are regularly organized under the auspices of these libraries. The public library workers knew, better than any one else, that these cultural programmes could appeal to the sentiments of the people and capture the attention of the public. The main item of the cultural programmes was dramas which could go deep into the mind of the people. Through cultural programmes, the public libraries actually created a silent social change in the society. At the same time, it gave popularity to those who were behind the cultural activities.

Kalasamitis and Sports Clubs were attached to all the libraries. It gave the people, especially the younger generation, an incentive to develop their taste in cultural and sports activities. The people of Kerala occupy an important position in these fields mainly because of the influence of the sports and arts centres affiliated to the libraries. In the field of drama, libraries of the state had provided enormous help and encouragement. This argument is sustained by the fact that the eminent play wrights of Kerala owe a deep debt of gratitude to this movement even now.

The Sanghom and its libraries have been discharging an excellent service in the field of adult and continuing education. The libraries are institutions for "education by self or education without a teacher." In recognition of its activities in the literary field, the UNESCO gave an Award to the Sanghom in 1975. Since the formation of public library system the adult education programme has been one of the accepted programmes of every library. The Sanghom took initiative in giving scientific guidance to the libraries in this matter. It helps very much to increase the literacy rate of the state. Moreover, it paved the way for the "Total Literacy Programme" (1990-91), through which the state received world wide reputation. The Opinionnaire Survey also shows that the public libraries of the state are functioning as non formal educational agencies and they actively involved in the literacy programmes of the state. It is the school for the deschooled. In the slums, in the trial colonies, and in the under developed areas, the libraries have conducted literacy camps. The Sanghom brought out publications for giving continuing education to the neo-literates and the drop- outs.

The adult education and non-formal education programmes were not limited to the imparting of basic library skills and eradication of illiteracy. A variety of programmes for specific target groups were being organized both in rural and urban areas. The Prorgrammes with special emphasis on the development of skills, agriculture and related issues, health and community leadership, were highly appreciated by all sections of the people.

With the intention of promoting reading habit among the people, Mobile Library Service, Bell Cycle Programme, Family Reading Programme and library services in Jails and hospitals were conducted by the Sanghom. Special sections for women and children were also opened in almost all the libraries. Books for developing desirable feelings, good habits and humanitarian values influenced and inspired the people. The library workers of the state were convinced that though reading appears to be a personal activity it was also a part of the social process.

The availability of good literature in the libraries sharpened the taste of the people. Men of letters in the state were active public library workers too. Libraries conducted literary activities with the guidance of the K.G.S in co-operation with the association of men of letters. The people have got enough opportunities to involve in literary activities and develop their taste in literature. The Opinionnaire Survey also indicates that libraries helped very much for the development of Malayalam literature. The public libraries of the state may be considered as the main 'consumers' of the books published in Malayalam language, and thereby the libraries helped the growth of publishers and indirectly the literary men. This is very obvious from the relation between the K.G.S and the S.P.C.S.

In the scientific front also the Sanghom evinced enough interest. In order to inculcate scientific awareness among the public, science classes, seminars, and demonstrations were conducted in different libraries. An Agricultural Book Corner was organized to help the agriculturalists. By organizing medical camps and attending sanitation works the Sanghom and the libraries were really discharging great service to the society. The Kerala *Sasthrasahithya Parishad* and the Sanghom jointly conducted many programmes for creating scientific awareness among the public. This continues to be so even today.

The library workers also gave much importance to the environmental issues. They celebrated Forest Festivals and conducted Forest Book Corner in every library with the guidance and advice of the K.G.S. Seminars on environment and deforestation were also held. Most of the libraries have maintained good gardens and clean atmosphere which attracted the public to these institutions and their activities.

The public libraries of the state are the capillaries of social activities in each village. Mass participation in the library activities maintained social contact devoid of discrimination on any basis. The libraries have helped considerably in pampering communal harmony in the state.

The need for public libraries so conceived has been felt in Kerala after the formation of the K.G.S. The people understood that reading would widen their horizons of understanding beyond the barrier of space and time. In democracy every one enjoys sovereignty, and in order to exercise it wisely it is necessary that every one should be well informed and trained to discriminate right from wrong. Reading of books opens the window of the mind and enables the readers to see problems steadily and see them whole. The public libraries of the state not only aim at creating more readers and reading materials, but also bringing the readers together. They bridged the gap between the increased number of readers and the increased number of books. Students were instructed to help themselves to acquire knowledge and they were expected to carry on this process, not till the end of their prescribed course, but to the end of their lives. The libraries of the state were par excellence the institutions for this kind of education.

The libraries are the centres for the dissemination of information and the exchange of ideas. They are undoubtedly a multipurpose agency which serve information, community recreation in the field of social, civic and utilitarian education. Reading relieved the people from parochial outlook and widened the horizon of knowledge. It reduced social tension and helped the people overlook the fictitious differences made by vested interests to make religious and communal disharmony among people. The Opinionnaire Survey also shows that the libraries played a prominent role for social change. They kept people out of the morass of ignorance and illiteracy, and redeemed people from the grip of superstitious practices.

As a democratic institution, operated by the people and for the people, access to the libraries of the state was rendered equal to all members of the community, regardless of occupation, creed, class or sex. They offered children, young person, women, labourers to educate themselves continuously, helped them keep abreast of the developments, in all fields of knowledge, and develop critical and constructive attitudes towards issues of public importance. They also helped making them socially and politically better citizens of the country and developing the creative potentialities and powers of appreciation in arts and letters.

The activities of the Sanghom were mainly centred around the rural libraries of the state. It gave an opportunity for the rural folk to involve in the various programmes of the Sanghom. It enabled them to form their opinions on the social, political and economic problems of the society. Moreover, they used these institutions as a reliable agency for promoting their self education and also as the media of mass communication. Infact, the libraries of the state played a vital role in reducing the gap between the rural and urban people in the society.

The K.G.S and its libraries contributed much to the elegance of the social fabric of Kerala. Public libraries creats social awareness against the curse of poverty, illiteracy and other social problems. All the libraries used to celebrate the important National Days and Birth Days of the National and International personalities. It enabled the public to recall these days, and their lives. The library workers co-operated with the constructive programsmmes of the state and the central government as part of national building.

Eventhough the Sanghom was not a statutory body, the state was actually meeting its recurring expenditure.

This was quite a unique thing, because in no other state in India, a library association had received such government owned libraries, support and assistance. The government owned libraries, in recognition of the merit of the Sanghom were handed over the Sanghom for public use. This was a remarkable phenomenon peculiar to Kerala. The Sanghom had given to some extent a certain pattern to the library system in the state. It enabled to enlist the service of numerous people for the development of libraries and to create library consciousness among the public.

The libraries, especially rural libraries, are the meeting places of villagers, where seminars and discussion on different issues, including political subjects were often held. The Opinionnaire Survey also shows that the libraries helped in understanding much the political situations prevalent in the state. The political parties, therefore, used these institutions as centres of their activities. No other institutions, save some public libraries in the state, have got the rare opportunity to witness the unique political events happened in this state. The workers of both the Congress and the Communist parties used the libraries to propagate their political ideas. The communist party workers took special interest in the movement and contributed much to the spread of the library movement. Often the political parties instructed the workers to involve actively in the movement. This has led to an unhealthy trend in the field of public library movement. It was this state of affairs that finally led to the take over of the K.G.S by the government in 1977. The Opinionnaire Survey indicates that enough books containing communist ideology are available in the libraries of the state. But the libraries were not controlled by them nor did they function according to the whims and fancies of the communist party. The democratically disciplined libraries under the Sanghom have succeeded in creating democratic awareness among the masses. The periodic elections in the Sanghom and libraries provided an opportunity to experience the democratic process. It was also a part of democratization. When the democratic institutions had begun to grow up, the libraries, an essential ingredienct of democratic setup further established its strong position in the state.

The progress of the public libraries in the state depends to a large extent on the service of politicians. They have encouraged the formation of new libraries throughout the state. The involvement of politicians in the library movement had been visible from the very outset. The Chief Ministers and political leaders have acted the President of the Sanghom on many occasions. P.N. Paniker served the Sanghom, as the General Secretary for a long time. He was a follower of the Indian National Congress, before the formation of the Sanghom. But after the assumption of Secretaryship, he did not involve himself in the mainstream of the state politics. Most of the Presidents of the Sanghom were top leaders of the Congress Party in the state. When the President was busy with the activities in the state politics, the functions of the Sanghom were usually carried out by the Secretary. Thus P.N. Paniker the Secretary, became an unquestionable functionary of the Sanghom. At the time of the rule of Communist party (1957-59) the Government tried to take over the Sanghom through legislation. They strongly contended that P.N. Panikar was not qualified enough to lead the movement.

Compared to the K.G.S., the Government owned, L.L.A has not done anything for the bolting and blooming of the library movement and the socio-cultural upsurge in the state. The journal of the K.G.S was widely accepted and it had a high position among the standard journals of the state. Other publications of the Sanghom also were widely acclaimed. The Book Selection Committee of the Sanghom helped the libraries to select good books. The novel programmes introduced by the Sanghom gave an impetus to the public libraries in the state.

Despite the progress made in the public library system, it must be said that some major defects are still persisting. The noticeable deficiency is that the state doesn't have a well-integrated library system. Also, though there is quantitative expansion in terms of the number of libraries and the number of books, the corresponding improvement in the quality is lacking. Besides, even the addition of books are also steadily on the decline except in a few libraries. Books on literature, especially fictions comprise the bulk of the collection. Sub-standard books were heaped in libraries with a view to demonstrate the superiority of libraries in terms of their quantum. Little has been done for the acquisition of books on the vocational needs of the community. Now the Sanghom is engaged in curbing the influence of Painkili Sahityam (trash literature) in the libraries of the state.

The second drawback is that most of the libraries are not scientifically organized; for instance, the failure in the implementation of the classification and cataloguing systems in most of the libraries. It should be remembered that even small libraries would be able to function better, if its documents are well orgasnised. The emphasis hitherto has been on the mere increase in the number of libraries without proper attention to infra-structural services. In the case of rural libraries, all librarians are honorary workers, while in the case of major urban libraries they are paid employees. The Sanghom is against permanent librarians and it pursued a policy of "untouchability" towards the qualified librarians . It viewed that the periodical training for library workers is necessary to conduct the daily routine of the libraries. In fact the Sanghom gave more importance to other activities of the libraries than the traditional ones. But qualified librarians are inevitable in every library to improve the quality of the present library services.

So far, the library movement in Kerala has been a source of pride to the people of the state. To make it more attractive and purpose-oriented, a comprehensive library legislation was essential. The demand for library legislation emerged in the state even before independence. But the first step in this regard was taken by the first communist government (1957-59) that came into power in the state. After that many governments have take steps to introduce a library legislation. Most of these acts were unacceptable to the Sanghom because they did not give proper place to the Sanghom and were against the existing democratic framework of the libraries.

At last, the long awaited library legislation in the state of Kerala became a reality in 1989, when the Left Democratic Front Government took the initiative in passing "the Kerala Public Libraries (Grandhasala Sanghom) Act 1989". It is the materialization of a long cherished dream in the chequered history of the library movement in the state. The K.G.S., since its formation, has struggled to pass a library law based on democratic principles, keeping up the peculiar fractures of the library movement in the state. The present act is proposed by the government after full consultation with the K.G.S and the library workers of the state. The Act is a unique one, in comparison with the previous library bills of the state and the library laws existed in the country. Now the library act is at the stage of implementation, and as per the Act, the K.G.S is expected to be converted in to the Kerala State Library Council.

The libraries are actually a barometer to measure the cultural attainment of people. The libraries, in other countries, are the focus of cultural activities. Free library service is a well recognized principle all over the world. The responsibility for providing funds for library development falls upon the government. The neglect of libraries really means the stunting of the social and cultural development. Hence it is the duty of the government to take more pragmatic steps for the efficient functioning of the public library system. Though a fabulous amount (31.5%) is provided in the budget for education, a very small amount (below 1%) is being spent for the promotion of public libraries. The government has to come forward in a big way in financing the public libraries, so that the latter would be in a position to cater the needs of the society and the state.

The information collected through the Opinionnaire Survey shows that the readers do not like the politicalization of library activities. A separate fund for library purpose in every library is very necessary (The Kerala Public Libraries Act on 1989 has a separate section in this regard). Likewise, it is desirable to have audio-video activities in all the libraries, specially in the rural libraries. The service of the library workers may be availed by the government in the constructive programmes and the K.G.S may conduct cultural and sports festivals every year with the active participation of all the libraries of the state.

However the public library system and the libraries can serve the people better, if only the necessary warming up is attempted on many a direction.

1. Library service should be free to each and every citizen of the State.

2. It is desirable to have an independent Directorate of Libraries. It can look after the entire field of the libraries in the state. It may conduct constant evaluation of library services in the state, and be in charge of the administration of the libraries.

3. There should be an All Kerala Library Advisory Committee consisting of officials, library experts, library workers and the representative people. They should periodically meet and review the works of the libraries of the state and recommend necessary changes in the policy matters of the library.

4. The state government should encourage the setting up of a Book Bureau in the state capital and from there libraries shall select and buy their books avoiding mediators.

5. An informal organization consisting of library users may be formed in every library and they form reading circles and study groups in the library and among libraries. They will also help to carry out the message of a library consciousness among the public. They can also communicate the essentials of library morality among their friends and the users of the library.

6. The public libraries of the State may co-operate with one another. And the libraries in schools and colleges, Departmental libraries, Research libraries and libraries in the University also should follow suit.

7. Each library may have a trained librarian who will be the Executive Officer of the library.

8. The elected members of the library may be the policy makers of the library. The librarian may be a permanent staff in the library.

9. The libraries of the state may act as effective and efficient information centers in each village.

10. Classification and cataloguing of the available resource in the libraries and a union catalogue may be prepared.

11. A Director of Libraries may be appointed as the Chief Technical Officer of the libraries. He shall be provided with all kinds of technical advice about the libraries in the state.

12. More facilities and encouragements may be given to libraries as centers of adult and continuing education.

13. A meeting of the library workers and the social workers would be summoned occasionally, which will be helpful to one another to understand the fields of activity.

14. To understand the taste and trend of the reading habit of the people of the state a detailed survey research is needed.

15. The infrastructural facilities of the libraries may be modernized.

16. Library Associations are essential for the development of library movement, and the state government should encourage development of strong library associations.

There were instances when the state government tried to suspend the powers given to the Sanghom. It was strongly criticized by all because they know that the functions of the government departments are not smooth and uninterrupted. And so it would not be healthy to hand over the activities of the K.G.S. to a department of government. The Sanghom efficiently discharges the duties entrusted with it. At the same time the activities of the L.L.A. proved that the government owned libraries could not function effectively.

At present, the involvement of the youth in the library field is on the decline when compared with the experience of the past. Once they were pillars of this movement. It shows that the present activities of the libraries are not suited, to attract the young generation. Likewise, the introduction of electronic media particularly the audio visual things reduce the reading habit of the people. People spend more time to watching the television instead of reading books. The prevented influence of those media has been appalling. The reading habit and the thinking capacity of the people also have been adversely affected by this trend.

Though the Sanghom started a crusade against the trash literature 'produced' by money minded publishers it hasn't so far succeeded in warding off the menace from the libraries. The newspapers of the state exercise a strong Keralite wakes up with a newspaper in hand or he may go to the nearest public library for it. The newspapers open-up a day's topic of discussion and thought for him. He is sometimes provided with false versions of facts. This is alarming, and it also reduces his natural capacity for thinking. The Sanghom and the library workers may organize a strong public opinion against such psychological exploitations.

The literacy programmes of the Sanghom have received world wide acclamation. The libraries are, undoubtedly , the schools of the neo-literates and they function as the centres of adult education. Now the government has started certain new centres in the name of "Jana Shikshan Nilayam" for adult and continuing education. However, it would be better if the libraries are made the centres for the implementation of the programme. If other oganisations are set up to discharge the present functions of the libraries, it would be a great loss of wealth and energy. Actually the libraries of the state are capable of carrying out such programmes.

Many things that give strength and sustenance to our culture have withered in recent years and the library movement also followed suit. Places that used to be vibrant with activity have become mere shadows of what they used to be. The libraries of the State are facing acute shortage of funds. There is no increase worthy of mention in the stock of books. The employees are disgruntled and the number of library users are on the decline. Once the cultural activities of the libraries were the nerve centres of the society but today they seem to have relapsed in to inaction. The Kerala Public Library Bill, it is hoped, will be a panacea for relieving the libraries of their present position.

The progress made by the Sanghom during the last forty five years has not helped it to keep away from the clutches of the Government and the bureaucracy. Despite this fact, the Sanghom has been given legal recognition and support by the Government. At present the libraries under the Sanghom are not in a way inferior to the libraries of the Local Library Authorities.

With the adoption of the new Act, the Kerala Grandhasala Sanghom would vanish, for it will be eliminated from the scene of activities by resorting to alternate arrangements, But the pioneer work of the K.G.S., with a galaxy of selfless and dedicated activists at the helm of affairs, has certainly left an indelible imprint on the field of social, cultural and educational achievements of the state. Receiving nothing but pittance by way of remuneration, the early workers put their heart and soul for the success of the movement. Their insight and social commitment unbridled by petty political motives, is actually a very important phase in the sphere of socio-cultural and educational evolution of the state.

Appendix - A

First Sircar Grant to the Trivandrum Public Library Neettu Dated 5 Kanni 1012 issued by Maharaja Swathi Thirunal

This is the royal writ issued by Maharaja Swathi Thirunal to inform that a letter from Mr. Robert, the library Secretary, dated 14 September 1836, requesting a grant of Rs. 1000 (One thousand only) for the Trivandrum Public Library was received. Letter to Thanma Peruma Pillai, the Treasurer of the District Treasury, directing him to release Rs. 1000 (One thousand only) for the above purpose is herewith enclosed. A writ has been issued to Diwan Subha Rao on 30 chingam 1012 ME that His Highness is pleased to authorise him to effect the payment accordingly. (Translated from Malayalam).

Appendix - B

Introduction of Rural Library Scheme and change in the TPL Rules Order Thereon R.DIS No. 386 of 35/ EDN., Dated 9th March 1935.

1. His Highness Government have given their careful consideration to the above proposals.
2. Government consider that steps should be taken to develop and expand the library movement in the state with a view to prevent lapses into illiteracy to provide facilities for adult education. The necessary funds may be provided by the Director of Public Instruction in the Education Budget for 1111 ME. The rural Libraries section will be attached to the office of the Director of Public Instruction and the Education Museum and Bureau will also be transferred there. Arrangements should be made for the transfer of superfluous books, old magazines etc., from the public library to the Rural libraries section.
3. In regard to improvement in the public library, Government consider that open shelves should be replaced by closed shelves.
4. The rules regarding affiliation are revised as below:-
   (a) Rules I(d) is deleted.
   (b) The following is substituted for the first sentence in Rule V. "A Mofussil library shall on affiliation pay a monthly subscription of Bh. Rs. (1) one a month, or Bh Rs. 5 five a half-year, or Bh. Rs. 9 nine per annum, all payable in advance.

(c) The following is added as paragraph (2) at the end of Rule V. "Libraries that are not in receipt of grant-in-aid from government shall have to deposit a sum of Bh. Rs. 10 ten against the value of books or arrears of subscription, which will be returned after deducting all dues to the library when they cease their affiliation.

(d) The following is substituted for Rule XVI.

In the case of grant-in-aid libraries, arrears of subscription and the cost of lost or damaged books will be reported to the Director of Public Instruction who shall realise the same from the grant.

In the case of libraries that are not in receipt of grant-in-aid from the Government, the arrears of subscription and the cost of lost or damaged books will be recovered from the deposit and the balance, if any, from the person in responsible charge of the affiliated library".

5. The suggestion to amend the rule restricting the weight of books and periodicals lent out each month to an affiliated library, is approved. The History Secretary, Trivandrum Public library, is requested to send up necessary amendments to the existing rules on the subject for the approval of government.

(By Order)

Sd/-

Chief Secretary to Government

To the Honorary Secretary, Trivandrum Public Library (TPL)

To The Account Officer, Trivandrum

To M.O. Thomas Esq.

To P.K. Narayana Pillai Esq.

To The Director of Public Instruction, Travancore

To The Gazette.

To The Press Room

Appendix- C

The Travancore Government Gezette 17 September 1946 (1 Kanni 1122 M.E)

Proceedings of the Government of His High Highness the Maharaja of Travancore

Read:

1. Letter dated 30th Vrischigom 1121 from the President All - Travancore library committee, submitting to Government certain proposals for the betterment and progress certain proposals for the betterment and progress of the library movement in the State.
2. Letter No. 163/ III dated 9th May 1946 from the Director of Public Instruction forwarding his remarks on the proposals of the All - Travancore Library Committee.
3. The memorandum submitted by the deputation of the Library Association at their interview with the Dewan on 6th August 1946 requesting certain facilities.

Order R.O.C. No. 6065/ 45 / Edn. Dated Trivandrum 12th September 1946.

It has been brought to the notice of Government that out of about 148 libraries known to exist in Travancore, 71 have been already affiliated to the All-Travancore Library Association and that almost all the remaining libraries have applied for affiliation. The Association has also started a survey of the libraries in the State, in course of which they have revived seven defunct libraries and opened four new ones.

4. Government have carefully considered the proposals submitted by the Association for the betterment of the library movement in the State. In view of the usefulness of the movement and of the good work done by the All – Travancore Library Association, Government consider that the Association, Government consider that the Association deserves encouragement. They therefore propose to place at the disposal of the Association an initial grant of Rs. 250 per mensem for appointing a body of enthusiastic workers. Government further propose to enhance the maximum annual grant payable to library from Rs. 200 to Rs. 240, the actual amount to be paid to each library being decided by the continued usefulness of the institution as judged and certified by the Department of Public Instruction. Government wish to make it clear that it will be the duty of the Association to organize the library movement in the state on sound and uptodate lines and to see that the libraries are well-manned and properly equipped. The question of recognition of the Association by Government will be taken up after it is duly registered.

(By order)

M. Padmanabha Pillai
Secretary to Government

To

The President, All – Travancore Library Association, Evoor.
The Director of Public Instruction
The Accountant - General
The Press Room
The Gazette

Appendix - D

The Memorandum Submitted by the Akhila Thiruvithamcore Grandhasala Sanghom office bearers to the Dewan of Travancore on 10 October 1947.

As per Travancore Company Act (Act No. IX) of 1114 ME (1938-39) the All Travancore Library Association was registered in May twenty seven1947, with Register Number 118. It may be approved by the Government. In order to appoint full – time library workers the grant to the Sanghom may be raised to rupees five hundred. The recognition of Sanghom as the spokesman of libraries, it may be allowed to recommend grant and correspond with, on behalf of them. Section (1) (194) of the Travancore Education Code laying the condition for sanctioning grant to libraries are not satisfactory for the present conditions. Hence it may be amended suitably and timely. Now the libraries of the State are working under different departments like Education, Dewaswom, Village Revenue and Harijan Welfare. These libraries may be brought under administrative control of the All Travancore Library Association. Kerala University may start a library science course for giving scientific training in the field of library.

Appendix D

Appendix - E

Kerala Grandhasla Sanghom Niyamavali (Malayalam)
(Kerala Grandhasala Sanghom Bye-Law)

Kuttayadasthu (Mal.) (Memorandum of Association)

I. The name of this society is Kerala Grandhasala Sanghom.

II. The registered office of this society is in Trivandrum Taluk.

III The objectives of this society are given below:

1. To function as an apex body of all the libraries in Kerala.
2. To promote adult education.
3. To save the neo-literate from plunging into ignorance.
4. To establish libraries and reading rooms through out the state.
5. To enrich the libraries functioning at present.
6. To start night schools.
7. To persuade the government to start a library Department and to do the needful for that.
8. To campaign for the introduction of a law governing the functioning of libraries.
9. To do the needful for providing training to the library workers.
10. To publish materials connected with library works.
11. To work for the development of the mother tongue.
12. To establish one main library in each Taluk.
13. To do all the statutory and remined things to achieve the above said objectives.

14. Purchase or lease land and buildings for the requirements of the society.
15. To help and enrich those companies, and firms the objectives of which are akin to the Sanghom and take over their power & or rights.
16. To engage in very lawful act which is helpful in meeting the financial needs of the society.
17. To establish branches and unions of the Sanghom in various parts of the country, on the basis of requirement, to achieve its objects.
18. To arrange for the payment of salary, bonus, allowance, to the workers of the society.
19. To meet the objectives of the Sanghom, money may be raised either by borrowing or by issuing debentures or by other means. The excess money be deposited with bank as per the decision of the Sanghom.
20. To borrow money, as said above, the Sanghom can sell or pledge or lease the whole of or a part of both the movable and the immovable property of it in accordance with the discretion of Director Board.
21. To do all the lawful things for the development and progress of the society.

IV. The assets of the society and the income from them however they should be spent only for meeting those objectives of the society as mentioned in this memorandum of association.

No part of the assets or income can be directly or indirectly divided among the members as dividend, bonus or in any other manner.

But this law will not be applicable for providing remuneration to the employees or workers of the society for the work they have done for the society.

V. The Sec. IV of this memorandum of association is a condition for issuing a license to the society from the government as per sec. 28 of the Travancore Companies Act, (the 9th act of 1114.)

VI. The liability of the members are limited.

VII. If the society ceases to exist during the period of membership of a member or within a period of one year from the extinction of his membership, each member of the society will be responsible for the liabilities and losses incurred by the society till the extinction of membership, expenses towards the closure of the society and expenses towards the declaration of rights of the members.

VIII. At the time of dissolution, the balance of property if any after deducting the liabilities, like loan, etc. should not be given to the members, or shared among them and this balance should be kept for those societies or institutions which have objectives similar to that of the society. The members of the society have the power to decide in this regard at the time of dissolution or prior to it. If they don't exercise this power, assets should be dealt with in accordance the decision of the District Court which has jurisdiction over the place of registered office of the company.

IX. Proper accounts should be kept for all the income and expenditure and assets and liabilities of the society and any member of the society should be allowed inspect these accounts subject to the reasonable conditions introduced by the society from time to time. Preparation of balance sheet , income and expenditure account, filing etc should be done in accordance with the sections 165 to 170 of the Travancore Companies Act, (Act 1114 of Travancore).

Appendix- F

Proceedings of the Government of His Highness The Maharaja of Travancore

Read:

1. O.G. R.D.C No. 6065/45/Edn. Dated the 12th September 1946 granting certain facilities to the All Travancore Library Association for the reorganization of the library movement in the State.
2. Letter No. 1 dated 1st Chingom lies from the All Travancore Library Association requesting grant of additional concessions.
3. letter No. 402/ III dated the 19th September 1947 from the Director of Public Instruction requesting the appointment of a committee to review the work done by the All-Travancore Library Association.
4. Memorandum submitted by the Library Association on 24th Kanni 1125 regarding the work done by them and requesting grant of additional facilities.
5. G.C. R.O.C No. 8360/47/Edn. Dated the 16th December 1947 sanctioning the appointment of a committee to review the work done by the Library Association.
6. Letter No. 250/III dated the 23rd April 1948 from the Director of Public Instruction forwarding his remarks on the report of the Committee appointed to review the work of the Library Association.

Order R.O.C. No. 8358/ 47/Edn. Dated Trivandrum the 12th July 1948.

From the report submitted by the Committee deputed to review the work of the All-Travancore Library Association. It is seen that the Association has resurrected 99 defunct libraries and opened 39 new ones. The Association has become a registered body.

It has affiliated more than 500 libraries as its members and organized Taluk Library Unions with a view to the consolidation of the library movement. The organizers under the Association have inaugurated adult education work in certain libraries. It is also seen that the Association is arranging to compile accurate Library statistics.

Government appreciate the good work done so far by the Association for the expansion and organisation of the library movements in the state and are pleased to sanction:

(i) that the All Travancore Library Association be recognized by Government

(ii) that all the libraries in this state be advised to get themselves affiliated to the Association, and

(iii) that the monthly grant of Rs. 200/- be raised to Rs. 500/- from the year 1185.

(By order)
Sd/-
M. Padmanabha Pillai
Secretary to Government

To

1. The President, All Travancore Library Association, N. Farur.
2. The Director of Public instruction
3. The Registrar, University of Travancore
4. The Accountant General
5. The Gazette
6. The Press Room

Appendix - G
Opinionnaire Survey

Given below are certain statements prepared to study the contributions of the public libraries in Kerala to the Social, economical, political educational and arts and sports fields of our social life and the problems that the libraries are now faced with. After reading each statement, you may please note your opinion according to the directions given below:

At the end of each statement three English letter (Y,N;U) are given. If you comply with the given statement you may put a circle around the letter 'Y' (Y). If you do not agree with the statement put a circle around the letter 'N' (N). In case you have no particular opinion you may put a circle around the letter 'U' (U). Please record your personal opinion on each statement. The details contained in these statements are intended for the purpose of research only .

1. Name :
2. Sex : Male / Female
3. Address :

4. Age :
5. Education Qualification :

6. Profession :
7. Yearly income :
8. Place of residence :
9. Name of your library :

Place:
Date:

(A)	1.	This library conducts discussion on current political affairs	Y.N.U
	2.	The politicians in this area work for the progress of the library	Y.N.U
	3.	These libraries helps a great deal to bring about an understanding of the political situation of the country	Y.N.U
	4.	This library contain sufficient publications of the political parties	Y.N.U
	5.	This library has been used as a place for conducting the meetings of the political parties	Y.N.U
(B)	6.	This library has several publications on communist ideology	Y.N.U
	7.	Different political parties in this area contest in the elections to the office bearers of the library	Y.N.U
	8.	The local leaders of the Communist Party are among the office bearers of this library	Y.N.U
	9.	The workers of this library do not have any special interest in organizations having communist leaning	Y.N.U
	10.	Discussions are conducted in this library on the teaching and theories of the great communist philosophers	Y.N.U
(C)	11.	This library helps to promote unity among various group of people	Y.N.U
	12.	The members of the minority communities make very little use of this library .	Y.N.U
	13.	This library has contributed much to the social changes in the locality	Y.N.U

	14.	The members of this library oppose to the superstitious believes of this area.	Y.N.U
	15.	The members of this library resist the activities of anti-social elements in this area.	Y.N.U
(D)	16.	It used to conduct art exhibitions like Cinema show dramas, etc. to raise the necessary fund for the library.	Y.N.U
		Due to financial difficulties the library cannot accomplish the following:	Y.N.U
	17.	To purchase a TV	Y.N.U
	18.	To carry out maintenance work.	Y.N.U
	19.	To organize public programmes conductive to knowledge	Y.N.U
	20.	To make the library more spacious.	Y.N.U
(E)	21.	This library functions as a centre for non-formal education.	Y.N.U
	22.	This library plays a key role in the promotion of literacy.	Y.N.U
	23.	The people in the locality get easy access to knowledge through the Radio and TV kept in the library.	Y.N.U
	24.	Newspapers and current publications encourage the people in the vicinity in the acquisition of knowledge.	Y.N.U
	25.	The librarian in this library is not qualified in Library Science	Y.N.U
(F)	26.	There are plenty of scientific	Y.N.U

publications in this library.

27. This library helped to enhance my scientific knowledge. Y.N.U
28. This library takes adequate interest in promoting awareness of health and hygienic among the people. Y.N.U
29. Scientific news are displayed in the notice board with special emphasis. Y.N.U
30. This library has helped to create a scientific attitude among the people nearby area. Y.N.U

(G) 31. I was not succum to a mental tension by reading "Painkili Sahityam' (trash literature) from this library Y.N.U

32. There are plenty of "Maa' publications in this library. Y.N.U
33. The library plays for the growth and expansion of Malayalam Literature. Y.N.U
34. Many men-of-letters in 'this area are workers of this library. Y.N.U
35. There are many precious books in this library. Y.N.U

(H) 36 The library is a cultural centre of the area Y.N.U

37. The library conducts competitions and gives away prizes to the winners. Y.N.U
38. With the efforts of this library, the talented in the spheres of art are identified and fostered to show their mettle. Y.N.U

	39.	Under the auspices of this library athletic competitions are held.	Y.N.U
	40.	There are many famous athletes around this area who have been by the library.	Y.N.U
(I)	41.	This library is a member of the Kerala Grandhasala Sanghom	Y.N.U
	42.	The library gets financial assistance from the Grandhasala Sanghom on time.	Y.N.U
	43.	The membership of the library increases.	Y.N.U
	44.	The Kerala Grandhasala Sanghom stands for the progress of this library.	Y.N.U
	45.	The library implements each programme of the Grandhasala Sanghom as quickly as possible.	Y.N.U
	46.	My reading habit is enhancing, as I am a member of this library.	Y.N.U
	47.	It enabled me to acquainted with the men of litters and their works through this library.	Y.N.U
	48.	The library encourages to start a new library.	Y.N.U
	49.	The library helps the selling of books and magazines.	Y.N.U
	50.	The library helps to evolve popular opinions on national problems.	Y.N.U
(K)	51.	Do not politicalize the functioning of this library	Y.N.U

52. For the functioning of this library a fund should be raised by various means. Y.N.U
53. This library should purchase a TV and a Radio. Y.N.U
54. The efforts members of the library should be included in the constructive works of the Government . Y.N.U
55. In each year, the Grandhasala Sanghom should organize competitions on sports and arts. Y.N.U

Any other matter: **Dr. A. Paslithil**

Sd/-

Appendix - H

Personal Interview Schedule

It is a set of questions which are asked and filled in by the researcher in a face to face situation with another person. The wording of the question is almost same for all the respondents. The main objectives of the researchers is to secure the respondent's consent to the interview, to motivate him to give full and honest answers, to ensure that the respondent's answer is relevant to the question and to record the answer.

1. Would you please comment upon the present functioning of the Kerala Grandhasala Sanghom and its affiliated Libraries ?
2. Can you elaborate the activities of the Kerala Grandhasala Sanghom for the Library movement in the State ?
3. Do you think that the functions of the Local Library Authorities intensified the Library movement in the State ?
4. In 1977, the Kerala Grandhasala Sanghom was taken over by the Government, what are the circumstances behind the take-over ? Do you have any comment upon this ?
5. What is your opinion on the political involvement of the Kerala Grandhasala Sanghom and its affiliated libraries ?
6. What is your attitude towards the different Library bills introduced in the Kerala Legislative Assembly ?

7. How will you comment upon the provisions of the new library bill enacted by the Kerala Legislative Assembly in 1989 ?
8. What were the problems and difficulties facing the library movement in the State ?
9. Can you mention the contribution made by the Kerala Grandhasala Sanghom in the social cultural developments in our society ?
10. Will you please explain your role in the development of Library movement in Kerala ?

Depending on the varieties given by the different subjects, certain clarifications to the questions are made on certain items. Some additional questions are to be against certain question, when the interviews failed to understand the meaning.

References

1. William J Goode and Paul K. Hatt, *Methods in Social Research*, Tokeyo, Mcgraw Hill, 1952, P. 133.
2. Alam Orestein, and William R.F., Philips, Understanding social research : An introduction, Boston, Allyn and Vacon Inc. 1978, P. 223.
3. Maurice B. Line Mafla, Library Surveys, An Introduction to their use, planning, procedure and Presentation, London Clive Bingley, 1967.

Bibliography

Primary Sources (Unpublished)

Aikya Thiruvithamcore-Cochin Grandhasala Sanghom, *Audit Report,* 1955-56, Trivandrum : A.T.C.G.S., 1957.

Akhila Thiruvithamcore Grandhasala Sanghom *Working Committee's note,* (Mal.), Ambalapuzha: P.K. Memorial Library, 1946.

Akhila Thiruvithamcore Grandhasala Sanghom *Yoga Nadapadi Book,* Ambalapuzha: P.K. Memorial Library, 1945

An *Agreement between the Sircar of Travancore and the subscribers* of the Trivandrum Public Library, Trivandrum : Public Library, 1856.

Anil, G.R., *Social and Economic Development of Travancore under Sir C.P. Ramaswamy Iyer,* Calicut University : Department of History, Unpublished Doctoral Thesis, 1986.

Copy of the *Memorandum* (Mal.), submitted to the Chief Minister C. Achuthamenon on 7 March 1976, Trivandrum : Kerala Grandhasala Sanghom.

Dairy of P.N. Panicker dated 4-10-1951, 3-11-1949 to 8-3-1951, 24-5-1956, 1-1-1965 – 12-12-1973.

File No. 149/29 Edn. 28 January 1929, Trivandrum : Directorate of State Archives, Kerala.

File No.C.F of 3286/33/Edn., Trivandrum : Directorate of State Archives, Kerala.

File No.C.F. of C345/34/Edn., Trivandrum : Directorate of State Archives, Kerala).

File No. R. Dis. 1633/34, Press Note, 14 April, 1934 Edn., 2 October 1934, Trivandrum: Directorate of State Archives, Kerala.

File No. C. 349/ 34/ Edn., Trivandrum: Directorate of State Archives, Kerala.

File No. R.O.C. No. 1918/43/Edn. 24 November 1943, Trivandrum : Government Secretariat.

File No. 2384/47/Edn., 15 September 1947, Trivandrum : Government Secretariat.

File No. ROC.HO.5353/47/Edn., 12 July 1948, Trivandrum: Government Secretariat.

File No. D.Dis. No. 441/51 EHL, 12-5-1951, Trivandrum : Government Secretariat.

File No. Ed (D) 3-6110/57 EDHD dated 30-4-1957 Trivandrum : Government Secretariat.

File No. E1/81/55 dated 15-3-1956 by the Director of Panchayat, Trivandrum: Government Secretariat.

File No. ED (D) 4-6110/57, G.O dated 30-4-1957, Trivandrum : Government Secretariat.

File No. 2910/57 G.O. dated 15-2-1957, ED (E) 2-2910/ 57/ EHD, Trivandrum : Government Secretariat.

File No. G.O. (MS) No. 429/Edn. D 25/7-61 and G.O (MS.) No. 48/Edn. Dated 25-1-1963, Trivandrum : Government Secretariat

File No. G.O. Rt. 418, 18 February 1958, G.O.Rt. No. 2793/ 67/Edn. 31 October 1962, Trivandrum : Government Secretariat.

File No. Gradation Committee, File No. G.O. Rt. 375/76/ H.Edn. dated 21-2-1976, Trivandrum : Government Secretariat.

File No. G.O.M.S. 41/86/ Home dated 28-2-1986, Trivandrum : Government Secretariat.

Government *Memorandum* No. 44, 472-A(Edn.), 21 September 1944, Trivandrum : Directorate of State Archives, Kerala.

Koshy, *M.J., The History of the Growth of Legislature in Travancore and Cochin upto 1956.* Trivandrum : Kerala University, Unpublished Doctoral Thesis, 1966.

Letter No.D.D.F. 12.29/75/HE-1 (NF FE.1, dated 20-10-1975) by Government of India, (Delhi: Central Secretariat).

Letter No. 9003/ 111 of detail dated 21-12-1947 (Trivandrum : D.P.I).

Letter No. 3666/C-3/75 H.Edn. (C) Dept., Tvm dated 10-11-1975, Trivandrum: Government Secretariat.

Ordinance No. 5 of 1977, on 16 March 1977, Trivandrum Government Secretariat.

P.K. Vilasam Library *Yoga Natapadi Book*, Minutes Book, (Mal); Ampalapuzha : P.K. Memorial Library, 1938.

Resolution introduced by K.M. Chumar, D.C.C President, in the D.C.C meeting held at Kottayam, (Mal.), supported by Antony Joseph, (Palai: Prakash Press, 3 February 1958.

Speech delivered by D.C. Kizhakkemuri on 15 September 1990 in connection with 45th Kerala Grandhasala Sanghom State Conference held at Ernakulam, Mariya Complex.

Speech delivered by T.K. Ramakrishnan in connection with the Annual Library Conference held at Ernakulam in 14 September 1990.

Trivandrum Public *Library Minute of Special General Meeting*, 15 October 1854, Trivandrum : Public Library.

Travancore Grandhasala *Sanghom Meeting Minutes* Book,(Mal); 1947, P.K. Memorial Library, Ambalapuzha.

Travancore, Maharaja Swathi Tirunal, *Nittu,* Trivandrum : State Archives, 1012 M.E.

Travancore, Maharani Parvathi Bai, *Nittu*, Trivandrum : State Archives, 992, M.E.

(Published)

Administrative Report, Education Department 1120 M.E., (1944-45), Ernakulam: Cochin Government Press.

Administrative Report of the Education Department – 1976-77, Trivandrum : Government Press, 1978.

Akhila Thiruvithamcore Grandhasala Sanghom, *Grandhasala Manual*, (Mal.), Trivandrum : Akhila Thiruvithamcore Grandhasala Sanghom, 1948.

Akhila Thiruvithamcore M.S. Book, Ambalapuzha: P.K. Memorial Library, 1944.

Annual Report of the Akhila Thiruvithamcore Grandhasala Sanghom – 1948, (Mal.), Trivandrum : A.T.G.S.

Annual Report of the K.G.S., 1971-72; 1972-73; 1973-74; 1974-75; 1975-76; 1976-77; (Mal.), Trivandrum : 1973, 1974, 1975, 1976, 1977, 1978, K.G.S.

Annual Report of the Travancore Cochin Grandhasala (Mal); Sanghom – 1951, Trivandrum : A.T.C.G.S.

Annual Report of the Young Mens' Association and Social Library Trivandrum : Chackai, October 1990.

Census of India - 2001, Series-3, Kerala, Trivandrum : Director of Census Operations, 2001.

Census of India – 1991, Provisional Population Totals Series-1, India, Delhi : Government of India, Director of Census Operations, 1991.

Copy of the *Accountant Generals' Report of 1977-78*, Trivandrum : A.G's Office.

Government of India, *Report of Advisory Committee for Libraries*, Delhi : Ministry of Education, 1959.

Government Proceedings, Current No.E 115 M.E., Trivandrum : Directorate of State Archives, 1904.

Innes, C.A. and Evans, F.B., (ed.), *Madras District Gazetteers*, Madras : Government press, 1951.

Joseph Mundassery, *Kozhinja Elakal : Athmakadha* (Mal.), Kottayam: D.C. Book, 1978.

Kerala Budget Estimate, 1957-58; 1958-59, 1959-60; 1960-61; 1961-62; 1962-63;1963-64; 1964-65; 1965-66; 1966-67; 1967-68; 1968-69; 1969-70; 1970-71; 1971-72; 1972-73; 1973-74; 1974-75; 1975-76; 1976-77; (Trivandrum : Government Press, 1958; 1959; 1960; 1961; 1962; 1963; 1964; 1965; 1966; 1967; 1968; 1969; 1970; 1971; 1972; 1973; 1974; 1975; 1976; 1977.

Kerala Gazette, (Extra ordinary), Vol. XXII, No. 169, 16 March 1977, Trivandrum.

Kerala Gazette (Extra ordinary), Vol. XXXIV, No. 452, Trivandrum : Government of Kerala, 18 Mary 1989.

Kerala Grandhasala Bill- 1970, Trivandrum : Kerala Legislative Assembly, 1971.

Kerala Grandhasala Sanghathinte Bharana Report – 1985-86, (Mal.), Trivandrum : Government of Kerala, 1990.

Kerala Grandhalaya Sanghom, *Kerala Grandhalaya Sanghom : Oru Samkshiptha Vivaranam 1943 muthal 1945 December vare,* (Mal.), Calicut : Mathrubhoomi Press, 1946.

Kerala Grandhasala Sanghom, *Election Notification* – 1976, Trivandrum : Kerala Grandhasala Sanghom, 1976.

Kerala Grandhasala Sanghathile Prathisandhi Enthukondu? (Mal.), A Notice issued by the Signatures on 27 December 1976, from Trivandrum.

Kerala Public Library Bill of 1971, Trivandrum : Legislative Assembly, 1971.

Kerala Public Library Bill 1971, vol. II, *Proceedings of the Select Committee held on August 8,9,16,19 and 21, 1974 and September 26, 1974 at Cannanore, Calicut, Trivandrum, Palghat, Ernakulam and Memorandum received from various individuals and organizations,* Trivandrum : Government of Kerala, 1975.

Kerala Public Library Bill, 1977, The Seventh Kerala Legislative Assembly, Trivandrum: Kerala Legislative Assembly, 1977.

Kerala Public Library Bill, 1985 - Background Materials, Trivandrum : the Secretariat of the Kerala Legislature, 1987.

Kerala State Administrative Report 1957 – 58, Trivandrum : Government of Kerala 1958.

Kerala State Administrative Report – 1959, Trivandrum : Government Press, 1961.

Kesava Menon, K.P., *Presidential Address of North Malabar Library Conference,* (Mal.) Calicut, Spector Press, 1957.

Nagam Aiya, V. *Report of the Census of Travancore- 1891,* vol.I, Madras : Addition & co., 1894.

Nayanar, E.K., *My struggle: An autobiography,* New Delhi: Vikas Private House, 1982.

Proceedings of Her Highness Maharani, Regent of Travancore, G.O. No.E. 2157, Trivandrum, 18 August 1917, Trivandrum : Directorate of State Archives, Kerala.

Proceedings of the Government of His Highness, the Maharaja of Travancore, Order No. 12, D.C. No. 6065/ 45/ Edn. Dated, 12th September 1945, Trivandrum : Directorate of State Archives, Kerala.

Proceedings of the Government of the His Highness of Travancore, 21 March 1931, Trivandrum : State Archives.

Publication of Malayalam Manuscripts : Administrative Reports – 1104, Trivandrum : Government Press, 1929.

Ranganathan, S.R., *Kerala Public Library Bill – 1960,* Trivandrum : Legislative Assembly, 1960.

Report of Advisory Committee for Libraries, (New Delhi : Government of India, 1954).

Report of the Director of Public Instructions 1073 M.E., (1897-1898), Ernakulam : Cochin Government Press, 1898.

Report of the Travnacore Education Reorganisation Committee May 1945 (Trivandrum, Government Press, 1946).

Report on the Administration of Cochin – 1113 M.E., (1938), Cochin : Cochin State Government, Cochin Press, 1944.

Report on the Administration of Cochin – 1118 M.E., (1948), Cochin : Cochin State Government, Cochin Press, 1944.

Report submitted by the Committee appointed to inspect the work done by the All Travancore Library Association, Trivandrum 1949.

Samskarika Swathandriyam Samrakshikkan Urachuninnu Poraduka, (Mal.) Notice published by Kottayam D.C., Palai : Prakash Press, 24 March 1958.

Sankaran, Thayattu, *Ente Anukalika Diary,* (Mal.), Kottayam: N.B.S., 198).

Sankaran, Thayattu, *Notice,* (Mal.) issued on 5 July 1975.

Secret Bulletin, No. 31, 25 July 1934, (\Trivandrum : Directorate of State Archives, Kerala.

Shekar, N.C. *Agniveedhikal,* (Mal), Autobiography, Cannoor: North Kerala Printers and Publishing House, 1987.

Sreedhara Menon A., (ed.), *Kerala District Gazetteers : Vol. 1, Trivandrum District,* Trivandrum : Government of Kerala, 1962.

State of Cochin, *Report of the Director of Libraries,* Cochin: Cochin Government Press, 1948, 1949.

The Proceedings of the XXII All India Education Centre and the IV All India Adult Education Conference, Trivandrum: Government Press: 1947.

Travancore Administrative Report 1946-47, Trivandrum : Government Press, 1947.

Travancore Administrative Report 1123 M.E. (1947-48), Trivandrum : Government Press, 1947.

Travancore Budget Estimate, 1945- 46; 1946-47; 1947-48; 1948-49; Trivandrum : Government Press, 1946, 1947, 1948, 1949.

Travancore – Cochin Budget Estimate, 1949-50; 1950-51; 9151-52; 1952-53; 1953-54; 1954-55; 1955-56; 1956-57; Trivandrum : Government Press, 1950; 1951; 1952; 1953; 1954; 1955; 1956; 1957.

Travancore Gazette, 23 September 1917, Trivandrum : Directorate of State Archives, Kerala State.

Vasudevan, N., *Report of Local Library Authority,* (Mal.), Calicut : L.L.A, 1985.

Personal Interviews with :

1. Ahammed Kutty, Chakkeeri, 15-12-1990, Malappuram.
2. Antony, A.K., 01-09-1990, Trivandrum.
3. Balakrishnan, Thengamam, 08-10-1990, Trivandrum.
4. Bhanuvikraman Nair, K., 13-12-1990, Trivandrum.
5. Bhaskara Panicker, P.T., 11-01-1989, Trivandrum.
6. Beeran, U.A., (M.L.A) 24-06-1990, Trivandrum.
7. Chakrapani Warrier, 10-02-1990, Ambalapuzha.
8. Das, I.V., 28-08-1992, Calicut.
9. Govinda Pillai, P., 28-09-1990, Trivandrum.
10. Guptan Nair, S., 19-10-1990, Trivandrum.
11. Keraleeyan, K.A., 07-12-1990, Calicut.
12. Kunjan Pillai, Sooranad., 30-07-1990, Trivandrum.
13. Karunakaran Nair, V.K., 10-02-1990, Alappuzha.
14. Maheswari Amma, K., 10-02-1990, Ambalapuzha.
15. Mammu Mash, K.P., (M.L.A), 20-06-1990, Trivandrum.
16. Panicker, P.N., 09-07-1990; 16-07-1990; 17-07-1990; 19-07-1990, Trivandrum.
17. Paramu, A.M., (M.L.A.), 20-06-1990, Trivandrum.
18. Rajagopalan Nair, J., 29-10-1991, Trivandrum.
19. Sivadasan Pillai, K., 12-02-1991, Trivandrum.
20. Sujanapal, S., 06-12-1990, Calicut.
21. Surendranath, K,V., (M..L.A), 5-04-1990, Trivandrum.
22. Unni Raja, C., 06-01-1990, Trivandrum.

Secondary Source (Books)

Abrahanson, Mark, *Social Research Methods*, Englewood, U.S.A., Prentice Hall INC, 1983.

Achutha Menon. C., *The Cochin State Manual*, Ernakulam: Cochin Government Press, 1911.

Anne Auastasi, *Psychological testing*, 6th edition, New York : Mac Millon, 1988.

Augustine, C.A. and Devarajan, G., (eds.), *Public Library System in India*, New Delhi : ESS ESS Publication, 1980.

Balagopal, A., *Calicut Local Library Authority*, (Mal.), Calicut : L.L.A, 1974.

Balakrishnan, A., *Kesariyude Mukhaprasangangal*, (Mal.), Kottayam : N.B.S. 1961.

Balakrishnan, P.K., *Jathivyavasthayum Kerala Charithravum*, (Mal.), Kottayam: S.P.C.S. Limited, 1983.

Balakrishnan, P.K., *Narayan Guru*, (Mal.), Korrayam : N.B.S., 1954.

Best, John W., *Research in education*, (New Delhi: Prentice Hall Pvt. Ltd., 1982).

Damodaran, K. and Narayana Pillai. C., *Keralathile Swathantriya Samaram*, (Mal.), Trivandrum : Department of Public Relation, Government of Kerala, 1957.

Gangadhara Pillai, V., *The Public Sector in Kerala*, Trivandrum: Kerala Academy of Political Science, 1980.

Goode William J., and Hatt Paul, K. *Methods in Social Research*, Tokeyo : MacGraw Hill, 1952.

Gopalakrishnan, P.K., *Keralathinte Samskarika Charithram*, (Mal.), Trivandrum : State Institute of Languages, 1974.

Government of Kerala, *Library Movement in Kerala*, Trivandrum : Department of Public Relations, 1990.

Government of Kerala, *The Press in Kerala*, Trivandrum : Department of Public Relations, 1977.

Govindan, K.C., *Memories of an Early Trade Unionist*, Trivandrum : Centre for Development Stdueis, 1986.

Janakeeya Shasthram, (Mal.), Trivandrum : Kerala Shasthra Sahithya Parishath, 1988.

Jefferry, Robin, *The Decline of Nayar Dominance : Society and Politics in Travancore 1847-1908*, New Delhi: Vikas Publishing House, 1976.

Josechandran, N., (ed.), *Dynamics of State Politics – Kerala*, Delhi : Sterling Pulishers, 1986.

Kaul, Vimal, *India since Independence : Chronology of Events 1947-1977*, vol.II, Delhi: Sagar Publications, 1978.

Koshy, M.J., *Last Days of Monarchy in Kerala*, Trivandrum: Kerala Historical Society, 1973.

Krishna Iyer, K.V., *Zamorins of Calicut*, Calicut: Norman Printing Bureau, 1938.

Krishna Iyer, L.A., *Kerala and Her People*, Palaghat: Educational and Supplies Depot, 1961.

Kumar, P.G.S., *Indian library Chronology*, New Delhi: Metropolitan Book Company, 1977.

Kumaran , M.K., and Bhaskaran. T., (eds.), *Sree Narayana Yuga Prabhavam*, (Mal.), Varkala: Sree Narayana Guru Propagation committee, 1978.

Kunjan Pillai, Elamkulam, *Keralathinte Iruladanja Edukal*, (Mal.), Kottayam : National Book Stall, 1953.

Kunjan Pillai, Soornad, *Sree Swati Tirunal Ramavarma Maharajavu*, (Mal.), Trivandrum: Department of Cultural Publications, 1989.

Kurup, K.K.N., *Modern Kerala : Studies in Social and Agrarian Relations*, Delhi: Mittal Publication, 1988.

Kurup, K.K.N., *Swathandriya Samaram Kasarcode Talukil* (Mal.), Kottakal : Kalaniketan Publishers, 1984.

Kusuman, K.K., *The Abstention Movement,* Trivandrum : Kerala Historical Society, 1976.

Line Mafla, Maurice B., *Library Survey: An introduction to their use, planning, procedure and presentation,* London Clive Bingley, 1967.

Logan, William, *Malabar,* vol..1, Trivandrum : Charithram Publication, Reprinted, 1981.

Menon, P.K.K., *The History of Freedom Movement in Kerala (1885- 1938),* vol. II, Trivandrum : Regional Records Service Committee: Kerala State, 1970.

Mohamed Kannu, *Vakkom Maulavi,* (Mal.), Biography, Kottayam: National Book Stall, 1981.

Nàgam Aiya, V., *The Travancore State Manual,* vol.I & II, Trivandrum : Travancore : Government Press, 1906.

Namboodiripad, E.M.S., *Keralam Malayalikalude Mathrubhoomi,* (Mal.), Trichur : Current Books, 1964.

Namboodiripad, E.M.S., *Kerala Society and Politics : A Historical Survey,* New Delhi: National Book, 1984.

Namboodiripad, E.M.S., *National Question in Kerala,* Ernakulam : Prabhath Books, 1957.

Namboothiri, N.M., *Zamoothiri Charithrathinte Kanappurangal,* (Mal.), Edapal : Vallathol Vidhyapeedam, 1987

Nan Lieu, *Foundation of Social Research,* New York : McGraw Hill, 1976.

Narayanan, M.G.S., *Cultural Symbiosis in Kerala,* Trivandrum : Kerala Historical Society, 1972.

Narayana Pillai, C., *Pattom Muthal Panampallivare,* (Mal.), Kottayam : D.C. Books, 1976.

Nilakanta Sastri, K.A., *A History of South India from Pre-historic Times to the fail of Vijayangar,* Madras : Oxford Press, 1966.

Nossiter, T.J., *Communism in Kerala : A Study in Political adaptation,* Delhi : Oxford University Press, 1982.

Oomen, M.A., *A Study on land reforms in Kerala*, New Delhi: I.B.H. Publishing Co., 1975.

Orenstein , Alam and Philips, William R.F., *Understanding Social Research : An Introduction*, Boston, Allyn and Vacon Inc, 1978.

Padmanabha Menon, K.P., *History of Kerala*, vol. IV, (Cochin : Cochin Government Press, 1937).

Panicker, K.M., *History of Kerala 1498 – 1801*, Annamala Nagar, Annamala University, 1960.

Panicker, K.N., *Against Lord and State: Religion and Peasant uprising in Malabar 1836- 1921*, Delhi : Oxford University , 1989.

Panicker, P.N., (ed.), *Keralathile Grandhalaya Prasthanam*, (Mal.), (Trivandrum : steps, 1982.

Parameswara Iyre, Ulloor,S., *Kerala Sahithya Charitram*, (Mal.), vol.1, Trivandrum : Kerala University, 1952.

Pereira. J. Jerald., *Narayana Guru : A Social Education*, Varkala : R.R. Publishers, 1989.

Pillai, A.K., *Congressum Keralaum*, (Mal.), Trivandrum : Kerala State Congress Committee, 1982.

Pope. G.G., & Ellis, F.W., *Maladiar* : 318, Madras : South India Siva Sidhanta Works Publishing Society, Tirunelveli, 1958.

Pothuval, A.K., *Keralathile Karshaka Prasthanathinte Oru Cheruvivaranam*, Trivandrum : Prabhath Printing, 1969.

Prajamandala Charithra Rachana Committee., *Cochin Rajya Prajamandalam*, (Mal.), Kottayam : Current Books, 1985.

Prakasam, R., *Keralathile Trade Union Prasthanathinte* Charithram (Mal.), Trivandrum: Prabhath Book House, 1979.

Priyadershan, G., *Pathrapravarthanam : Prarambha Swaroopam* (Mal.), Trichur : Kerala Sahitya Academy, 1982.

Ramanath Iyer, S., *Progressive Travancore*, Trivandrum : Anantharaman Press, 1923.

Ramanujan Nair, P., *The Library Movement in Kerala : The need for reform and legislation*, Trivandrum : Tvm writers club, 1974.

Ravindran, T.K., *Asan and Social Revolution in Kerala : A study of his Assembly Speeches*, Trivandrum : Kerala Historical Society, 1972.

Sankaranarayan , K.C. and Karunakaran, P., *Kerala Economy*, (Delhi, Oxford , I.B.H., 1985).

Shungonny Menon, P., *History of Travancore from the Earlier Times*, vol. I & II, New Delhi : Cosmo Publication reprint, 1984.

Sivadasan Pillai, K., (ed.), *Kerala Grandhasala Sanghom*, Trivandrum : Kerala Grandhasala, 1981.

Sreedhara Menon, A., *Aadhunika Keralam*, (Mal.), Kottayam: NBS, Indian Press, 1988.

Sreedhara Menon, A., *Cultural Heritage of Kerala : An Introduction*, Cochin : East West Publication, 1978.

Sreedhara Menon, a., *Legacy of Kerala*, Trivandrum : Government Press, 1982.

Sreedhara Menon.A., *A Survey of Kerala History*, Kottayam: National Book Stall, 1967.

Syalvey, Edward., *Delhi Public Library Project*, New Delhi : Ministry of Education : UNESCO Project, 1953.

Thomas, K. Kurian., *Trivandrum Public Library*, Historical Perspective, Kottayam : Archana Printers, 1987.

University of Kerala, *Handbook 1977-78.*, Trivandrum : Kerala University, 1977.

Velayudhan, P.S., (ed.), *Kerala Charithram*, (Mal.), Vol. I & II Ernakulam : Kerala History Association, 1973.

Velu Pillai, T.K., *The Travancore State Mannual*, Vol. 1-3, Trivandrum : government of Travancore, 1940.

Vijayan, N., (ed.), *Keralathinte Moonnu Dashakangal*, Trivandrum : Language Institute, Government of Kerala, 1982.

Viswanath, C.N., *An Introduction to Public Library Organization with Special Reference to India,* Bombay : Agricultural Publishing House, 1961.

Walker, Helen. M., and Leve Joseph, *Elementary Statistical Methods*, Calcutta: Oxford, IBH Publishing Co, 1976.

Periodical & Journals

Current Book Bulletin, Kottayam (Mal.), Vol.10 (94), 1990

Economic Review 1981, Trivandrum : State Government of Kerala, 1982.

Grandhalokam, Trivandrum: (Mal.),Vol. 1(1-7), 1948 : Vol. 2(9), 1950; Vol. 3(1-8), 1951; Vol. 4 (1-7), 1952; Vol. 5(3), 1953; Vol. 6 (1-8), 1954; Vol. 7(11), 1955; Vol. 8(1), 1956; Vol. 10(2-12), 1958; Vol. 11(11), 1959; Vol. 12(7-12), 1960; Vol. 13(1), 1961; Vol. 14(2), 1962; Vol. 15(8), 1963; Vol. 16(5-7), 1964; Vol. 17 (7-12), 1965; Vol. 18(6-12), 1966; Vol. 19(1-12), 1967; Vol. 20 (2-5), 1968; Vol. 21(6-8), 1969; Vol. 22(4-10), 1970; Vol. 23 (12), 1971; Vol. 24(2-8), 1972; Vol. 25(2), 1973; Vol. 26(1-5), 1974; Vol. 27 (4-10), 1975; Vol. 28 (4-12),l 1976; Vol. 29(1-8), 1977; Vol. 30 (1-9), 1978; Vol. 32(1-9), 1980; Vol. 33 (1-3), 1981; Vol. 34(1-8), 1982; Vol. 35(1-7), 1983; Vol. 36(2-9), 1984; Vol. 37(3-8), 1985; Vol. 38(1-8), 1986; Vol. 39(3-6), 1987; Vol. 40 (3-10), 1988; Vol. 41(1-11), 1989; Special Issue September 1990; Vol. 42(1-5), 1990; Vol. 43(2-6), 1991.

India Today, Madras: (Mal.), Vol. 1(17), 1990.

International Library Review, London: Vol. 5-12, 1973-1978.

Janapadham, Trivandrum: (Mal.), Vol. 22(2), 1991.

Kerala Calling, Vol.9(10), Trivandrum : Public Relations Department, 1989.

Kala Kaumudi, Trivandrum: (Mal.), 26 June 1976., 7 June 1987.

Lucknow Librarian, Lucknow: Vol. 5-10, 1973-1978.

Library Herald, Delhi: Vol. 10-18, 1970-1978.

Mathrubhoomi Weekly, Calicut: (Mal.), Vol. 51(68), 1973; 68 (29), 1990 Calicut : Mathrubhoomi Press.

Sakshara Keralam, (Mal.), Vol. 5(33), Trivandrum: K.G.S. 1976.

Thiruvithamcore Krishi Vyavasaya Masika, (Trivandrum), (Mal.), Vol.14 (4), 1934 January – February.

Social Scientists, (New Delhi), Vol. 16(8), 1988.

Souvenirs

Chowa Thozhilali Yuvajana Vayanasala and Grandhalayam, Suvarna Jubilee Souvenir, (Mal.), Kannoor: Chowa Thozhilali Yuvajana Vayanasala and Grandhalayam, 1986.

Deshaposhini Suvarnna Jubilee Souvenir, (Mal.) Calicut : Deshaposhini Library, 1988.

Golden Jubilee Souvenir of Sengupta Library 1958, (Mal.), Calicut: Sengupta Library, 1958.

Hundred years of Legislature bodies in Kerala (1888-1988), Centenary Souvenir, Trivandrum : Kerala legislature, 1990.

KANFED's 8th Anniversary Souvenir, (Mal.), Trivandrum : Saksharatha Bhavan, 1985.

KANFED's 13th Anniversary Souvenir, (Mal.), Trivandrum : Saksharatha Bhavan, 1990.

Kerala Grandhasala Sangom Rajatha Jubilee Souvenir, (Mal.), Trivandrum : Kerala Grandhasala Sangom, 1971.

Kottayam Public Library Souvenir, (Mal.), Kottayam: Indian Press, 1967.

Sree Chithira Thirunal Golden Jubilee Souvenir, (Mal.), Trivandrum : Sree Chithira Thirunal Library, 1966.

Sree Chithira Thirunal Libaray Upahara Grandham, (Mal.), Trivandrum : Sree Chithira Thirunal Library, 1976.

Souvenir of the XXV All India Library Conference held at Trivandrum in May 14-18, 1979, Trivandrum : Geo Printer, 1979.

Souvenir of the Sashtiabdapurthi of Sachivottama Sir C.P. Ramaswamy Iyer, Trivandrum : AVR Press, 1940.

Souvenir of the Temple Proclamation Memorial, Trivandrum: Temple Entry Proclamation Committee, 1942.

Souvenir Published in connection with 40th Anniversary Celebrations of the Sahitya Pravarthaka Co-operative Society, (Mal.), Kottayam: College Book House, December 1985.

Trivandrum Public Library Platinum Jubilee Souvenir, Trivandrum : Government of Kerala, 1974.

Venmani Shashtiapta Mahamaham, (Mal.), Vellarapalli: Mangalodayam Press, 1120 ME (1944-45).

Seminar Papers

Chandran, Manayath, Kerala Grandhasala Niyamum : Pashchathalaum Prathyekathakalum , (Mal.), Paper presented in one-day seminar on 25 September 1989 at V.J.T. Hall in Trivandrum sponsored by Kerala University.

Narayna Pillai, G. Manalil, *Grandhasala Prasthanaum Saksharathayum,* (Mal.), Paper presented the 45th Library Conference held at Ernakulam, on 16 September 1990.

Ramakrishnan, M.N. *Kerala Public Libraries (K.G.S.) Act 1989*: An Over View, Paper presented in one-day seminar on September 25, 1989 at V.J.T. Hall in Trivandrum sponsored by Kerala University.

Sivadasan Pillai, K., *Librarikal Ennale, Innu, Nale,* (Mal.), (Paper Presented in the Kottayam District Seminar of the K.G.S. February 1975.

Newspapers (Malayalam)

Chandrika, Calicut: Daily, (Mal.), 22 June 1962; 30 December 1980.

Deepika, Kottayam: Daily, (Mal.), 20 May 1952; 16 June 1962; 27 December 1970.

Deshabhandu, Kottayam: Daily, (Mal.), 3 August 1958; 19 June 1962.

Deshabhimani, Calicut: Daily, (Mal.), 26 November 1960; 23 June 1962; 31 December 1970; 16 February 1973; 24 January 1977; 11 February 1977; 19 March 1977; 19 August 1989; 30 August 1989.

Dinamani, Quilon: Daily, (Mal.), 8 August 1956.

Express, Trichur: Daily (Mal.), 19 May 1957; 31 August 1958; 19 February 1973.

Janatha, Ernakulam: Daily, (Mal.), 23 August 1958.

Janayugam, Quilon: Daily, (Mal.), 26 April 1960; 28 June 1962; 28 December 1970.

Keralabhooshanam, Kottayam: Daily, (Mal.) 20 June 1962; 29 December 1970.

Kerala Kaumudi, Trivandrum: Daily, (Mal.), 30 May 1952; 7 April 1958; 5 September 1958; 4 Janurary 1961; 27 July 1962; 30 December 1970; 20 February 1973.

Malayala Manorama, Kottayam: Daily, (Mal.), 3 June 1891; 22 May 1952; 21 October 1956; 5 July 1957; 5 September 1958; 26 October 1960; 15 June 1962; 16 June 1962; 21 May 1965; 24 February 1973; 27 December 1970.

Malayala Rajyam, Quilon: Daily, (Mal.), 5 October 1956; 30 December 1970.

Mangalam, Kottayam: Daily, (Mal.), 6 March 1990; 30 April 1990.

Mathrubhoomi, Calicut: Daily, (Mal.), 15 March 1936; 13 June 1937; 15 June 1956; 16 august 1956 ; 8 October 1956 ; 9 May 1957; 6 July 1958; 14 August 1956; 8 October 1956; 9 May 1957; 6 July 1958; 14 August 1960; 27 October 1960; 19 June 1962; 27 October 1962; 26 May 1965; 27 December 1970; 22 September 1972; 5 April 1985.

Pothujanam, Trivandrum: Daily, (Mal.), 8 May 1957; 7 June 1962.

Veekshanam, Ernakulam: Daily (Mal.), 4 December 1976.

(English)

Indian Express, Madurai: Daily, 5 March 1961.

Indian Express, Cochin: Daily, 21 April 1990; 14 July 1990.

Index

A

Achuthamenon, C, 155, 156
Administrative Reforms, 24
Adult Education, 50, 51, 55, 79, 100, 179
  Boards, 101
  Centres, 78, 100, 233
  Program, 45, 80, 90, 100, 101, 222
  Training, 101
Adult Literacy Centres, 165
Advait Vedanta Philosophy, 17
Advisory Committee for Libraries, 123
Agrarian Relations Act, 135
Agricultural Book Corner, 223
Aikya Thiruvithamcore Cochin Granthasala Sanghom, 89, 91, 98, 102-05, 119-121
Akhila
  Malabar Kisan Sanghom, 52
  Thiruvithamcore Granthasala, 219
  Thiruvithamcore Granthasala Sanghom, 73, 77, 78, 82, 89, 91-95, 219, 241
  Thiruvithamcore, 97, 98
All Cochin Library Association, 70
All India
  Library Congress, 61
  Library Conference (4th), 45
  Travancore Library Association, 48
All Kerala
  Granthasala Sanghom, 119
  Trade Union Congress, 57
All Travancore
  Cochin Library Association, 100
  Library Association, 67, 70, 74-78, 80, 96, 98
  Objectives, 78
  Library Conference (2nd), 79
Ambalapuzha Library Conference, 73
  Resolutions, 73-74
Anand Pradayani Library Alleppey, 181
Arabian Sea, 15
Arabs—Chinese, 16
Aryan Culture, 17
Aryanization, 17

Athmavidhya Sangham, 35
Atmavidyan Sanghas, 37
Ayyankah, 31

B

Backward Classes, 28, 30, 31
Bakkalan—Eranjoli, 47
Basic Library Skills, 222
Besant, Annie, 37
Bharana Samiti, 175
Block Union, 142
Book Selection Committee, 91, 176, 228
Brahmanism, 16
British Book Clubs, 26
British Museum, 25
Brown, John Allan, Astronomer Travancore Sircar, 27
Buddha Viharas, 16
Buddhism, 16

C

Cadogan, Edward, Col., 25
Cannore Municipal Councils, 68
Cannore—Alleppey, 57
Caste System, 17, 18, 32
Casteless Community, 16
Central
  Association for Libraries Cochin, 70
  Libraries Association of Kerala, 157, 196
  Library Committee, 123
  Social Welfare Board (CSWB), 184
Charitable Act, 67
Cheru Line of Rulers, 16
Cherai Public Library, 34
Child Welfare Council, 177
Christian Missionaries, 19, 24
Church Councils, 126
Church Mission Society, Kottayam, 24
Chattampi Swamikal, Social Reformer, 31, 32
Circulating Libraries, 106
Civil Obedience Movement, 46
Cochin Act, 1938, 55
Cochin and Malabar, 218
Cochin and Malabar Areas, 96
Cochin Tenancy Act, 57
Cochin, Cranganore and Vaipinkotta, 19
Communism, 106
Communist
  Parties, 226
  Party of India, 46, 58, 106, 134
  Party Workers, 226
Congress Party, 37, 46, 54, 58, 107, 155, 226, 227
Congress Socialist Party, 57, 58
Constitutional Reform Committee, 89
Continuing Education, 141, 233
CPI (M), 134, 155, 156, 158, 160-164
CPP Library Panmana (Quilon), 32
Cultural Renaissance of Kerala, 30

D

Devadar Malabar Reconstruction Trust (DMRT), 38
Devadar, DK, 38

Devadasis System, 18
Dewan Nam Pillai Memorial
    Library, 51
Director Public Instructions,
    49, 50
District
    Board Palghat, 68
    Library Board, 197
    Library Committee, 174
    Library Council (DLC),
    198, 200
Dravidians, 16

E

E Raman Menon—A
    Balagopal, 55
East India Company, 23, 27,
    28
Education, 17, 27, 28, 32, 69,
    76, 217
    and Learning, 19
    and Literature, 18
    Free and Compulsory, 60
    Informal, 32
    Non-Formal, 29
    Policy, 60
    Reorganization
    Committee, 100
Educational
    Institutions, 17, 18, 28,
    31, 32, 54, 60
    Policy, 135
    System, 217
Emergency, 160
English Education, 24
English Schools, 27
Ernakulam Public Library, 34
Ernakulam Sahitya Parishad,
    99
Eviction Procedures Act,
    1967, 135
Ezhava Community, 32

F

Farm Information Business,
    184
Farm Labourers, 156
Feudalism Society of Kerala,
    31
First World War, 37
Five Year Plan (1st), 105
Free Education System, 29
Freedom Struggle, 218

G

Gandhi, (MK), 56
Gandhi, Indira, 155
Gopalan, AK, 46
Gopalan, KPR, 46
Gopinathan Nair, TN, 72
Gouri Lakshmi Bai, 23
Gouri Parvati Bai, 24
Govinda Menon, Panampoli,
    120
Govt. of India Act 1935, 58
Gradation Committee, 94, 95,
    120, 131
Grades and Grants, 144
Granthasala Sanghom, 117
Granthasala Union, 196

H

Harijan Welfare Dept., 103
Hindu Temples, 17
Hinduism, 17

I

Indian
  Adult Education Association, 123, 180
  Granthasala Association (ILA), 68, 196
  Law Commission, 143
  Library Association (ILA), 46
  National Congress, 47, 56, 58, 61, 124
Information Community, 224
International Children Year, 177

J

Jail Library Services, 185
Jainism, 16
Jains' Pallis, 16
Janapradayani Library, 33
Janmi Kudiyan Regulation, 56
Jayasankar Award, 177
Joint Family, 31
Joint Family System, 56

K

K Damodaran—Kerala, 53
Kala Samitis, 118, 123, 221
Kanakakunna Palace, 180
Kelu, MK, 47
Kenyaraman, 48
Kerala Granthalaya S, 122, 124-126
Kerala Granthalaya Sanghom, (KGS), 67-70, 99, 107, 118, 120, 127, 130-132, 134-137, 139, 140, 142-145, 155-162, 164-166, 171-188, 195-197, 211, 213, 219-222, 223-230, 232, 234, 243
  Act, 197
  Control Board, 195
  Details, 243-245
  Silver Jubilee Celebrations, 136
  Structural Frame, 176
Kerala
  Granthasala Bill, 1920, 142, 143
  History Congress, 70
  Legislative Assembly, 142, 143, 155
  Legislature Association, 197
  Library Act, 121
  Library Association, 67, 196
  Library Committee, 48
  Pradesh Congress Committee, (KPCC), 37, 54, 57
  Public Library Act, 229, 230
  Public Library Bill, 142, 195-197
  Public Library Bill, 1971, 143
  Salient Features, 142, 197-199, 234
  Sasthrasahitya Parishad, 223
  Society, 31, 32 see under Society also
  State Library Council, 229
  University Library, 90
  University, 185

Keraleeyan, KA, 46, 47
Kesava Dev—Joseph Mundassery, 107
Kingdoms of-, 18
  Calicut, 18
  Cochin, 18
  Travancore, 18
KL Chacko—Gopala Menon, 45
Kodungaloor Public Library, 34
Kolacherry Kisan Union, 52
Kottayam
  Conference, 79, 80
  District Congress Committee, 124
  Public Library, 33
Koyithumpuram, Kerala Varma Valiya
Krishna Iyer, VR, Justice, 143
Krishnavilasom Mahila Vayanasala, 35
Kulasekharas, 17, 18
Kunjaraman, Susreevan, 47
Kunjuraman, Kundajerry, 47
Kurup, M Krishnan, 97

L

Labour Union, 57
Lalitha Kala Academy, 196
Land Reform Act, 135, 156
Left Democratic Front Govt., 197, 229
Liberalism and Enlightenment, 24
Libraries
  and Kala Samitis, 173
  Elections, 159, 160
  Election Schedule, 159, 163
  Development, 212, 213
  Distributing, 158
  District, 156, 157
  Economic Conditions, 208
  Education Role of-, 209
  Growth of-, 37
  Malayalam/Tamil, 51
  Of Kerala, 217
  On Scientific Field, 209
  Political Activities, 206
  Private Subscriptions, 26
  Private, 25
  Public, 49, 225, 228
  Relations with Communist Parties, 207
  Relations with KGS, 211
  Role in Culture/Sports, 210
  Rural Libraries Grant, 51
  Rural, 49, 50, 51, 97, 98, 102, 103, 156, 180
Library
  Advisory Boards, 120
  Bill, 49, 124-27, 134
  Building, 36
  Cess, 50
  Committee, 45
  Conference, 72
  Conference (2nd), 49
  Conference (3rd), 51
  Deshaposhini Library, 172, 173
  Executive Committees, 171
  Executive Committees, Powers, 171-172
  Grants, 121, 122, 131, 134, 157, 195
  Jail, 55
Legislation, 50, 80, 197, 229

Mahila, 55
Movement, 23, 29, 37, 38, 45-51, 61, 68, 69, 95, 103, 117, 121, 127, 130, 131, 134, 140, 143, 159, 221, 227, 229
Basic Principles, 50
In Kerala, 25, 49, 140
History of-, 67, 70
Spread of-, 45
Organizations, 67, 107
Organizers, 187
PK Vilasam Library, 71
Princes, 55
Public, 55, 56 see under Public Libraries also
Records, 172
Sahitya Panchanan Library, 70, 71
Workers, 53, 67-69, 76, 119, 127, 140, 161, 195, 218, 223, 228, 229, 233
Literacy, 15-17, 28, 181, 182
Campaigns, 161
Centres, 141, 178
Functional, 180
Growth, 182
Program, 180
Rate, 29
Local Library Authority, 118, 119, 121, 122, 125, 135, 156, 166
Lock, Chief Judge, 34

M

Madras
Library Act, 126, 132
Library Act, 1948, 119
Library Bill, 1948, 118
Local Board Act, 1834, 28
Presidency, 28
Tenancy Act, 57
University, 27
Malabar, 28, 46, 47, 52, 53, 58, 60, 68
Aided Teacher Union, 57
and Cochin State, 45
and Cochin, 27, 69
Coast, 19
District Congress, 37
District Board, 58
Library Association, 54
Library Conference, 53
Library Movement, 97
Local Library, 182
Vayanasala Sanghom, 55, 67
Malayalam
Language, 17-19, 29, 30, 46, 217, 223
Literacy Men, 77
Writers, 77, 91
Literatures, 19
Mappila Peasantry, 38
Mappila Revolt, 38
Marxists, 159
Mattancheri, 27
Menon, Ambat Sivaram, 55
Menon, AR, 55
Menon, AS, 45, 47
Menon, MP Sivadasa, 68
Ministry of Education, 178
Missionaries, 7, 30, 31
Educational Activities, 31
Modern Education, 25
Modern English Policy, 24
Muhammad Hebubullah, 50
Municipalities and District Boards, 28
Munro, Col., 23, 28

Munthankare Sankeravilasom Library, 33
Muslim League, 126
Mysore Public Library, 132
Mysorean Invasion, 23

N

N Gopala Pillai—KM Kesavan, 80
N Narayanan Kurup—P Madhavan, 74
Nadesh K Krupskaya Prize, 179
Nagercoil, 24
Nair Service Society, 126
Nair, Gopinath, TN, 173
Nair, KN Damodaran, 177
Nair, VGN—Pillai Vayanasala, 70
Namboodiripad, EMS, 46, 57, 117, 124, 134, 135, 155
  Coalition Ministry of-, 155
Namboodiripad, Ghali SV, 57
National Central Library, 105
National Library Week, 186
National Movement, 56, 69
Night Schools, 55
Non-Formal Education Agencies, 222
North Kerala Library Conference, 118
North Zone Library Conference, 119
Nursery Education to Children, 177

O

Opinionnaire Survey, 203-214, 221, 223, 224, 226
  Text, 249
Organization of Libraries, 75

P

Panampani Govinda Menon—K Thomas, 101
Panchayat Library Union, 142
Panchayats, 120, 121, 156
Panicker, PN, 70-72, 78, 80, 90, 94, 96, 97, 99, 102, 103, 140, 158-160, 165, 166, 227
Panicker, VG, 181
Partition of Bengal, 37
Peasant and Labor Movement, 53
Personal Interview Schedule, 255
Pillai, K. Ramakrishna (Editor), 30
Pillai, M Govinda, 48
Pillai, P Krishnan, 46
Pillai, PA Thanu, 89, 91
Pillai, Pattom A Thanu, 131
Pillai, PK Narayanan, 49
Pinarai Vivekananda Library, 58
PK Memorial Library, 70
Political Parties, 56
Polyandry, 31
Portuguese and Dutch, 19
Pottakad, SK, 131
Praja Socialist Party (PSP), 155
Princely State of Kerala, 28
Printing Presses in Kerala, 19
Printing Technology, 217
Private Forest, 156
Progressive Writers Association, 107

Prominent Play Writers, 172, 173
Public Libraries
 of Kerala, 67
 of Malabar, 219
Public Libraries, 135, 156, 218-20, 222-23
Public Library, 25, 38, 50, 230, 234
 Bill, 125
 Building, 26
 Concept, 25
 Movement, 229
 System, 228, 230

Q

Quit India Movement, 59

R

Raghavan, PC, 53
Raj, MK, 68, 70
Raja Raja Library, 33
Rajagopalachari, C, 58
Rajya Samacheva, (Tellichery), 30
Ramakrishnan, TK, 176
Ramaswamy Iyer, Sir CP, 49, 58, 60, 72, 81
Ranganathan, SR, Great Library Scientist, 46, 69, 79, 81, 124, 126, 127, 132, 134
Reading
 Clubs, 27
 Habits, 222
Reforms in Travancore, 24
Resource Sharing, 49
Robert, J, 26
Royal Proclamation, 27, 30
Rural
 Development, 100
 Libraries, 56 see Library also
 Library Engandiyoor, 34
 Library Schemes, 237-238
 Library System, 51

S

Sahitya
 Academy, 196
 Pravarthaka Sahakarana Sanghom, 77, 99
Samitis, 173
Sahyadri Hills, 15
Salane, Sir Hans, Founder of British Museum, 25
Samasthi Kerala Pusthakalaya Samithy, 48
Sangam Period, 16
Sangeetha National Academy, 196
Sankara, Hindu Saint, 17
Sanmargha Darshini Library—Sen Gupta Library, 52
Sanskrit and Tamil, 17
Satyagraha, 58
Science and Philosophy, 18
Seaty, AF, 34
Select Committee, 195
Seminaries and Colleges, 19
Sinha, KP, 123
Slave Trade in Travancore, 24
Slavery, 28
Slaves, 31
Slogans of National Movements, 176

Boycott Foreign Clothes, 176
Eradication of Untouchability, 176
Upliftment of Harijans, 176
Social and Educational Development, 34
Change in Malabar, 37
Cultural Movement, 35
Development in Kerala, 37
Development, 217
Education, 176
Order, 32
Reform Movement, 23, 31, 34
Reforms, 30, 56
Regulation Acts, 56
Cochin Nair Act, 56
Mappila M Act, 56
Nair Regulation Act, 56
Service Program, 52
Transformation in Travancore, 24
Transformation of Kerala, 31
Workers, 140, 180
Socialist Party, 126
Society, 221, 225
Kerala, 19, 135, 217
Of India, 18
Pre-Historic, 17
Socio-Cultural Relations of Libraries, 203
Socio-Political Movement, 45
Socio-Religious Movement, 31
Sports Clubs, 221
Sree Chithira Thirunal, 89
Sree Chithira Thirunal Library, 49, 172, 173
Sree Harshan Library, 47, 52
Sree Mulava Tirunal, 27, 32
Sreenarayan Vilasom Library, 35
State
Central Library (ies), 106, 156
Education Conference, 69
Institute of Languages, 184
Library Authority, (SLA), 50, 124, 134, 196, 197, 199, 200
Library Union, 142
Public Library Bill, 197
Reorganization Act, 117
Stathan, KM, 49
Swathi Thirunal, Royal Writ, 235
Swawti Thirunal, Maharaja, 24, 25

T

Taluk
Central Libraries, 92
Libraries, 106
Library Union, 95, 198-200
Unions, 123, 174, 175
Unions of Libraries, 126
Tamil Language, 17
Technical Training, 79
Tehran Conference, 180
Temple Entry Proclamation, 27
Tenancy Act, 57
Textbook Committee, 51
Thanoor Mahila Library, 119
Thunchath Ezhuthachan, 68

Tipu Sultan (Mysore), 27, 28
Tirur Grama Bandhu Library, 53
Total Literacy Program, 22
Town Implementation Act, (1865), 28
Trade, 16
Training Camps for Library Workers, 118
Travancore, 23-25, 27, 29, 30, 33, 37, 49, 50, 55, 56, 58, 60
  and Cochin, 30, 217, 218, 219
  Company Act, 78
  Congress Committee, 100
  Education Reforms Committee, 49
  Educational Rule, 28
  Joint Stock Companies Regulation, 27
  Library Association, 95, 96
  Memorial, 32, 33
  Public Library Committee, 26
  Public Library Reorganization, 50
  State Congress, 71, 72, 89
  University, 60, 100
Travancore-Cochin Unification, 107
Treaty of Srirangapatam, 28
Trichur, 48
Trichur Public Library, 34
Trivandrum, 26, 29, 31, 35, 49, 80-87, 89, 141, 178
  Public Library, 25, 27, 90, 125
  Public Library Society, 26, 27
Trivandrum—Kalicut, 181

U

UNESCO, 102, 178, 179, 222
United
  Taluk Library Association, 93, 100
  Travancore-Cochin Lib. Association, 89, 117, 119, 120
  Trivandrum Ass. 182
UNO, 183
Untouchability, 17, 56

V

Vaghbadanandan, Social Reformer, 35, 37
Vaghdanemde, 31
Varma Chithira Tirunal Balarama, Maharaja of Travancore, 56
Vernacular Primary Schools, 24
Village Uplift Committees, 103
Vinjana Sandajan Library, 34
Visakam Thirunal, 34
Voluntary
  Agencies, 177
  Organization, 98, 102, 137

W

Wanchu, NN, 165
Western Ghats, 15
Women's Centres, 180
World War II, 58, 60